FOOD IN THE ANCIENT WORLD

FOOD IN THE ANCIENT WORLD

JOAN P. ALCOCK

Food through History

Greenwood Press
Westport, Connecticut • London

Library of Congress Cataloging-in-Publication Data

Alcock, Joan P. (Joan Pilsbury)
  Food in the ancient world : / Joan P. Alcock.
    p. cm.
  Includes bibliographical references and index.
  ISBN 0–313–33003–4
  1. Food habits—History. 2. Food—History. 3. Civilization, Ancient.
I. Title.
  TX353.A47 2006
  641.30093—dc22   2005026303

British Library Cataloguing in Publication Data is available.

Library of Congress Catalog Card Number: 2005026303
ISBN: 0–313–33003–4
ISSN: 1542–8087

First published in 2006

Greenwood Press, 88 Post Road West, Westport, CT 06881
An imprint of Greenwood Publishing Group, Inc.
www.greenwood.com

Printed in the United States of America

∞™

The paper used in this book complies with the
Permanent Paper Standard issued by the National
Information Standards Organization (Z39.48–1984).

10 9 8 7 6 5 4 3 2 1

The publisher has done its best to make sure the instructions and/or recipes in this book are correct. However, users should apply judgment and experience when preparing recipes, especially parents and teachers working with young people. The publisher accepts no responsibility for the outcome of any recipe included in this volume.

For John Marshant,
an excellent friend and stimulating
colleague

CONTENTS

ACKNOWLEDGMENTS

I am most grateful for the help that is always freely given by the librarians of the Institute of Classical Studies, University of London. David Allen and Caroline Brick of the Horniman Museum Library, Forest Hill, London, provided help with the Egyptian literature and produced books with their usual courtesy. Professor Emeritus Bryan Reuben, London South Bank University, made valuable suggestions for the improvement of the text.

I am especially grateful to Wendi Schnaufer at Greenwood, who allowed me extra time to complete this book, which was delayed through a series of accidents and misfortunes. Her patience has been exemplary.

INTRODUCTION

The interest in food in its historical content has increased enormously since the early 1990s, and food studies have become an important part of history and literature. People have to eat, and become curious to know what and how our ancestors ate, especially in more distant ages. Historical studies of food help to satisfy that curiosity. This book discusses food grown, produced, and eaten from the beginnings of the Egyptian predynastic civilization, about 4000 B.C., to the end of the Roman Empire, in the fifth century A.D. It concentrates on four civilizations: the Egyptians, the Greeks, the Romans, and the Celts. Each of these civilizations developed in a different way and each had its own individual history, the Egyptians developing a unique and outstanding civilization based on kingship, the Greeks evolving the concept of democracy, and the Celts ranging across Europe, extolling a warrior aristocracy whose prowess was honored by heroic deeds in battle. These three civilizations were eventually conquered by the superior military might of Rome, and if this book concentrates more on Roman methods and practice, it is because Rome subsumed these three other civilizations, concentrating on molding them into a coherent whole.

The history of Rome is that of a controlled, politically organized republic becoming an ambitious expanding empire, consisting of 40 provinces, which at its zenith straddled the Mediterranean and expanded into central Europe. United under a competent, centralized government, the Roman administration allowed the civilizations it conquered to retain many of their individual characteristics and native laws and customs. At the same time, it enhanced the development of food production and distribution by means of the introduction of new farming techniques and opportunities for trade. At its best, the Roman Empire provided strong government, established a network of roads along which goods could be carried, and provided conditions in which trade could flourish while under the protection of a disciplined regime. Toward the end of the fourth century A.D., this protection was menaced by the invasions of barbarian hordes, which both the Greeks and the Romans had despised.

Yet though the empire disintegrated and the trading network collapsed, the legacy of Rome was available to successive ages through the writings of Greek and Roman scholars. In addition, Greek and Roman writers interpreted Egyptian and Celtic customs. These have been used to provide firsthand evidence in this book. Egyptian culture is illustrated by hieroglyphics and scenes painted and carved on Egyptian tombs. Additional knowledge of the Celts comes from archaeological evidence and legends and mythologies, which have been passed down orally or were written down by scholars from the fifth century A.D. onward. Archaeology has provided an enormous amount of material, ranging from discoveries in tombs, paintings and carvings in pyramids, and discoveries in buried cities to more humble artifacts in the form of dining and kitchenware. Modern archaeological techniques have revealed food remains, eating habits, methods of cooking, and the circumstances in which meals were eaten. All this evidence allows a considered estimate to be made of food produced and eaten in four great civilizations of the ancient world.

There are other factors to be considered. Over the period of time considered in this book, society moved from a hunter-gatherer one to one preferring settled agriculture. This occurred at different times in different areas, but it began in the Near East about the ninth century B.C. and spread through Egypt, the Mediterranean, and northward throughout Europe. The result was a change from gathering wild plants to cultivating new ones in tended plots, from hunting animals to better breeding techniques. this in turn led to a more settled existence, an increase in population, organized societies, and a determination to keep and protect land, with the inevitable result of ensuing conflict.

The four civilizations met and controlled this agricultural revolution in different ways, some more efficiently than others. They also expanded their knowledge of food by experimenting with preparing and cooking it and broadening their taste horizons. This was obvious with the expansion of the spice trade, importing new textures and flavors from different areas of the world and enhancing food experience. Curiosity is only one of the aspects by which human beings expand their knowledge; obtaining new foods and experimenting in food cultures allowed them to do this.

Not everyone was able to enjoy this experience. For many in society, life was a hard existence dependent on climate, the state of the land, and the growth or failure of the harvest. Obtaining enough food to live at a subsistence level could be a struggle, especially during the winter months. Crop failures, poor or rotten food, food poisoning, and eating of plants with little value to humans were part of daily life. Many sought a protector or patron who would ensure a regular food supply or relied on private or public charity. In the Roman Empire at least half the population of the city of Rome was dependent on the state handout of grain, much of it shipped from Egypt and taken from the peasant society there. At the other end of the social scale were those having an ample supply of food with a wide variety of products and tastes. They could indulge or overindulge their appetites in a variety of ways, some seemingly bizarre to modern taste. This book considers both these aspects of society as well as those who grew or gained sufficient food to live an uneventful life. It was during this period that urban life developed, resulting in a society that was a consuming, and not a producing, society. This group had to be fed, and arrangements were needed to do this. The result was improved trading methods, covering everything from transport to monetary calculations.

This book also mentions other areas, such as the Near East and northern Europe, when comparisons need to be made or when new foods and cooking methods appear. It is written for the nonspecialist who wishes to know what food products were available, how they were cooked and served, what people ate, and how they ate then. It touches on the enjoyment, and sometimes disgust, that food gave to people. It relies, as indicated, on written and pictorial evidence supplemented by archaeological data, and where possible sets the food into its historical context. The texts are referenced, but other references are kept to a minimum. More detailed studies will be found in books and articles mentioned in the bibliography. This book hopes to stimulate an interest in food in the ancient world and to encourage readers to further explore this fascinating subject.

CLASSICAL AUTHORS MENTIONED

Boldface text within entry refers to main entries in this chapter.

Aelian (ca. A.D. 170–235). Greek rhetorician who taught in Rome. His most well-known work, *On the Characteristics of Animals,* is a collection of excerpts and anecdotes of a moralizing nature in 17 books.

Ammianus Marcellinus (ca. A.D. 330–395). Roman historian. He was a Greek native of Antioch and became an officer to the Roman general Ursicinus in 354. He joined the Emperor Julian's invasion of Persia in 363 and later visited Egypt and Greece. In the late 380s he wrote a history of Rome continuing the history of **Tacitus** from A.D. 69 to his own day. The first 13 books have been lost; the remainder cover the years 354–378.

Anon. Author of the "Moretum," one of a group of short Latin poems in a collection called *Appendix Virgilana* dating from about **Virgil's** time. The "Moretum," or "The Salad," deals with a peasant's preparation in the early morning of his meal, then setting out for the day's work.

Anon. Anonymous Greek traveler of the first century A.D. who authored the *Periplus Maris Erythraei,* a work describing the coasts of the Red Sea and the Arabian Gulf as well as showing knowledge of parts of India and East Africa.

Anthimus (active A.D. 474–511). Greek doctor who was attached to the court of the Emperor Zeno. He became involved in treacherous activities and fled to the court of Theodosius, who sent him on a diplomatic mission to the Franks. Some time after A.D. 511 he wrote a handbook on dietetics called *De Observatione Ciborum Theodoricum Regem Francorum Epistula*. This was half medical text, half cookery book.

Antiphanes (fourth century B.C.). Greek dramitist who wrote mainly comic plays.

Apuleius (active ca. A.D. 155). Apuleius's *Metamorphoses* (or *The Golden Ass*) is the one Latin novel that survives in its entirety and gives many details of popular life. The hero is accidentally turned into an ass and undergoes a series of adventures.

Archestratus (mid-fourth century B.C.). Born in Gela in Sicily. Some of his *Hedupathia* (also called *Opsopoiia* or *The Life of Pleasure*), a culinary tour of the Mediterranean, was preserved by **Athenaeus**.

Aristophanes (ca. 457–ca. 385 B.C.). Poet of Attic comedy who wrote at least 43 plays, of which 11 survive, together with fragments. He laid down a structure for plays and led change in comedy in the early fourth century B.C., making use of parody, satire, and exaggerated fantasy. He did not hesitate to attack ruthless, self-seeking men, but displays sympathy with men of independent means who enjoy traditional pleasure.

Aristotle (384–322 B.C.). Greek philosopher who taught in Athens at the Academy. His works cover every branch of philosophy and science known to his day and had a great influence on late antiquity and subsequent eras.

Athenaeus (active ca. A.D. 200). Egyptian Greek born in Naukratis in Egypt and author of the *Deipnosophistae, (The Deipnosophists)* a tale of 16 men dining together in Rome and discussing a broad variety of topics, including food and medicine. His comments are drawn from a large number of literary sources.

Ausonius (ca. A.D. 310–395). Latin poet, born in Bordeaux, who became a teacher of rhetoric. After 30 years he was summoned to the imperial court of the emperor Valentinian to teach the emperor's son

Gratian. When Gratian became emperor in A.D. 375, Ausonius became praetorian prefect of Gaul, but after Gratian's murder in A.D. 383 he retired to Bordeaux. He wrote a considerable amount of poetry, the best-known poem being the *Mosella*, a description of the river Moselle and the fish caught in it.

Caesar (100–44 B.C.). Roman statesman, general, and dictator. He subdued Gaul between 61 and 56 B.C. and invaded Britain twice, in 55 and 54 B.C. His *De Bello Gallico* (*Commentaries on the Gallic Wars*) was written in the third person to indicate his belief that this was an objective, truthful record of events.

Cassiodorus (ca. A.D. 490–585). Politician and writer who became prefect of the court of King Athalaricus in 533. Two years later he retired and devoted himself to writing. His works include the *Chronic*, a history of Rome up to A.D. 519; a history of the Goths; *Institutiones*, dealing with the customs of the monks; and *Variae*, an edited collection of state papers on the structure, ideology, and culture of the late Roman government.

Cato (234–149 B.C.). Roman statesman and moralist. His literary works included *Origines*, a history of the origins of Rome and the Italian cities, together with the more recent Punic wars. His *De Re Rustica*, also known as *De Agri Cultura*, is concerned mainly with the cultivation of fruits, olives, and vines. He wrote from his own experience and was mainly concerned with the practical necessities of running an estate.

Chrysippus of Tyana (ca. 280–207 B.C.). Stoic philosopher who taught in Athens. He elaborated the doctrines of Zeno into a unified system.

Cicero (106–43 B.C.). Roman statesman and orator, whose prolific writing included poems, letters, and prosecution and defense speeches. His numerous letters included many to his friend Atticus. His political career included the governorship of Cilicia.

Columella (active A.D. 60–65). Spaniard who served in the Roman army. He composed a treatise on farming, *De Re Rustica*. This covers all aspects of running an estate, including livestock, cultivation, gardens, and the duties of a bailiff and his wife.

Diocles of Carystus (late fourth century B.C.). Greek physician whom **Pliny the Elder** called the next after **Hippocrates** in time and fame. Only fragments of his work have survived, however, dealing with all aspects of animal physiology, anatomy, and botany.

Diodorus Siculus (active ca. 60–39 B.C.). Greek historian who wrote a world history in 40 books centered on Rome. These are based on ancient sources and are a useful, but uncritical, compilation of legends, social history, and mythology. He was the first to write an herbal on the medical use of plants.

Dioscorides (active first century A.D.). Greek physician who served with the Roman army; he wrote *Materia Medica* in five books. The subject matter included the medicinal properties of plants and drugs. It listed more than 700 plants and 1,000 drugs.

Euphron (mid third century B.C.). A Greek poet.

Euripides (ca. 485–406 B.C.). Greek tragedian who played little part in public life but wrote about 80 plays, of which 19 survive intact. After his death his plays were revered and regularly revived.

Frontinus (ca. A.D. 30–ca. 104). After serving as consul in A.D. 73 or 74, he was governor of Britain 74–78. He wrote *Strategemata,* a manual on war strategies for the use of officers, and *De Aquis Urbis Roma,* dealing with the history, technicalities, and regulation of the aqueducts of Rome.

Galen (A.D. 129–199). Born in Pergamum. Greek physician who rose from being a gladiator doctor in Asia Minor to being court physician to the emperors Marcus Aurelius, Commodus, and Septimius Severus. He lectured, demonstrated, and wrote on every aspect of medicine and anatomy. His books had enormous influence and formed the basis of many later medical works.

Gildas (died ca. A.D. 570). British cleric and author of *De Exidio et Conquestu Britanniae,* ca. A.D. 540, a short history of Britain that gives insight into the Dark Ages.

Heracleides of Syracuse. A Greek cookery writer who is mentioned five times in Athenaeus.

Herodotus (ca. 484–ca. 425 B.C.). Greek historian, born in Helicarnassus, who traveled in Greece, Egypt, and the Near East. He wrote and lectured extensively. His aim was to write a history of the Greco-Roman world, but in doing so he wrote widely on the history and customs of these areas together with Persian customs. Most of the information is firsthand or from eyewitnesses.

Herophilus (early third century B.C.). Born in Chalcedon, and one of the great founders of a school of medicine at Alexandria. He studied anatomy based on human dissection. His writing includes the origins of diseases and studies of organs and parts of the body.

Hesiod (ca. 700 B.C.). Worked as a shepherd on Mount Helicon, where he said he received a calling that he should write poetry. His main surviving works are *Theogony,* dealing with the origins of the gods, and *Works and Days,* giving advice to the workingman.

Hippocrates (ca. 460–ca. 370 B.C.). Probably the most famous figure in Greek medicine, whose name is attached to the Hippocratic Corpus, 60 treatises dealing with medicine, surgery, and health.

Horace (65–8 B.C.). Roman poet whose complete published work survives. The *Epodes* and the *Satires* were written about 30 B.C. and the *Odes* in 23 B.C. He also wrote the *Epistles* and *Carmen Saeculae,* the latter dealing with the Secular Games of 17 B.C.

Josephus (A.D. 37–after 93). Jewish historian who wrote a history of the Jewish Revolt against Rome, which began in A.D. 66. The work contains one of the best descriptions of the Roman army.

Juvenal (active second century A.D.). Probably the greatest of the Roman satirical poets, writing 16 bitter, humorous satires portraying life in second-century Rome.

Libanius (A.D. 314–ca. 393). Greek from Antioch who studied at Athens and taught at Constantinople. He wrote an autobiography called *Orations,* a funeral oration of Emperor Julian, and several hundred letters.

Livy (59 B.C.–A.D. 17). Born in Padua and the author of a history of Rome in 142 books, the last 22 of which deal with events in his own time.

Lucian of Samosata (ca. A.D. 120–180). Traveler and lecturer who moved to Athens and developed public recitations. Later he moved to Egypt and accepted a post in Roman administration. Author of 80 writings, chiefly dialogues, which illustrate contemporary life and manners.

Lucretius (ca. 99–ca. 55 B.C.). Roman poet and philosopher. Author of *De Rerum Natura,* a poem dealing with the system of Epicurus and demonstrating that fear of the gods is groundless and that the world and everything in it is governed by the mechanical laws of nature.

Marcellus (first century A.D.). Physician from Asia Minor living during Nero's reign whose writings may have been incorporated into those of Apicius.

Martial (ca. A.D. 40–103). Spaniard who worked in Rome after A.D. 64 and relied on his poetry for a living. Between A.D. 86 and 98 he wrote 11 books of epigrams, short poems, each of which pithily expressed a concept, with the subject matter ranging across the whole spectrum of Roman life.

Maximus of Tyre (A.D. 125–185). Sophist and the author of 41 lectures who lectured at Athens and Rome in the age of Emperor Commodus.

Oribasius (ca. A.D. 320–390s). Born in Pergamum. Became physician to Emperor Julian about A.D. 351. At the emperor's request he wrote four books of medical compilations, taking extracts from **Galen, Athenaeus,** Rufus, **Diocles,** and other writers. After the emperor's death in 361 he moved to the court of the emperor Theodosius and wrote two abridgments of his work.

Ovid (43 B.C.–A.D. 14). Poet born in the valley of the Apennines, east of Rome, who traveled around the Mediterranean. His poetry aroused the displeasure of the imperial court, and he was banished to Tomis on the Black Sea. His main poems are the *Ars Amatoria, Tristia, Fasti,* and *Metamorphoses.*

Palladius (active fourth century A.D.). Latin author whose main treatise on agriculture, *Opus Agriculturae,* in 14 books contained general information on setting up and managing a farm and the work to be done each month.

Pausanias (flourished ca. A.D. 160). Greek geographer who wrote at least 10 books on the history and topography of a number of countries.

Paxamus. Greek (Hellenistic) author who wrote in Rome. His most well-known books are *On Cooking* and *On Farming*. He was cited by Athenaeus.

Persius (A.D. 34–54). Uncompromising Stoic who wrote letters satirizing characters who were either aged or immature tutors and students.

Petronius (died ca. A.D. 69). Roman satirical writer and author of the *Satyricon,* a novel of which the most well-known part is Trimalchio's feast, an ostentatious dinner party to which a motley crowd are invited as guests or gain admittance.

L. Flavius Philostratus (third century A.D.). Wrote during the reign of the Emperor Septimius Severus. He wrote a life of Apollonius of Tyre and a number of minor works including one on athletic training.

Plato (ca. 429–347 B.C.). Greek philosopher born in Athens. He studied under Socrates and after Socrates' death traveled in Italy and Sicily for the next 12 years. On his return to Athens in 388 B.C., Plato established the Academy, which he presided over for the next 40 years of his life. His philosophy revealed the influence of Heraclitus and the Pythagoreans. His writings were in the form of dialogues from which his views have to be deduced. Plato does not appear by name and much of his philosophy is conveyed through Socrates as the main speaker.

Plautus (ca. 250–184 B.C.). Roman dramatist born in Umbria who wrote about 130 comedies, of which 29 have survived. Although having many stock characters, the plays deal with contemporary life and social settings.

Pliny the Elder (A.D. 23–79). Prolific writer on natural history. His 37 books cover most aspects of natural history, ranging through natural phenomena, medicine, botany, zoology, geography, and minerals. His death during the eruption of Mount Vesuvius is recorded by his nephew. (Unless otherwise stated, references to Pliny in this book refer to Pliny the Elder.)

Pliny the Younger (A.D. 61–113). Adopted by his maternal uncle, **Pliny the Elder**. He became an administrator, holding several offices of state, including that of governor of Bithynia-Pontus on the Black Sea, where he died. He wrote many letters, which cover a wide variety of subjects, personal and official.

Plutarch (ca. A.D. 50–129). Mestrius Plutarchus of Chaeronea visited Athens, Egypt, and Italy and eventually lectured at Rome. For 30 years he was a priest at Delphi. He wrote more than 200 books, including a group of rhetorical works, a series of dialogues, and Roman and Greek questions dealing with religious antiquities. He also wrote *Parallel Lives,* exemplifying the virtues and vices of famous men.

Polybius (ca. 200–118 B.C.). Greek historian who lived in Rome. He wrote a history of Greece in 40 books, covering the period 264–146 B.C. He focused on military and political affairs and provided eyewitness accounts of events.

Poseidonius (ca. 135–50 B.C.). Historian, scientist, and philosopher born in Apamea in Syria. He spent most of his time in Rhodes, becoming head of the Stoic school. He wrote 52 books on history, covering the period 146–81 B.C. This included customs of barbarian races.

Procopius (A.D. 500–after 562). A Byzantine Greek historian, secretary to Belisarius, general of the Emperor Justinian. Wrote the *History of the Wars of Justinian* in eight volumes.

Propertius (c 50 B.C.–after 16 A.D.). Roman poet who wrote elegies and other poems with an intense visual imagination.

Seneca the Younger (ca. 4 B.C.–A.D. 65). Roman politician, philosopher, and dramatist, who was born at Corduba in Spain and came to Rome to study rhetoric and philosophy before setting out on a political career. He was chief advisor to Emperor Nero but in 65 was implicated in the conspiracy of Piso and forced to commit suicide. He wrote voluminously on many subjects, including rhetoric and philosophy. His *Naturales Quaestiones* dealt with natural phenomena. He also wrote 20 books of *Epistulae Morales ad Lucilium*, an artificial correspondence.

Sidonius Apollinaris (c A.D. 430–480). Gallo-Roman poet and later Bishop of Augustonemetum (Clemont-Ferrand), capitol of the Averni region in Gaul. He published numerous poems and letters detailing local customs and mythological allusions.

Soranus (second century A.D.). One of the greatest Greek physicians, who studied in Alexandria and practiced in Rome during the reigns of Trajan and Hadrian. He wrote 20 books on medicine and terminological problems. Two of his works have survived in their entirety, a treatise on fractures and another on gynecology.

Sosipater (third century B.C.). Greek poet.

Strabo (64–after 24 B.C.). Greek geographer who came to Rome several times after in 44 B.C. and traveled widely in the Mediterranean region. His 17 books, the *Geography*, covers the chief provinces of Roman world and other inhabited regions around the Mediterranean.

Suetonius (born ca. 69 B.C.). Wrote widely on antiquities and natural sciences, but the work that survives is his *Lives of the Caesars*, an account of Julius **Caesar** and the 11 subsequent emperors.

Tacitus (A.D. 56–ca. 117). Born in Gaul, he eventually became a Roman senator and governor of Asia. He married Agricola's (Governor of Britain A.D. 78–84; was previously military tribune in Britain in A.D. 58–61 and commanded Legion XX in A.D. 70–74) daughter and wrote a life of his father-in-law, published in A.D. 98, which gives a much-quoted description of Britain. In the same year he wrote the *Germania*, dealing with the history and customs of the German tribes north of the Rhine and the Danube. His major works, the *Histories*, dealing with the period A.D. 69–96, and the *Annals*, covering the period A.D. 14–68, are invaluable for the events in the first century A.D.

Tertullian (ca. A.D. 160–220). Latin Christian writer who was born in Carthage and trained as a lawyer. He converted to Christianity about A.D. 195 and then devoted himself to Christian writings, including defending the church against charges of atheism and magic.

Theophrastus (ca. 376–ca. 287 B.C.). Greek philosopher, born at Eresus in Lesbos, who followed Aristotle as head of the Peripatetic School in Athens. He wrote on a great variety of subjects, including inquiries into plants (*Historia Plantarum*), metaphysics, and different types of characters.

Thucydides (ca. 455–400 B.C.). Greek historian who collected material for a history of Greece during the Peloponnesian War from 431 B.C. His narrative breaks off in 411 B.C. He is usually to be relied on for the accuracy of information. He said that in writing the history his purpose was to provide posterity with a warning as to how men may behave in the future.

Valerius Maximus (early first century A.D.). Roman historian who accompanied Sextus Pomponius, the younger son of Pompey, to Asia in A.D. 27. On his return he wrote nine books of historical examples illustrating moral and philosophical points, mainly drawn from **Cicero** and **Livy**.

Varro (116–27 B.C.). Prolific writer who is said to have written more than 600 books. Of these probably the most important was *De Lingua Latina,* a treatise on Latin grammar, and *De Re Rustica,* in three books, which was intended as a practical manual of running a farm for the benefit of his wife, Fundania.

Vegetius (active ca. A.D. 379–395). Military writer who wrote a manual, *Epitoma Rei Militaris,* on military training and the organization of the Roman Legion.

Virgil (70–19 B.C.). Roman poet born in Cisalpine Gaul who studied philosophy in Rome. About 42 B.C. he began the composition of the *Eclogues* while he was living in the Campania. This was followed by the *Georgics* and the *Aeneid.* After his death he was regarded as one of the greatest of the Latin poets, and his works and his tomb, outside Naples, became the objects of a cult.

Xenocrates (active 339–314 B.C.). Head of the Athens Academy and a disciple of **Plato** who wrote on philosophy, the nature of the gods, and the teachings of a practical morality.

Xenophon (ca. 428–354 B.C.). Athenian historian who joined the expedition of Cyrus the Younger, (423–401 B.C., Persian commander who made a famous march "up country") described in the *Anabasis.* After leading back the Ten Thousand he served the Spartan king and under two Spartan generals before returning to Athens. He wrote on numerous subjects, civil and military, based on his own experiences.

ABBREVIATIONS FOR NOTES

AF. Galen. *De Alimentorum Facultatibus (On the Properties of Foods).* Translated as *Galen on Food and Drink* by Mark Grant (London: Routledge, 2000).

CIL. Corpus Inscriptiorum Latinarum. 21 volumes with parts and supplements (Berlin: Apud Georgium Reimerum/de Gruber, 1888–ongoing).

D. Athenaeus. *Deipnosophistae (The Deipnosopophists).* Translated and edited by C. B. Gulick, 7 volumes (London: Loeb Classical Library, 1927–1941).

DA. Cato. *De Agri Cultura.* Translated and edited by W. Davis (London: Loeb Classical Library, 1934).

MM. Dioscorides. *Materia Medica. The Greek Herbal of Dioscorides.* Illustrated by a Byzantine A.D. 512. Translated into English by J. Goodyer A.D. 1655. Edited by R. T. Gunther (Oxford: Oxford University Press, 1934).

NH. Pliny (the Elder). *Natural History.* 10 volumes. Translated and edited by H. Rackham, W.H.S. Jones, and D. E. Eichholz (London: Loeb Classical Library, 1938–1963).

OA. Palladius. *Opus Agriculturae.* Edited by R. H. Rodgers (Leipzig: Teubner, 1975).

OC. Anthimus. *De Observatone Ciborum Theodoricum Regem Francorum Epistula (On the Observance of Foods).* Translated and edited by Mark Grant (Tontes, England: Prospect Books, 1996).

RR. Columella. *De Re Rusticae.* Translated and edited by H. Boyd Ash, E. S. Forster, and Edward H. Heffner (London: Loeb Classical Library, 1941–1955).

RR. Varro. *De Re Rustica.* Translated and edited by W. D. Hooper (London: Loeb Classical Library, 1934).

SF. Galen. *De Simplicium Medicamentorum Temperamentis ac Facultatibus (On the Properties of Simples).* Text and Latin translation, volume 11, by C. G. Kuhn (Leipzig: Teubner, 1833).

TIME LINE

ca. 12,000 B.C.	Einkorn and lentils collected from the wild in Syria.
ca. 11,000	Barley gathered from the wild in Greece. Franchthi Cave occupied. Finds included animal and fish bones, shellfish, snail shells, lentils, and nuts.
ca. 10,000	Wild boars tamed in Egypt.
ca. 9000	Emmer known to have grown wild in Near East and to have been cultivated at Jericho. Sheep domesticated in the Near East.
ca. 8000	Chickpeas grown in Palestine; wild peas domesticated in Near East. Oxen and cattle domesticated in Egypt. Einkorn cultivated at Jericho.
ca. 7000	Oxen, cattle, and pigs domesticated in Near East.
ca. 6000	Settled communities in Greece cultivating peas and beans, domesticating animals, and growing emmer, einkorn, millet, and barley.
ca. 5500	Predynastic period of Egyptian history began. Hunter-gatherers began settling in agricultural villages in Egypt. Growing of grains and other domesticated crops began.
ca. 5000	Millet grown in the Caucasus; domestication of date palm began. Sheep and goats known to have been herded in Egypt.

ca. 3200	Beginning of hieroglyphic writing in Egypt.
ca. 3100	Beginning of Egyptian Archaic Period. Egypt was divided into Upper and Lower Egypt, both areas having a hunting, fishing, and agricultural economy. Pyramid building begins.
3100	Narmer founds the First Egyptian Dynasty.
2686	Beginning of the Old Kingdom in Egypt. Domestication of wild animals increased.
2589–2566	Building of Khufu's pyramid. Workers' wages partly paid in onions, garlic, and beer. Increased variety of diet. Wine produced in large quantities.
2181–2040	First Intermediate Period. Low floods in Egypt. Radical measures taken to ensure irrigation so that crops were grown.
2056	Beginning of the Middle Kingdom in Egypt. Procedure of irrigation well established.
ca. 2000	Minoan civilization began in Crete.
1650–1570	Second Intermediate Period in Egypt.
1570	Beginning of the New Kingdom. Egyptian diet widens considerably. Egypt emerges as an imperial power.
1473–1458	Reign of Queen Hatshepsut. Expedition sent to the land of Punt.
1450	Beginning of the Mycenaean Period in Crete.
1417–1379	Reign of Amunhotep III. Vineyard planted at Luxor.
1336–1327	Reign of Tutankhamen.
1198–1160	Reign of Ramses III. Vineyards were planted in oases.
1100	Destruction of the Mycenaean Period in Crete.
1070–656	Third Intermediate Period. Egyptian state begins to lose control over the peasantry. State decentralization and fragmentation of the kingdom.
1050	Migration of Greeks to the coasts of the Aegean and Asia Minor in order to colonize the coastal regions.
ca. 850	Greeks begin extensive trading relations with peoples of the Near East.
776	Conventional date of emergence of Greece as a country and the holding of the first Olympic Games. Rise of Greek city-states.

ca. 700	Beginning of the Celtic Halstatt culture.
753	Traditional date for the founding of the city of Rome.
735	Greeks colonize Sicily and begin to develop a wine industry.
720	Sparta invades Messenia and enslaved its people as helots.
ca. 700	Greeks begin to explore Black Sea and realize its value as a provider of fish for their markets.
650s	Greeks begin to trade with Egypt.
616	Traditional date for the beginning of Etruscan rule in Rome.
594	Beginning of the rule of Solon in Athens. Export of corn and other agricultural products forbidden in order to prevent famine. All debts canceled.
ca. 530	Hochdorf tomb in Baden-Württemberg region of Germany.
ca. 525	Archimedes' screw introduced into Egypt.
525	Persian domination of Egypt. Nile to Red Sea canal completed by Darius I.
510	Traditional date of the founding of the Roman Republic after the Etruscan kings were driven out.
ca. 500	Vix tomb in France.
ca. 500	Emergence of the Celtic La Tène culture.
499–480	Persian Wars eventually lead to the Athenian defeat of the Persian navy at Salamis.
482	Discovery of silver deposits at Laurium in Greece leads to the building of an Athenian fleet, used partly for defense and partly for trade.
480	Athenians defeat the Persian king Xerxes at the naval battle of Salamis.
477	Persian army defeated after the foundation of the Delian League.
461–429	Pericles establishes his rule in Athens, thus ensuring that the population secured sufficient food.
431	Sparta invades Athenian territory, leading to the Second Peloponnesian War.

425	Sparta attacks Pylos. Thucydides comments on Spartan rations.
404	Sparta defeats Greece but does not destroy the city of Athens.
ca. 400	Pepper first mentioned in classical Greece.
ca. 400	Invasion of northern Italy by the Celts.
390	Celtic Gauls sack Rome.
359	Philip II becomes King of Macedon.
338	Philip defeats a coalition of the Greek states at Chaironeia. Macedonian rule established over Greece.
336	Murder of Philip. Succession of his son, Alexander.
334	Alexander invades Persia.
332	Invasion of Egypt by Alexander the Great leads to the collapse of Persian rule and the founding of the city of Alexandria. Ptolemaic period began in Egypt.
331	Alexander defeats the Persian king Darius, leading to the burning of Persepolis and the murder of Darius.
326	Alexander reaches India and opens the way for traders to bring back more spices from the East.
324	Death of Alexander in Babylon.
312	First essential Roman road built between Rome and Capua, allowing trading communications to be expanded. First Roman aqueduct, the Aqua Appia, built, enabling fresh water to be brought into Rome.
279	Galatians invade Greece and attack Delphi. Furthest expansion of Gallic territory, after which the Gauls are on the retreat.
264	First Punic War between Rome and Carthage begins over control of Sicily. Carthage is defeated and cedes Sicily to Rome in 241 and Sardinia and Corsica in 237. These islands soon become noted for the production of their wines. Conquest of Carthage allows the Romans to indulge in the more exotic tastes provided by trade.
225	Celtic invasion of Italy defeated by the Romans at the Battle of Telamon.
218	Outbreak of the Second Punic War. Hannibal invades Italy, defeats the Romans at the Battle of Trasimene,

	and soon controls southern Italy but not the city of Rome.
202	Battle of Zama. Hannibal is defeated and Rome absorbs Spain into the Roman Empire.
189	Booty brought to Rome after Gnaeus Manlius Vulso's campaign in Galatia includes couches, precious hangings, furniture, gold and silver vessels, and even cooks.
148	Macedonia becomes a Roman province.
146	Defeat of the Achaean League. Greece absorbed into Rome. Total defeat of Carthage results in Africa becoming a Roman province.
121	Southern Gaul (Gallia Narbonensis) becomes a Roman province.
74	According to Pliny, Lucullus introduces the cherry tree to Rome.
58	Julius Caesar begins the conquest of Gaul.
55 and 54	Julius Caesar invades Britain.
51–30	Reign of Cleopatra in Egypt.
49	Pliny says that Fulvius Lippinus was the first to fatten snails in Italy.
48	Battle of Pharsalia, in which Caesar defeated Pompey. Caesar ensures Cleopatra's rule in Egypt.
41	Meeting of Cleopatra and Mark Antony.
31	Battle of Actium, leading to suicide of Antony and Cleopatra. Augustus Caesar assumes kingship of Egypt, beginning Roman total control of the country. Egypt becomes a major grain-producing area for Rome.
9 A.D.	Massacre of three Roman legions in the Teutonic forests leads to the frontier of the Roman Empire being established on the Rhine.
14	Death of Emperor Augustus.
43	Invasion of Britain on orders of Emperor Claudius. Britain becomes a Roman province.
47	According to Pliny, the cherry tree introduced into Britain.
54	Death of Emperor Claudius, almost certainly from eating poisoned mushrooms.

70	Roman tastes become more exotic as produce flows into Rome from all areas of the empire and the Far East after the sailing conditions are established by the *Periplus Maris Erythraei*.
79	Destruction of Pompeii, Herculaneum, and surrounding villas by eruption of Mount Vesuvius.
84	Emperor Domitian gives a great banquet in the Coliseum.
101–106	Emperor Trajan conquers Dacia and extends the boundaries of the empire in eastern Europe.
117	Beginning of the reign of Emperor Hadrian, who establishes the boundaries of the Roman Empire. The Rhine and Danube Rivers delineate the northern limits.
166	Roman merchants reach the Han capitol in China, thus ensuring continuation of spice trade with Rome.
284	Diocletian becomes emperor and attempts to stabilize the currency by introducing a gold coinage.
301	Emperor Diocletian's Price Edict, which attempts to eliminate inflation. This proves impossible and is ignored.
312	Constantine becomes emperor of the Western Roman Empire.
313	Edict of Milan ensures toleration in the Roman Empire for the Christians.
324	Emperor Constantine begins the building of Constantinople.
406	Invasion of the Vandals, Sueves, and Alamanni into the Roman Empire, leading to the collapse of the Roman frontier in Rhineland and of Roman rule in Britain and Spain.
408	Goths besiege Rome and demand 3,000 pounds of pepper as tribute money in addition to gold and silver.
410	Rome sacked by Alaric.
451	Huns invade the Roman Empire.
473	Last Roman emperor deposed by the German mercenary Odoacer, who founds a new Germanic empire based on Italy.

CHAPTER 1
HISTORICAL OVERVIEW

POPULATION

Modern scholars have found it difficult to assess the population of the ancient Egyptian, Greek, Celtic, and Roman civilizations. Population figures have an impact on the economy and environment of an area, and over the course of several hundred years they may alter considerably. There were few official censuses, and those there were could not be considered accurate.

Throughout the centuries, in spite of war, disease, and plague, the population of the ancient world increased until the second century A.D. This was because of increased quantities of food, improved agricultural practices, better breeding of livestock, and control of plant disease. In turn this would lead to population expansion into marginal areas once decreed unsuitable for agriculture. Desert regions were cultivated, swamps drained, heavy soils plowed, and woodland reclaimed.

Calculations of population in Egypt rely on estimations of cultivated areas and yield of crops. It has been estimated that there might have been about 350,000 inhabitants in predynastic times, 870,000 in the time of Egyptian unification (ca. 3000 B.C.), and 1.6 million in the Old Kingdom (about 2500 B.C.).[1] With the introduction of the *shaduf,* which allowed increased use of land, the population probably reached two million in the New Kingdom. Increased acreage in the Ptolemaic period would support a larger population, possibly up to four or five million. Contemporaries gave their own estimates. Diodorus Siculus, a Greek historian who lived in Rome, suggested three to seven million, while Josephus, a Jewish historian who lived in the first century A.D., estimated a population of seven million.[2] Alexandria, one of the largest cities, probably had more than 100,000 inhabitants in the Ptolemaic period.

Estimation of the population of Greece is even more difficult. *The Cambridge Ancient History* commented that "no figures for the total population of the ancient Greek world are available at in any period in its history and evidence for individual cities is scattered and fragmentary."[3] There was one census in the fourth century B.C., taken on the orders of the Macedonian governor. This, according to Athenaeus, an Egyptian Greek active ca. A.D. 200, recorded a population for Athens of 21,000 citizens, 10,000 *metics* (foreign settlers), and 400,000 slaves.[4] This last figure seems a decided overestimate. By the next century the population had increased. Fifth-century Athens is estimated to have had a population of 40,000 citizens and a further 20,000 *metics*. Woman and children may have added another 200,000.[5]

According to the Greek historian Herodotus, Sparta had 8,000 fighting men in 480 B.C., 5,000 of whom were to fight at the Battle of Plataea in 479 B.C.[6] Many men were killed in the earthquake of 454 B.C. A century later there were only 1,200 fighting men, 700 of whom fought at Leuetra in A.D. 371. There the casualties numbered 400.[7] The Greek philosopher Aristotle reported that in his day (late fourth century B.C.) the number had dropped to under 100 of the male population: "Sparta could not succeed in enduring a single blow, but was destroyed by the smallness of her population."[8] From then on Sparta was forced to rely on Helots (labor force of Sparta) to fight its battles. Aristotle concluded that the Spartans had been decimated, because although the state held out inducements for the citizens to have as many children as possible, the practice of dividing the land among all the sons resulted in many men being poor and thus not able to keep up their strength.

The Roman Empire was more widespread, and thus calculations of its population are more difficult. Karl Beloch began a serious study of the population in 1886, and his calculations, on the whole, have stood up to modern evaluation. The population of Rome and its surroundings in the fifth century B.C. was probably about a million, but its governable territory in Italy was only about 4,500 square miles. At the time of the Punic wars the population of the city of Rome was about 100,000–150,000 and that of Carthage about 40,000. The Roman Empire tried to assess the population for taxation purposes. The most famous is perhaps that recorded in St. Luke's Gospel (2: 1–3) when "the decree went out from Caesar Augustus that all the world should be taxed" and so "all went to their own city" to be counted.[9] On the death of Augustus in A.D. 14 the Greek east had a population of 20.4 million and the Latin west had 25.1 million, giving a total population for the empire of 45.5 million. The city of Rome alone then numbered 750,000 and was soon to reach over a million. By the mid-second century the population of the Greek east of the empire had increased to 23.1 million and the Latin west to 38.2 million, giving an overall total of 61.4 million. This seemed to have been the zenith of the empire. The increase in population probably led to an increase in the price of foodstuffs and of land, particularly in the west, which was more heavily cultivated. It was noticeable that there was an increase in the price of wheat in Egypt by about 50 percent. Already, however, there were checks on the increase in population because of a decrease in marriage and fertility rates, and disease was taking its toll. Contact with the Far East through trading routes seemed to have introduced plague, possibly smallpox, into at least Egypt, Syria, Asia Minor, Gaul, Germany, and Greece, taking a heavy toll on human life.[10]

There were constant reoccurrences of this and other diseases, as there seemed to be little immunity. The result was a 10 percent drop in the population of the closely packed cities and military camps, and the decline continued for the rest of the empire. This makes calculations for the rest of the period of the empire totally impossible, and any calculations seemed to be based on individual cities. In A.D. 450, for example, the capital of the eastern empire, Constantinople, was estimated to have between 300,000 and 400,000 people. But a century later it was so devastated by plague that Procopius (a sixth-century A.D. historian) reported that 10,000 people were dying each day.[11]

In one part of the empire, Roman Britain, serious calculations have been attempted, although the figures have varied greatly since the 1920s. The population was first calculated at about half a million, and raised to a million and a half in the 1930s. This figure was obviously too low given the calculation for the population of Iron Age Britain. Present research, based on the discovery of a large number of new sites, suggests that the population may have been between four and six million, and this would include legionaries and auxiliary troops billeted within the province.[12]

The total Celtic population is even more difficult to assess. The population of Britain at the end of the first century B.C. has been estimated at three to four million, based on the fact that the land was studded with settlements, isolated farmsteads, and *oppida* (hill forts), which may have been primitive towns. The population of Gaul has been estimated to be between six to eight million, based on rapid growth in the last two centuries B.C. because of increased food production and migration from central Europe. In A.D. 14 the population of Gaul and the outlying German area was estimated to be 5.8 million. By the late Roman period the population of Gaul alone had probably risen to 12 million.[13]

AGRICULTURAL PRACTICES

The Egyptians

Agricultural practices varied greatly in time and country depending on the type of land available, the climate, agricultural practices, and the political regime. In Egypt cultivation of crops depended on the inundation of the Nile caused by rainfall in central Sudan, which caused an increase in the level of the White Nile. A few weeks later rains in Ethiopia raised the level of the Blue Nile, and the combination of the two rainfalls increased the flow of water into Egypt. The fertile area was confined to a narrow strip on either side of the Nile. This was called the Black Land, from the deposits of black silt brought down the river in flood time. The desert was the Red Land, a district to be distrusted apart from the oases where date palms grew. This was a region subject to a scorching wind, which raised clouds of fine dust and dried out the fields.

So dependent were the Egyptians on the Nile flood that Nilometers along the river registered the level of the water to monitor its progress. These were steps leading to below the water surface and marked on a scale of cubits and fractions of a cubit. The Egyptians dated their year from the first months of inundation, which was then followed by months of sowing and harvesting. The river had a seasonal cycle, which Egyptian poets likened to colored cloth. From January to March there was a green cloth when the crops were growing. From April to June the cloth was gold as the crops ripened, and in July and August there was a black cloth of mud, ready for the planting of the next crop. In less prosaic terms there were three seasons. *Akhet* was the inundation when the river flooded and deposited a fertile layer of silt over the land, *Peret* was the emergence of the land, and *Shemu* was the lack of water or the dry season.

The Nile began to rise in mid-July at Aswan and continued to flood Upper Egypt at different heights at different places until August and Lower Egypt until mid-September. By then the force of the water was

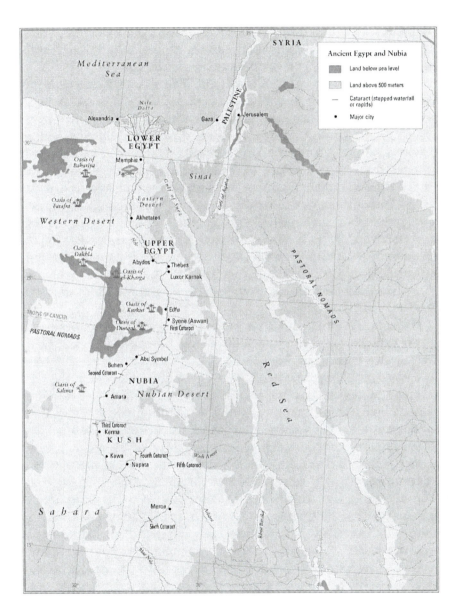

Ancient Egypt and Nubia.

spent as it entered the flat alluvial plains of the northern reaches, and the Egyptians had to react swiftly to get the water onto the land as well as to move their flocks to higher land. In November the water was dropping, but administrators quickly recorded the boundaries of land, partly to prevent legal wrangles over ownership of property and partly to prepare for assessment of taxation later in the year.

Systematic construction of canals and irrigation channels probably began during the First Intermediate Period (2081–2020 B.C.) when a series of low floods occurred that meant radical measures had to be taken to ensure crops were grown. By the time of the Middle Kingdom (2056–1650 B.C.) the procedure was well established. The water was directed from breaches made in the levees into outflow channels and then to fields and plots, far beyond the immediate reaches of the flood. The outflow was controlled by dams, which could be opened and closed when required. When the flood receded, leaving the rich deposit of mud, work began on the land. Irrigation works were implemented, dykes repaired, canals dredged, and weeds cleared. A bonus was that fish entered the plots when the Nile waters covered them so that they could be scooped up to provide a welcome addition to the food supply.

The land was loosened with a hoe or plowed and cross-plowed with a two-handled wooden plow shod with a bronze blade. The fields were strewn with seeds, in quantities carefully allotted to each farmer by an overseer. Sometimes seeds were cast at the same time as the land was plowed so that the plow planted the crop. At other times cattle or pigs trampled seeds into the ground, in addition contributing their own manure to the rich soil. Hard work was required day after day. When the emmer (corn), barley, and flax crops ripened, the assessor scribes arrived to check the probably yield of the harvest, which would be compared with the actual yield after threshing had been completed. The crops were cut with sickles, usually made of wood or an animal jaw spiked with flint teeth, and women and children collected the sheaves in baskets. No attempt was made to weed the fields, so weeds were mixed in with the grain. Cattle trampling on the grain did threshing. Winnowing meant throwing the grains into the air so that the chaff was blown away. The grain was then placed into sacks, and sweepers made sure that every bit of grain was collected.

Scribes now further assessed the quantity of grain, which was usually taken by skiff or punt along the canals to be stored in granaries. These usually took the form of a round-based cone, made of wood or mud bricks, with a domed top. Trapezoidal-shaped granaries held the grain for the next season's sowing so that future crops would be assured. Temples would have their own granaries. At Ramses II's funerary temple at Thebes, the granaries took the form of rows of mud-brick corridors with barrel-vaulted roofs having filling holes in them. The regularity of the floods and this careful husbandry of grain meant that Egypt could feed the population, even in famine conditions, and have a surplus to sell to foreigners, thus gaining a huge profit for the state.

Water was lifted from irrigation channels by buckets carried across the shoulders on a yoke. At the end of the Eighteenth Dynasty the *shaduf* was introduced into Egypt, probably from Mesopotamia. This was a bucket placed on the end of a pole and lifted by means of a counterweight placed at the other end. It allowed a greater amount of water to be lifted on the fields but could be as monotonous and wearisome a job as watering with the buckets. In Ptolemaic times, a cattle-manipulated water wheel (*sahkian* or *saqqieh*) supplemented the *shaduf*. As a far more efficient method of raising water, it continued to serve farmers even after the *tanbur*, Archimedes' screw, was introduced into Egypt about 525 B.C. during the Persian period.

Detail from a wall painting in a tomb at Thebes. A man lifts water from the Nile by means of a *shaduf*. Redrawn from Sir John Gardner Wilkinson, *The Manners and Customs of the Ancient Egyptians*, 1837.

Once the grain harvest was over at the end of March, a second crop could be grown. There was sometimes another cereal but more often pulses, which were especially regarded as fertilizing the land. These crops enrich the soil with nitrogen. In addition, rectangular beds surrounded by low dykes that could be used as paths were used to grow vegetables. Plots at the fortress of Mirgissa covered areas of 13 square meters (42.6 square feet) with small irrigation channels. In these were grown vegetables for home consumption or sale. The tax collectors assessed these also, and Horemheb (a general and advisor to the pharaohs in the eighteenth dynasty), for example, forbade his officials to plunder the land by taking the best vegetables and keeping them for their own use. Strict rules were laid down to prevent anyone from obstructing another person in the use of water or blocking a neighbor's supply. More and more land was brought into use, allowing Egypt to become one of the richest food-producing areas in the ancient world. By the Twelfth Dynasty the delta had been drained and part of the Fayum reclaimed, with Lake Moeris being used as a reservoir. The final extension of cultivated land in the Fayum had to wait until the Ptolemaic period.

The Egyptians also had many orchards that needed artificial irrigation, either from a well or a pool. These were walled to keep out thieves or animals. The ground could be flooded, although care had to be taken that the water did not reach too far up the trees. An Egyptian proverb, "If the gardener becomes a fisherman, let his trees perish," may refer to this. The orchards contained a variety of fruit trees, including date and doum palms and carob, apricot, Egyptian plum, and fig trees. The Eighteenth Dynasty tomb of Ana had a list of trees, which seems to have included almost every tree known at the time. The trees were planted in rows with the water channels running between them. Water might also be preserved, for aesthetic purposes, in square pools surrounded by brick or mud walls. Trees were planted for shade and for their association with deities, while flowers were grown purely for the enjoyment they gave. Vines were grown supported by trellises, both for their shade and for their fruit. In addition, garden plots were tended both for culinary and nonculinary plants. For the poor they could include pens for geese; for the wealthy they might hold a menagerie.

Tomb paintings show the gardeners bringing produce to the owners of the gardens. An inscription from one tomb instructed the gardeners to "take great care, hoe all the land, sieve the earth with a sieve, hack with your noses in the work."[14] The hard work needed in a garden and an orchard was recorded in a poem, for many gardeners, like field workers, were bound for life to the owner:

> The gardener carries a yoke.
> His shoulders are bent with age;
> There is a swelling on his neck
> And it festers.
>
> In the morning he waters vegetables,
> While at noon he toils in the orchard.
> He works himself to death,
> More than in all other professions.[15]

All land in Egypt was owned by the state, either by the pharaoh directly or by the temples and the nobles who had received land as a gift from the pharaoh. The laborers were peasant farmers, who were allotted a plot that they rented through taxation, mainly in kind, and to which they were tied for life, with most of the produce going to the landowner or the state. Stewards superintended these. If peasants could not pay their taxes, they were mercilessly punished, as revealed by tomb paintings, which show them being beaten by overseers. In the New Kingdom (1570–1069 B.C.) this tight control lessened. Land was divided into large estates and smallholdings, which could be bought and sold. By the Third Intermediate Period (1070–656 B.C.) the state had almost lost its authority over the peasantry. Land became part of inheritance and could sold with ease.

Probably about a third of the population was involved in agriculture, which was regarded as a gift from the god Osiris, although people could have more than one job. In addition, there were herdsmen who looked after cattle and sheep belonging to estate owners and temples, but their status was regarded as a low one, with criticism being made of their rough clothing, lack of personal hygiene, and habit of living in reed huts that were easily built and dismantled. They moved their animals about to get better pasturage, often feeding them by hand. Many herds were driven to the delta from the upland areas to obtain better grazing. Usually herdsmen specialized in tending only one type of animal—sheep, long-horned cattle, goats, pigs, or horses. Herds were very large, which may have led to overgrazing, but large herds were regarded as necessary to provide an emergency food supply. Herdsmen had to ensure that the cattle were fed and to brand them for identification, usually on the horns. During the dry season the herds were driven to the marshland of the delta. Livestock breeders had a higher status because they fattened beef cattle, and taste and quality were appreciated.

Some men tended flocks of geese on special poultry farms, and in paintings on Middle Kingdom tombs there seems to be evidence for crane farming. As these animals and birds were also assessed for taxation purposes, the care taken for their welfare had to be as vigilant as that of the farmer for his crops. Animals were held in high regard. Some, as Herodotus said, were part of the household, and great care was taken of them.[16]

Fishermen were also regarded as being of low status, partly because fish smelled and went bad easily, so that the smell often clung to their garments. One tomb recorded, "behold my name stinks more than a catch of fish on a hot day."[17] Fish, however, caught in the Nile and its canals as well as on Lake Moeris provided protein for the Egyptian diet. Paintings in the tomb of Kagemni at Saqqara show fishermen taking their catch from the sea, having it recorded by scribes, and giving some to local officials as a tax. The remainder was presumably traded. Marketing scenes indicated their value. One fish equaled a loaf of bread or a jar of beer. Fish were caught by rod and line, in traps, and by teams using a dragnet. Fishermen's work was especially dangerous, for much of the water was home to hippopotamuses and crocodiles.

The Greeks

The Greeks included not only those living in the Balkan peninsula but also those settled in Asia Minor, Sicily, southern Italy, southern France, and the numerous Aegean islands. They recognized a common language, religious beliefs, and kinship and regarded those living without those attributes as "barbarians." The name *Greece* or *Hellas* for the land had little or no significance in the ancient world, for Greece was not regarded as an entity or a country. The Greeks never formed a nation or country as a united whole until conquered first by Macedonia and then by Rome. Rather, the country was divided into city-states, of which the three greatest were Athens, Sparta, and Thebes. Each city-state was resolutely determined to remain independent, with its own legal and political institutions, coinage, and system of weights and measures.

This was basically a result of the Greek landscape, which was less accommodating toward its people than that of the Egyptians. Greece is a mountainous land, having sparse vegetation and few trees, although

Ancient Greece.

the land was probably more wooded in ancient times than it is now. The mountainous regions have been estimated to cover at least four-fifths of the landmass. There is little constant water, for although the rivers may be full to overflowing in spring and winter, they dry up in summer. Only a few rivers, such as the Peneus in Thessaly, retained a constant flow. The prominent mountain ranges, which cut off one area from another, accounted for the individualism of the different areas of Greece and the lack of unity between those areas. The city-states were founded on the small basins, plains, and coastal creeks existing between the mountains. Until the Roman subjugation, there were few roads to link these, and they were merely narrow, badly maintained dirt tracks. When there were threats from outside, such as the Persian invasions, the Greeks formed alliances, which soon disintegrated once the danger had passed.

The climate also shaped the Greek character, making it seem harsh and uncompromising to those who did not accept the conditions by which the city-states were governed. Hot, dry summers gave way to wetter conditions in the autumn, with more rain falling in the west from the prevailing winds than in the east. Winters could be cold, with bitter north winds, and the mountain peaks were covered with snow. Hesiod, a Greek poet of the sixth century B.C., remarked in his poem *Works and Days* that his father came from Cyme in Asia Minor to Boeotia and settled in "a miserable hamlet called Ascra." Hesiod worked as a shepherd on Mount Helicon and therefore experienced climatic conditions: "bad in winter, oppressive in summer, good at no time."[18]

Greece has a long jagged coastline with few really good harbors. The sea was also regarded as an enemy, hostile and indifferent to the fate of men. In Homer's *The Odyssey*, Odysseus found this out as he tried to make his way back to Ithaca, a journey that took nine years. Homer's details of the hostility of the god Poseidon were intended to indicate the capriciousness of the elements. But the sea provided Greece with three benefits. First, as the inland roads were so bad, the Greeks preferred to travel by sea in the summer months, and thus built up resilience to the hostile elements. As the sea also penetrated inland in a series of creeks, this method of travel became both the natural preferred way of transporting goods and a means of obtaining food. Ships could take an average cargo of from 70 to 400 tons burden, and the *Syrakosia,* built under the supervision of Archimedes about 240 B.C., was reputed to have three decks and carry a cargo of 2,000 tons. Ships were even hauled across the Isthmus of Corinth to enable merchants to avoid the hazardous journey around the Peloponnese, a feat that allowed Corinth to take a toll for this.

The sea also provided fish, which played an important role in the diet of the coastal regions. The Athenians in particular relied on fish for their protein more than meat. Eventually the word *opson,* which covered everything eaten with bread, gradually came to mean fish and fish products, so that bread and fish became the staple diet of the population. Impromptu markets were set up where fish could be sold as soon as they were landed, and fish were swiftly conveyed to urban markets, especially that in the Athenian agora. Independent-minded fishermen therefore, in contrast to those in Egypt, were regarded with respect.

Although Greece lacked the soil and climate suitable for growing much wheat, parts of the country were rich in marble and minerals, especially lead and silver. These were exported particularly by Athenians, whose proximity to the seacoast allowed them to exploit the trade.

Athenian power was based on the fact that it was near the sea and could export marble and import wheat relatively easily. It thus became an innovative state, whereas landlocked Sparta remained conservative, lacking enterprise and strictly controlling its citizens, especially in food. The seagoing Greeks were able to use the sea to colonize other areas, especially the Ionian coastline in Asia Minor, the islands of the Aegean, and coastal areas in North Africa and Italy. This again increased their trading advantages, allowing them to import food, wine, and other goods.

The soil of Greece was relatively infertile, and crop growing was not helped by the frequent droughts. Attica in particular was bemoaned by ancient writers for its dry, stony soil. What this did mean, however, was that every piece of land in the narrow valleys was cultivated, and the Greek countryside was as carefully managed as the polis, the city-state, incorporating both the town and the surrounding rural area, so that landowning and obligations to citizenship were side by side. Often a small number of wealthy male landowners held the largest portions of land, while the rest was left to a majority of small landowners and the peasant class. Only in Sparta, and possibly Crete, did women have the right to own land. Land was often divided between sons, but it could be amalgamated by purchase or marriage, so there was constant change in ownership, leaving holdings scattered. This meant that the land could be more easily managed from a town or village than from a farmstead situated on one plot. Land could be let to tenant or peasant farmers or worked by laborers or slaves.

Slaves were often non-Greeks captured in war. This may have been the case in Athens but was particularly true of Sparta, which did not send out colonists and therefore had to rely more on its own produce for sustenance. Its only great colony was at Taras (modern Taranto in Italy). Wanting more territory, in about 720 B.C. it invaded neighboring Messenia and enslaved its people as Helots. Those men who were not, at first, drafted into the Spartan army were allowed to farm the land, but had to give up most of their produce to feed the Spartans. Later, individual Spartan households were linked to individual Helot households, in effect owning them so that they could pass them on to heirs or to other Spartans.

The main crops grown were the Mediterranean staples: cereals, olives, and vines. The cereal crop was mainly barley, which was suitable to the dry climate and could be grown almost anywhere. Millet was grown in northern Greece. The Boeotian Plain was one of the best areas for wheat. In the third century B.C., when Athens was under the domination of Macedonian kingship, the cities did not enjoy the freedom in democracy that they had had before. Certain material benefits were, however, conferred on cities. The most important of these, apart from a series of new building projects, was that there was a more reliable supply of food. When shortages occurred, the kings paid for wheat shipments, so that the citizens were not reliant on oats and barley and less nourishing crops.

The most popular tree was the olive, which, being very adaptable, could grow in poor conditions and produced both oil and an important staple food. The earliest vineyards had been planted in the third millennium B.C. when vines were brought from Asia Minor. Mostly there were small plots belonging to aristocratic producers and exporters. The poorer classes did not plant vines until Solon, the Athenian lawgiver, in the sixth century B.C. permitted them to do this. Dwarf vines were cultivated on small plots. Larger vineyards with better vines, grown on low cordons or layered along the soil to protect them from summer winds, were established on the plains. Some grapes were pressed for wine, with smaller estates joining together for the pressing, but many grapes were dried as raisins or eaten as fruit. Small garden plots grew vegetables and herbs, and orchards were established, one of the main crops being figs, another important staple. In some areas there was the risk of food running short in a very dry season, and Athens and other city-states had to rely on imports of wheat and wine to survive. Other important crops were legumes and fruit trees. The Greeks became adept at grafting and propagating trees and at cropping other crops between the trees, so that as much land was used as possible.

Cattle rearing could only take place in the valleys and on the coastal plains. The best pasturage was in Boeotia and Thessaly, where the homes of wealthy cattle barons were sited. Horse breeding also took place on the plains of Thessaly. As the hill soil was often poor and stony and covered with *maquis,* dense undergrowth sometimes up to four meters (13 feet) high, pigs, sheep, and goats were the most common form of animal husbandry, because they ate leaves, weeds, and scrubby vegetation. Holm oaks and Kermes oaks produced acorns on which pigs would feed happily. A by-product was the manure that all the animals produced, which helped to fertilize the land.

There was a romantic fondness for the countryside, which was obvious in classical literature. In the Greek poet Aristophanes' play *The Peace,* Trygaeus recalled his country life: "I long to be in the country and start hoeing my plot of earth. Recall the old life we once had, which Peace made possible for us—fresh and dried figs, myrtle and the sweet new wine, the bed of violets beside the well, the olive trees we miss."[19] Dicaeopolis, in Aristophanes' play *The Acharnians,* commented, "I gaze towards the countryside, yearning for my own place, loathing the city, missing my former village, where you never heard the word 'buy'; we never bought charcoal, cheap wine, oil or anything; our land let us 'buy' there."[20] Allowing for an element of poetic license, especially as Aristophanes is emphasizing the benefit of peace over war, there was possibly more than a grain of truth in the feeling that a countryman controlled his own lifestyle. One advantage the Greeks did have was in the wild regions. There was abundant game, so that hare, wild boar, and deer could be hunted for food, not for sport, and wild fowl, partridges, quails, and larks trapped.

The Greek agricultural year began in the autumn when the rains arrived. First, religious festivals for Demeter, the goddess of corn and the fruits of the earth, were held as being essential to ensure crops would grow. The most important of these was the *Thesmophoria,* in which the central element was the sacrifice of a pig. The land was cross-plowed with a wooden plow and the seeds sown at the same time between October and December—first barley and then wheat. Legumes could be sown at the same time. During this season vines and fruit trees were pruned. Trenches were dug around trees and other plants so that as much water as possible would get to the roots. Later the earth would be stacked around the trunks to conserve the moisture. Olive trees fruit once every two years, so during that time the olives were picked and pressed or made ready to eat. At the end of these activities, further festivals in honor of Demeter and Dionysus took place.

In February agricultural activities resumed, when more pruning was needed. Spring-sown cereals, vegetables, and legumes could be sown during March and April, with extensive raking and tilling of the land to get rid of sprouting weeds. Harvesting of wheat with iron sickles took place from May to July. The wheat was put onto stone threshing floors and trampled on by animals. Winnowing was done in the usual manner of throwing it in the air. The stubble was burned to help fertilize the land over which dung was spread. By now fruit picking was taking place, and there was a lull in the farming activity. More intense activity came in late August and September, when the grapes had to be gathered and dried or pressed into wine. Once this had been done the agricultural year began again. Sometimes the land was left fallow for one or two years to recover its fertility. On the whole the Greeks clung

to traditional methods, partly because the aristocracy despised technological improvements and partly because the vast amount of slave
labor encouraged them to follow what they believed to be their role in
political life rather than concentrate on agriculture. It was the Romans
who, in spite of retaining slavery, pushed forward new ideas that
helped to increase agricultural yield.

The Romans

Whereas the Greeks followed only one crop and fallow rotation, the
Romans progressed further in their agricultural matters, for they
developed a system of different crop rotations.[21] Winter wheat needed
rich soil, and so was sown every second year. Barley was sown in very
rich or very poor soil, as the Roman agricultural writer Columella suggested that "the land is weakened by this crop."[22] After cropping the
ground had to be manured. Beans and other pulses could then be
planted in rich soil between crops of wheat and barley. The Romans
might not have known about the nitrogen-giving properties of
legumes, but they realized the value of green manuring. Roman writers stressed the value of vines and olives. Those, together with grain
and vegetables, would allow a farm to become almost self-supporting.
Columella recommended growing wheat between olive trees, because
the trees bear a crop only in alternate years, and so the wheat would
provide a cash crop in the year when there were no olives.[23]

Improvements came in the form of agricultural implements: an
improved auger for bore grafting and the scythe to enable the corn to
be reaped more quickly. A more efficient plow was introduced with a
coulter, which turned the sod. The Roman agricultural writer Varro
mentioned an improved threshing sledge (*plostellum poenicum*) and the
Latin scholar and writer Pliny the Elder a hand-operated reaping comb
(*pectum manualis*), which would lead to the improved Gallo-Roman
vallus used in Gallo-Belgica.[24] Even the application of dung was given
serious consideration. As well as animal manure, pigeon dung, and even
human excrement, olive oil dregs were placed around trees, and lupine,
legumes, and compost were plowed into the soil. Near the seacoast
ground-up oyster shells were used to give the soil more aeration.
Better breeding of sheep and cattle enabled stock to be improved, and
new plants were introduced almost as soon as the Romans expanded
their empire into other areas. For the Romans, the working of the
agricultural year and the celebration of its accompanying festivals
were similar to that of the Greeks, although once the empire had

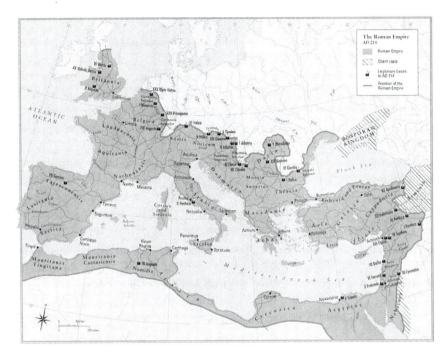

The Roman Empire.

expanded, times of sowing and harvest depended on the regions where farms were established.

As well as land use, what concerned the Romans was ownership. Land meant wealth, and the acquisition of it became a priority. Land also meant the rights to citizenship. The chief landowners in any city or town held positions on the ruling council or were elected to the main offices of power. But ownership, be it that of a peasant farmer or an aristocrat of great estates, also satisfied a need to be part of country life, to get back to rural roots. Even speculators and investors in land, whom Cicero (first-century B.C. orator and historian) referred to as preferring "an income from city property to one derived from the farm" (that is, investing the profits of their trade in land), felt this.[25] Most of the descriptions of country life, as in the Roman poet Virgil's *Georgics,* extol its virtues with more than a little poetic license—even sentimental idealism—but Cato in the second century B.C., Columella in the first century A.D., and Palladius (a fourth-century A.D. writer) in the late empire wrote practical manuals to help farmers and estate owners. Varro in the late first century B.C. wrote his manual when he was in his 80s as a guide for his younger wife, who had just bought a property. His advice, however, could be useful to any estate owner. Pliny the Elder's first-century A.D. encyclopedic *Natural History* gave useful descriptions of plant, animal, and inanimate forms. Possibly the manuals leaned heavily toward idealized estates, and Pliny the Younger's (a nephew of the elder Pliny who wrote a valuable collection of letters) description of his villa in Tuscany in the first century A.D. has suspicious similarities to these.[26]

The system of land ownership and working covered a wide variety of interests, partly because as the empire expanded it absorbed local agricultural customs. Land could be owned by the state or by owners living on the estate or in the town, leaving a bailiff to manage the property. Free peasants could own land and work the farm with their families. Other peasants would rent land but pay for it with part of their produce. There were peasants who hired themselves out to owners of large estates for long or short periods, essential at times of harvest. Sometimes these had a contract for a share of the harvest. In the Roman provinces there were many who hired themselves out to pay off debts. Agricultural slaves could be in bondage to their owners, either living permanently on the estate or being hired on contract when needed. The system of slavery meant that labor was always available when needed at busy times of the year. Cato's *De Agri Cultura* illustrated the ideal estate, situated probably in the Campania near to Rome, based on about 40 hectares (100 acres) of land operated with a freedman manager supervising about 50 slaves who could be fully employed throughout the year.

Tenant farmers were particularly important, as they provided a solution to the problem of an owner working an estate distant from his usual home, and which he visited infrequently. It was especially useful for those who lived in a town. There was always a risk that the tenant might not be able to pay his rent or neglect the property, or that the owner might dismiss the tenant at short notice. Therefore the system came to be carefully regulated in Roman law. It served both sides well except in times of unrest, as happened in the provinces in periods in the third and fourth centuries.

Peasant farmers were subsistence farmers in that they consumed almost all they produced. If there was any surplus, it was taken to the local market to exchange for essential goods. A careful control had to be kept on the type of crops grown to ensure they would feed the household or could be sold at a profit. If there was a drought or the weather was bad, resulting in a poor harvest, the peasants were near starvation. Unrest in the countryside meant the risk of having the crops taken by marauders, and, above all, the taxman had to be paid. Most peasants were satisfied with the minimum they could make utilizing any unexpected surplus as a cash crop that could avoid rural debt, which remained a problem throughout the Roman period. It was only the more ambitious who were willing to increase the surplus and invest in larger properties. When this happened they might find that they had become liable to higher taxation. All agricultural land was taxed, so the best use had to be made of it. Landowners had to supply the army with grain, hides, and produce or the tax collector with cash.

One difficulty was the laws of inheritance, which insisted that fathers had to provide for sons. Splitting the land could mean the eldest sons had the largest portion, so that younger sons might have to find themselves new jobs or properties. Many joined the army, thus proving a ready supply of manpower. But the empire produced another solution—expand to take on new land, which at first became state-owned land (*ager publicus*). Hence the remorseless conquest of other areas from the late republic period until the second century A.D., which allowed land to be taken over and bought by or given to the ambitious. Soldiers were settled in colonia and given land after 25 years' service. Colonia (colonae, pl.) were towns established first by the Emperor Augustus to settle veretans who were retired from the army. They were expected to set an example to Romanize the province when they were settled. This provided a solution to the problem of retiring veterans and also ensured that the concept of Romanization was part of political policy in most parts of the empire. In turn, because many of the veterans by the late first century had not been recruited in Italy, this produced a polyglot empire of different groups and "nationalities" united under Roman law.

The great landowners, many from the senatorial or equestrian ranks, had their own problems and ambitions. In the republic the ideal had been Cincinnatus, elected consul in 460 B.C., who negotiated in the struggle between the patricians and the plebeians and then returned to his farm. Called on again in 458 B.C. to fight the Etruscans and the Volscians, he helped to defeat them, refused to accept dictatorial power, and once again returned to his farm. In the empire, farms and villas were the homes of their owners, who viewed the estate as land for investment to provide a secure income, act as a status symbol, or assist in advancement to senatorial or other ranks. The estate was classified in the census, and neglect of it could entail punishment. Some men bought estates to provide pleasure and a relaxed life; others specialized in growing certain crops to provide a larger income. A villa might provide a retirement home after a career in public service. Some men helped other men to buy smaller estates, as Pliny the Younger did for his friend, the Roman historian Suetonius. Pliny, in fact, had not just one estate but, like many others, had acquired a number of them. Estates, large and small, acquired by purchase, gift, or inheritance, might be situated over Italy or even the empire; hence the need for bailiffs or tenant farmers. Sometimes land would be worked from a base inside town. At Pompeii and Herculaneum, large numbers of agricultural implements found in town houses, for instance in the House of Menander, seem to be too many to use in the attached garden. These could have been used by the household to cultivate land elsewhere. They may, however, have been stored there on a temporary basis or have been used for other purposes.

Not everyone owned a number of estates. For some owners, especially in the provinces, a villa was their only home; a working farm had to provide an income for the family. It still provided status in society. If the villa was expanded, and many were in the third and fourth centuries A.D., with magnificent dining rooms and other apartments, this was the reward for investment in the estate and also reflected the owner's social standing. For them the aim was profitability. Cato gave advice on this, and in doing so touches on the need for excellent storage, including a well-built barn and plenty of vats for oil and wine. This is because not only will the owner benefit from good prices, but also "it will redound to his wealth, his self-respect and his reputation."[27] Under no circumstances must the property decline in value, for this might have affected the displays of *liberalitas,* which were an essential part of public life. The surplus on the estate produced wealth for owners to provide gifts to the community in the form of public feasts and buildings.

Some officials and military men who bought villas introduced new plants, which they had brought back with them from their campaigns. The expansion of the empire also introduced new fruits, vegetables, and herbs. Better breeding methods were established in the provinces, thus benefiting local agriculture. But the villa owners were concerned only with their own properties. There was no wish to buy run-down properties to improve them. The most sought-after properties were prosperous ones, which provided a good income. What mattered was social standing as compared to the estates of other owners. Acquisition of land, no matter how poor the land, was valued more than improvement to increase the value of all estates.

The Celts

The Celts, whose area stretched from Spain and France in western Europe to the Balkans and as far as Turkey, were originally a tribal nomadic people. Caesar's (the Roman general and politician Julius Caesar who invaded and conquered Gaul in the first century A.D.) portrayal of the Gallic Celts described two "classes of people of account and dignity," which indicates the makeup of society.[28] One was the priesthood of the Druids; the other was the nobles. Some of the nobles had great power and had numerous retainers, warriors, and clients who served them and, in turn, were given protection. Land seems to have been held in common by the tribe, with grazing rights granted to individuals. Wealth centered on livestock, and it was the possession of the herds that mattered. There was therefore no state ownership of land and no general taxation in Celtic areas until their conquest by the Romans. Individual taxation and customs systems were under the control of a tribe or the local chieftain. The struggle for control of these and for land often led to unstable and violent politics.

Much of the land was well populated, with social groups based more on kinship and community than political structure. There were tribal centers, often hill forts, which were also used as refuges in war, where the hereditary or elected chieftain lived surrounded by his warriors and their families. Tribal subdivisions, usually kin groups, known later to the Romans as *pagi*, occupied smaller territories. Nomadic practices gradually gave way to settled villages, gathering places for religious use, and isolated long or round houses surrounded by fields, many of which have been revealed by aerial photography. Individual extended family and client groups owing loyalty to the tribal chieftain occupied these. In return for this protection, livestock and produce were provided as tribute. Wealth came from war, which had a key role in volatile Celtic society, and, as in other civilizations, persons captured in war were enslaved to serve nobles and wealthy families or even to be included among export commodities.

Society was rural, based on crops, herds, and land management. Fields and stockyards surrounded small villages and isolated farmsteads. Stone or earth boundaries of earth and stone, with abrupt linear slopes, known as *lynchets*, reveal the remains of fields. When the fields were plowed, heaps of stones were placed on the sides of the fields, creating higher boundaries, which defined the plots. The fields were square, being rarely more than 120 by 80 meters (400 by 260 feet) and often smaller. Their width was often greater in proportion to their length. This was necessary to help cross-plowing by the *ard*, a simple wood or stone plow that could not turn the soil, but scratched or broke up the earth. Some farmers used pigs to root up the soil. In the wetter areas of northern Europe, a heavier plow was developed, which turned the soil and led to longer strips of plow land. Celtic-Teutonic tribes living in the German areas first made these innovations, but they soon spread throughout Celtic Europe.

Once the ground had been prepared in the spring, seeds were sown, basically emmer and spelt, barley, and oats. Einkorn had been one of the earlier crops. Millet was a popular crop in Gaul, and rye in the more northerly areas. Sowing could be done by a dibbing stick, which made holes, or a sowing stick, which when drawn across the ground made a long furrow. After the seeds were sown, the earth was then scuffed over. Once the corn had ripened, it was cut with flint sickles, or more probably the ears were plucked off with fingers. It was then threshed with a flail or by allowing animals to trample on it and winnowed by the traditional methods. In some areas it was possible to sow emmer and spelt in the autumn, that is, winter sowing to produce an early spring crop.

Instead of silos and granaries, the Celts preserved their grain in pits, many containing an average capacity of one ton. Experiments carried out in Britain and elsewhere proved that grain can be kept successfully during winter months by this method. Grain was put into pits after harvesting, and the mouths were sealed with a clay or wood covering extending beyond the circumference of the pit. Provided the pit was airtight, the grain coming into contact with the damp clay, chalk, or basket-lined pit walls germinated using the available oxygen and releasing carbon dioxide. This halted further germination, preserving it in suspended animation, enabling it to keep almost perfectly for several months. The pit could be opened for some grain to be removed and then resealed. Pits were dug for individual households, and at some hill forts the occupants had cut hundreds of pits. Probably not all were in use at one time, for pits could become sour and had to be abandoned. But the large number suggests storage capacity on a huge scale. Careful layout of pits along tracks suggests the hand of an organizing authority. As well as pits, there were four-post structures covered with thatched roofs, which may have been used as granaries or to hold pottery jars filled with other commodities.

Other crops grown included beans, peas, and lentils. Vegetable plots were small, and much of the food was gathered from the wild. If there were tended orchards, they were small, and no evidence has been found to indicate growing on a commercial scale. Food was grown for household use, with some going as tribute to the aristocratic protector. Beer (resembling barley ale) was brewed, and wine (for which the Celts in Gaul soon developed an inordinate fondness) was imported into Celtic areas. Diodorus reported that the Gauls would exchange a slave for an amphora of wine.

The farmers tended individual herds, mainly sheep, cattle, goats, and pigs. All these animals were smaller than those bred in modern times. Sheep were exploited for their milk, cheese, and wool, which was plucked rather than shorn. These were akin to the modern Soay sheep, which still exists on the St. Kilda Islands in the Outer Hebrides in Scotland. The Celtic shorthorn cattle, now extinct, may have been akin to the small Kerry cattle found in Ireland. Pigs were also smaller and were allowed to roam wild in extensive woodlands, which were carefully managed as much for their timber and fuel as for the animals. Meat, especially pork, was an essential part of Celtic diet.

By the end of the Iron Age in the first century B.C. there was more extensive use of land. Woodlands were being cleared at an unprecedented rate, and the wetter heavy-clay valleys, which had been regarded as unproductive land, were being plowed with a heavier plow. Farming was no longer subsistence farming but was producing fairly reliable surpluses, which in turn supported the growing population. Surpluses would have been necessary, for although the Celts were not an urban population, by the end of the second century B.C. large straggling settlements, referred to by Caesar as *oppida,* had appeared in an area that stretched from middle Europe through central France and into southern Britain. The farming community would have to support people living in the *oppida* as well as craftsmen, metalworkers, and the nonproductive warrior class. Nevertheless, life was not secure. Crop disease was a problem, and soil erosion and depletion have been deduced in France and Britain. Caesar indicated that the crop failures and famine caused unrest in Gaul.

By the first century B.C. in Gaul, Greco-Roman culture was acting as a catalyst for change. Imports increased, and Rome and Massalia (Marseilles) were having an increasing influence as examples of urbanized government. Rome established trading and diplomatic links in Gaul and in Britain, so that central Gaul became partly Romanized, and later southern Britain became susceptible to Roman influence. By this time Rome was also becoming interested in the wealth of those areas. The vulnerability of the political system caused by the tribal feuding and unrest among powerful cliques gave Rome the opportunity for conquest.

Caesar's invasion of Gaul began the process of ensuring that the Celts were compelled to move, whether they wished it or not, toward an urban classical civilization, with its economy based on town life.

TRADE

Trade in the ancient world was based on local markets, providing opportunities for buying, selling, and bartering of local products, which were vitally necessary to landowners to obtain commodities they lacked or to raise money to pay off debts and taxes. Small landowners may have preferred gift exchange or bartering, as was the case in classical Greece, where ritualized friendship operated in the exchange of goods. Large landowners, however, might aim to have a surplus for sale to increase their wealth, rebuild part of the estate, or distribute among their clients. These markets could be established in towns or nodal points in the countryside. Occasional markets or fairs, often held at religious sites, were not only means of worshipping deities but additional opportunities for trading and feasting. These markets encouraged even small landowners to produce a surplus by which even a one-man farm could benefit. The poem "Moretum," written by an anonymous author in the early first century A.D., recounts how the lowly peasant Simulus, having prepared his sparse morning meal, goes to till his vegetable plot. The vegetables are not for his own use but to take to market. He goes to the city carrying on his shoulder a bundle of produce, which, having sold, allows him to return home with his pockets heavy with money. This is not barter or gift exchange, but the means of gaining cash for a cash crop.

Local markets could be set up ad hoc in Greece, but often the polis incorporated them into its agora. Roman emperors built huge buildings to house them—witness the impressive *marcella* (markets) that Trajan built in Rome. Rome also had its fish market, meat market, and wholesale market. Other cities and towns throughout the empire copied these, although on a smaller scale. Markets were so important in the Roman Empire that permission had to be secured from the local council and in Rome from the Senate. One of the main reasons for the control of markets was to protect existing markets from undue competition. Pliny the Younger recorded that a praetorian senator asked the permission of the Senate to hold a weekly market on his property, but representatives of the nearby town of Vicetia (modern Vicenza) opposed this because they feared it would take away their trade.[29] Inscriptions record that local markets were held in a traditional sequence to avoid a clash of dates.

Long-distance trade was more important. Egypt had established trading links with neighboring countries, and in the New Kingdom these increased as trade ceased to be a royal monopoly, even though the expedition that Queen Hatshepsut (1473–1458 B.C.) sent to the land of Punt was deemed to be one of the most significant features of her reign. Egypt established trading links with countries in the Middle and Near East, exporting grain, dried fish, cloth, and papyrus. In return, copper came from Cyprus, and ebony, ivory, cattle, and other animals from south of that region, links that were to continue.

Greece expanded its trade, basing this on the colonies it had established through the Aegean and to southern Italy and Gaul. Even the wealthier Celts sought trade with the Greeks and Romans, seeking luxury objects by which they could enhance their standing. Many handsome objects found in Celtic graves had come from those regions. In the last two centuries B.C., Gaul and to a lesser extent Britain had begun to import goods on a large scale. The Greek historian Strabo mentioned that Celtic Britain's exports included hunting dogs, cattle, hides, iron, precious metals, grain, and slaves.[30]

Many of the landowners refused or were reluctant to become associated with trade because of the risks this could entail. This allowed opportunities for middlemen to become involved in making contracts with the landowners to market or export their goods. The classical world built up a class of *negotiatores* who would carry out business deals and even supply manpower to an estate, such as that needed for picking and pressing grapes at the harvest. Many *negotiatores* were of high status, some from the *equites* class, other being wealthy freedmen. They could be based in Rome or in the provinces and were usually to be found in the major ports, where they used their connections with overseas markets to promote trade, set up deals, and see that they were completed. This was particularly important in dealing with shippers and with merchants who wished to hire part of the space in a ship for their cargoes. Many deals would have collapsed without their aid. This went beyond trading matters, for they were useful in securing land, collecting taxes, and even loaning cash. By the first century A.D. they were specializing, so that inscriptions record a dealer in oil (*negotiator olearius*) and a dealer in wine (*negotiator vinarius*). Their activities were strictly controlled by law, and Roman jurists were constantly involved with the minute details of commercial legislation.

Trade was not confined to the Roman Empire. Once the Romans had subsumed Egypt after 14 A.D., they had access to a vast emporium of spices, but they wished to go farther because they knew that spices came from more distant lands. The greatest advance in long-distance trade was made during the reign of Emperor Claudius (A.D. 40–54), when a Greek merchant, Hippalus, who sailed from the Red Sea to the Indian Ocean, elucidated the wind system of the monsoon. As the southwest monsoon prevailed from April to October and the northeast from October to April, it became possible to sail from the Egyptian port of Berenice to Calicut in India in 70 days and to make the return journey within the year. Ships would leave port in July and use the winds to reach the mouth of the Ganges or the Malabar Coast in south India, and then return in November loaded with the products of the East. Their cargo would then be transferred overland to Alexandria and other ports for shipment to Rome, from where it would be distributed elsewhere. The discovery of the route reduced the dependency of Rome on the Arabian overland route. Trade with India increased even more when an unknown writer in the first century A.D. published *The Periplus of the Erythraean Sea,* detailing the harbors, sea conditions, and safest routes to the East. The spice trade improved enormously, and Rome became the distribution center for the empire. In A.D. 166 Roman merchants reached the Han capitol in China, thus sealing Rome's contact with the East. Spices, especially pepper, flowed into Rome from China and India, together with ivory, pearls, gemstones, and silk.

Trade also resulted from two other causes. The first was that wheat had to be transferred to Rome to feed its population. The catch-phrase "bread and circuses" reflected the vital truth that the populace of Rome had to be fed and entertained to prevent popular unrest.[31] Almost half the population of Rome subsisted on imported wheat, much of it coming from Egypt, regarded as the breadbasket of the empire. *Negotiatores* were responsible for moving this load to Ostia, where great granaries had been built to store the grain before transfer along the Tiber to Rome and into other warehouses around the area of the Aventine. Emperor Claudius had been adamant that induce-ments had to be made to ensure traders had the ships to transport the grain. The second was the necessity of supplying the army, and from the late second century B.C., the state had to ensure that the army was fed. This entailed moving supplies to legions and auxiliaries in the provinces. Although the troops were eventually drawn from those provinces and might therefore be accustomed to eating their own type of food, the commissariat had to supply the garrisons with such items as wine, *liquamen,* and olive oil. This trade was again the work of *negotiatores,* and the success of their endeavors can be seen, for example, by the lists of goods that have survived on the wooden writing tables found at Vindolanda.

The vast array of local goods on sale is summed up by Cato: "Tunics, togas, blankets, smocks and shoes should be bought in Rome; caps, iron tools, scythes, spades, mattocks, axes, harness, ornaments, and small chains at Cales and Minturnae; spades at Venafrum; carts and sledges at Suessa and in Lucania; jars and pots at Alba and Rome; and tiles at Venafrum ... oil mills at Pompeii, and at Rufrius's yard at Nola; nails and bars at Rome; pails, oil-urns, water pitchers, other copper vessels at Capua and Nola; Campanian buckets from Capua will be found useful; pulley ropes and all sorts of cordage at Capua; Roman baskets at Suessa and Casinum ... at Rome will be found the best."[32] For international trade the words of the Revelation of St. John the Divine (Rev. 18:11 AV), believed to date from the end of the first century A.D., can suffice to sum up the products of Rome: "And the merchants of the earth shall weep and mourn over her; for no man buyeth their merchandise any more. The merchandise of gold, silver and precious stones and of pearls and fine linen, and purple and silk, all kinds of wood, and all manner of vessels of ivory; vessels of precious wood and of brass, iron and marble. And cinnamon, spices, ointments, frankincense, wine, oil, fine flour and wheat, beasts, sheep, horses and chariots and slaves and the souls of men" (Rev. 18:11 AV).

NOTES

1. Karl W. Butzer, *Early Hydraulic Civilization in Egypt* (Chicago: University of Chicago Press, 1976).

2. Eugen Strouhal, *Life of the Ancient Egyptians* (Liverpool: Liverpool University Press, 1996), 134–135.

3. M. M. Austin, "Society and Economy," in D.M. Lewis, John Boardman, Simon Hornblower, and M. Ostwald (eds.), *The Cambridge Ancient History,* vol. 6, *The Fourth Century BC* (Cambridge: Cambridge University Press, 1994), 535.

4. Athenaeus, *D* 272c.

5. Austin, "Society and Economy," 535–539; Robert Flacelière, *La Vie Quotidienne en Grèce en Temps de Périclès* (Paris: Hachette, 1959), 52.

6. Austin, "Society and Economy," 538.

7. Xenophon, *Hellenica,* 2 vols. Translated by C.L. Brown (London: Loeb Classical Library, 1985), 6.4.15.

8. Aristotle, *Politics.* Translated by H. Rackham (Cambridge, Mass.: Loeb Classical Library, 1950), 2.1270a.12.

9. All Biblical references are to the King James Bible, authorized version. Hereafter, AV.

10. Karl J. Beloch, *Die Bevölkerung der Griechiscch-Römishen Welt* (Leipzig, Germany: Dunker and Humblot, 1886); Bruce Pryor, "Demography," in Alan K. Bowman, Peter Garnsey, and Dominic Rathbone (eds.), *The Cambridge Ancient History,* vol. 11, *The High Empire AD 70–192* (Cambridge: Cambridge University Press, 2000), 787–816.

11. Bryan Ward-Perkins, "Land, Labour and Settlement," in Averil Cameron, Bryan Ward-Perkins, and Michael Whitby (eds.), *The Cambridge Ancient History,* vol. 14, *Late Antiquity: Empire and Successors, AD 425–600* (Cambridge: Cambridge University Press, 2000), 320–324; Procopius, *Wars* 11.22–23.

12. Peter Salway, *Roman Britain* (New York: Oxford University Press, 1981), 542–545.

13. Anne Ross, *The Pagan Celts* (London: Batsford, 1986), 76; Simon James, *Exploring the World of the Celts* (London: Thames and Hudson, 1993), 63, 147.

14. Quoted in Alix Wilkinson *The Garden in Ancient Egypt* (London: The Rubicon Press, 1998), 29.

15. Miriam Lichtheim, *Ancient Egyptian Literature: A Book of Readings,* vol. 3, *The Late Period* (Berkeley: University of California Press, 1980), 35.

16. Herodotus. Translated by A.G. Godfrey. 4 vols. (Cambridge, Mass.: Loeb Classical Texts, 1921–1924), 2.65.

17. Quoted in Douglas J. Brewer and Renée F. Friedman, *Fish and Fishing in Ancient Egypt* (Warminster, England: Aris and Phillips, 1989), 15.

18. Hesiod, *Works and Days,* translated and commentary for the social sciences by David W. Tandy and Walker C. Neale (Berkeley: University of California Press), 633–640.

19. Aristophanes, "The Peace," in *Plays,* translated by Jeffrey Henderson, 4 vols. (Cambridge, Mass.: Loeb Classical Library, 1998–2002), 569–579.

20. Aristophanes, "The Acharnians," in *Plays,* translated by Jeffrey Henderson, 4 vols. (Cambridge, Mass.: Loeb Classical Library, 1998–2002), 32–36.

21. Pliny, *NH* 18.187. (Unless otherwise stated, references to Pliny in this book refer to Pliny the Elder.)

22. Columella, *RR* 2.9.14.

23. Columella, *RR* 5.9.7.

24. Varro, *RR* 1.52.1.

25. Cicero, *De Officiis,* translated by W. Miller (London: Loeb Classical Library, 1951), 2.25.88.

26. Pliny the Younger, *The Letters of the Younger Pliny,* translated and edited by B. Radice (Harmondsworth, England: Penguin Press, 1963), 5.6.

27. Cato, *DA* 3.2.

28. Caesar, *De Bello Gallico (The Conquest of Gaul)*, translated and edited by S.A. Hanford (Harmondsworth, England: Penguin Press, 1951), 6.13–15.

29. Pliny the Younger, *Letters*, 5.4.

30. Strabo, *Geography*, 8 vols., translated and edited by H.L. Jones (London: Loeb Classical Library, 1917–1982), 4.5.2.

31. Juvenal, *The Sixteen Satires*, translated and edited by Peter Green (Harmondsworth: Penguin Press, 1967), 10.80.

32. Cato, *DA* 135.

CHAPTER 2
FOODSTUFFS

Not everyone in the ancient world was short of food. In the northern areas this might be the case, as food was often scarce in the winter months. If food was not available, people starved, and there would be no record of this. Some foods available today and from the time of the discovery of the New World would not be available to ancient civilizations. Tomatoes, potatoes, and maize, for example, became available only when Europeans exploited the abundance of the Americas. Many items, such as spices, became available once the trade routes to the Far East had been established. Substitutes were also available. Sugar was not readily available to the ancient world, so honey and other sweeteners, such as date palm syrup, took its place. There was great variety of game and fish, together with many edible plants. Vegetables, especially in Egypt, formed a large part of the ordinary person's diet. The Roman mastery of trade ensured that foodstuffs could travel to the farthest parts of the Roman Empire, and if a foodstuff, such as the essential *liquamen,* became unavailable, Roman initiative ensured that local produce filled the gap. Starvation was always a possibility, but ingredients available within the four ancient civilizations are indicated by the list given below.

GRAINS

Grain crops are the most important type of plant foods, as cereals for human consumption and as fodder for animals. Their chief value is in the provision of carbohydrates and as a source of B-group vitamins. As bread and pottage they are "filler foods" and so were an important part in the diet of all social classes. Egypt was widely known as a major grain grower throughout its history, and in the Roman period, the Fayum, irrigated by the water of Lake Moeris, was one of the main suppliers of grain to the city of Rome.

Wheat

The main crop of the northern Celtic world was einkorn (*Triticum monococcum*), which also grows wild throughout the Near East. It was known to have been collected from the wild as early as 12,000 B.C. in Syria, but it does not seem to have been gathered in Egypt. Later this was supplanted by emmer (*Triticum dicoccum*), which grew wild in the Near East by 9000 B.C. and soon became a major crop throughout the Mediterranean. Emmer was a major crop in northern Europe in the Neolithic and Bronze Age periods, but was less popular in Mediterranean lands, although it was a predominant crop in Egypt. It was the basis of a Roman thick porridge (*puls*), a traditional food to which could be added pieces of meat or fish. The Roman poet Ovid mentioned *puls fabracia,* or *puls* eaten with fat bacon, which was offered to the goddess Carna, who was reputed to subsist on foods native to Rome—"no voluptuary is she to run after foreign viands."[1]

Cato gives a recipe for what he calls "Punic porridge":

> Soak a pound of groats in water until quite soft. Pour into a clean bowl. Add three ponds of fresh cheese, half a pound of honey and one egg, mixing the whole thoroughly.[2]

Spelt (*Triticum spelta*) was grown in northern regions, as it grew well in a damp climate and could be sown as a winter crop. This grain was difficult to thresh, and the Romans preferred to cultivate club wheat (*Triticum compactum*), which had been developed from emmer and seemingly had been grown in the Middle Eastern regions as early as 8000 B.C. Club wheat was grown in parts of Greece but was often supplemented by durum wheat (*Triticum turgidum*), which produced *similago,* the flour for flat unleavened bread and common bread wheat, which when ground produced *siligo,* a fine white flour. Cato, in the second century B.C., assumed that all farm slaves would have the opportunity to eat wheat bread. The main variety of wheat in Egypt was emmer, but Egyptians also used barley for bread making. That Egypt was noted for its abundance of grain production can be seen in the biblical story of Jacob sending his sons to Egypt, for he had "heard that there was corn in Egypt" and that "they may buy for us from thence; that we may live and may not die" (Gen. 42:2 AV).

Barley

Barley (*Hordeum vulgare*) was a major cereal crop in the ancient world. Wild barley was gathered in Greece as early as 11,000 B.C., probably as a development of the crop known in the Jordan valley and southern Levant. Barley, in fact, has a major role in the biblical story of Ruth (Ruth 2:15–23 AV). There are two species of cultivated barley. The two-eared variety was the earlier version, but Egypt cultivated a six-rowed variety. It was grown from predynastic times, evidence of which dates from finds at Abu Simbel and Aswan ca. 8000 to 7000 B.C. Portrayed in tombs, it was the symbolic representation of the god Osiris. Each Pharaoh regarded himself as becoming Osiris when he died; therefore the representation indicated his concern for his provision of sustenance to his people.

Both Egypt and Greece used barley for bread making, but barley is less suitable for this process than wheat. The glumes that enclose the grain cannot be removed by one threshing. They need a double process, which in antiquity meant roasting the grain in its husks. This process destroys the gluten, making it unsuitable for leavened bread. Barley bread made as flat cakes was popular, probably because these need not rise and could be placed near a fire to bake. Barley bread was not appreciated in Rome, where it was used to make a kind of polenta or mixed with wine to make a drink.[3] In the Roman army, according to the Roman politician Sextus Julius Frontinus, eating barley bread was regarded as a punishment.[4] Barley bread seems to have been a useful food in the biblical story of feeding the five thousand (St. John 6:9 AV), but there is a hint of poverty in that Jesus was feeding the Galilean poor and that the miracle is enhanced by poor bread being multiplied and fed to the poor. The fourth-century A.D. Pergamum physician Oribasius, quoting the second-century A.D. Greek physician Galen, said that barley cake (which is baked under an earthenware cover) filled the stomach with flatulence and that it remained in the stomach for a long time, causing disorder. If honey was added, it encouraged the stomach to evacuate faster.[5]

Barley was, however, used for making a fermented drink. If barley is allowed to germinate and produce shoots, it develops an enzyme, diastase, that converts grain starch into fermentable sugars. To encourage this, the grain is spread out and dried to convert it to malt. Roasting can stop this malting process. The crushed malt is then steeped in water to produce a sweet brown liquid (wort), more like a barley wine than a light ale. Barley was also used as a fodder crop, and Pliny recommended it to increase the strength and enlarge the muscles of animals.

Millet and Sorghum

Millet was not generally known in the ancient world. Broomcorn millet grown in the Caucasus in at least 5000 B.C. spread to Greece and Rome and from there to western Europe. Its main use was in porridge or boiled and mixed with lard or olive oil when food was scarce. Pliny said that one variety, foxtail millet, was grown in Gaul.[6] Classical writers sometimes confused sorghum with millet.

Oats

Wild oats were gathered in the Mediterranean area as early as 11,000 B.C. The Celts used it as a basis for pottage. Pliny said that the German tribes made a kind of *puls* from them, but the main use of oats for the Greeks and Romans was as a fodder crop.[7] It could be eaten in times of scarcity, in which case it was used for a poor kind of bread or boiled and eaten with reduced wine or honeyed wine.

Rye

Rye was grown in the central and cool northern areas of Europe, being used for both human food and as a fodder crop. It was popular because it could be grown in poor soil. It was not grown in southern Europe, Greece, and Egypt. The Celts made a black bread from it, which both Galen and Pliny found disagreeable to the stomach.[8] Emperor Diocletian's Price Edict in A.D. 301 put the price of rye the same as barley, 60 denarii for a *castrensis modius*, while wheat was 100 denarii for the same measure.

Rice

Rice was little-used in the ancient world. It was domesticated in India, Southeast Asia, and China, and seems to have reached Greece after Alexander's expeditions. Some may also have reached Greece from Persia or been imported from India. This could have made rice very expensive; hence its seemingly little use. However, Apicius used it as a thickening agent, which gives a somewhat opposite impression, although its use may have been confined to wealthy households. Rice gruel made with goat's milk was recommended as part of medicinal treatment. Galen said that it can "check the stomach" and is harder to digest than groat.[9] The inhabitants of the Lower Nile valley may have known it in Egypt, but any rice in quantity would have been imported. Rice was not cultivated in Egypt on a large scale until after the Arab conquest, when it was sometimes used to make bread.

The late-fifth-century Greek doctor Anthimus, who said that rice is good after it has been properly cooked, provided a recipe, which resembles a rice pudding:

> Boil rice in fresh water. When it is properly cooked, strain off the water and add goat's milk. Put the pot on the flame and cook slowly until it becomes a solid mass. It is eaten like this, hot not cold, but without salt and oil.[10]

LEGUMES

Beans

The broad bean or fava bean was a major crop for all social classes in the classical world. It was cultivated from a wild variety found in the Near East and became prolific in southern Europe during the prehistoric era. Beans could be eaten raw, boiled, roasted, or in the pod, which would provide fiber. The Roman poet Martial commented that "if the pale bean bubbles for you in the pot, you may decline the dinner of rich hosts."[11] Beans could be ground and added to bread flour, but as their skins were tough they were often skinned and split, ready for thick soup. Classical authors warned that eating them could lead to flatulence. Apicius mentioned beans from Baiae, which indicates that they were prized.

> Boil, chop finely. Serve with rue, green celery, leeks, oil, *liquamen,* a little *caroenum* or *passum.*[12]

In both Greece and Rome beans had a role in ritual, being offered to the gods and used in ceremonies. Pliny remarked that eating beans "clouds the vision," and it is known that beans can produce favism, a hemolytic disorder common among Mediterranean people.[13] Herodotus claimed that the Egyptians hated beans: "as for beans they cannot bear to look on them, as they imagine they are unclean."[14] Beans, however, have been found in Egyptian tombs. A pale variety was made into rissoles, while the smaller brown bean was stewed with oil, garlic, and herbs and served with bread.

Chickpeas

Chickpeas were one of the oldest and most used pulses of the Near East, being grown in Palestine about 8000 B.C. They were first gathered from the wild but quickly became cultivated. The Egyptians cultivated the chickpea, which could be ground and added to bread to increase its weight and density. They have been found in Egyptian tombs and, as they have a little protrusion, the Egyptians called them hawk-faces. They were ground into a paste resembling modern hummus or used in bread dough. The Greeks served them as part of *tragemata* eaten fresh, roasted, or dried, and served them at symposia. When boiled they were used in soup; in Rome this was a cheap food, bought from street sellers. Seasoned with oil and salt, they were used as a vegetable. Aristophanes mocked the name, giving it a double meaning as "glans penis," and noted its tendency to cause flatulence.[15]

The Greeks and Romans preferred the black-eyed pea or cowpea. Chickpeas, being cheap to buy, could make a good soup for the poor and thereby had an inferior status. Martial said a helping cost one *as*.[16] Anthimus warned that, when eaten raw, they caused violent flatulence, bad indigestion, and diarrhea, but they were diuretic and hence good for the kidneys.[17] Green chickpeas might be used as a laxative.

Fenugreek

Fenugreek was regarded as a both a fodder plant and one for human food. It was sometime eaten at the beginning of a meal with *liquamen*, as it was believed that this would act as a laxative. Its juice was mixed with honey for that purpose. The seeds, with their distinctive curry smell, were used to flavor sauces in Rome and butter in Egypt. In Egypt it has been found in the tombs of predynastic dynasties, indicating early knowledge; it was also found in Tutankhamen's tomb. Pliny said that an unguent of fenugreek was the most celebrated of its kind in the time of Menander in the second century B.C.[18]

Lentils

Lentils were a major part of diet in the ancient world. Wild lentils were known in Syria in 7500–9200 B.C., and from there they passed to Greece and Rome. In Greece they were a staple food; in Rome less so, as the Romans believed they could render men indolent and lazy. They were a major food for the working class in Egypt. They have been found in the stomach of predynastic bodies dating to 3150 B.C. in Egypt, and the Egyptians used them as a trade commodity for cedar wood from Lebanon. Pliny noted that there were two species available in Egypt, both of which were intensively cultivated.[19] The main use for lentils was as a base for soup or pottage, which could be flavored with spices or herbs. The soup could be made with a base of barley soaked overnight, together with seasoning of pennyroyal, savory, dill, and chopped leeks. Anthimus suggested flavoring with vinegar or sumac.[20] Their constant use among the peasant class indicates that they constituted probably the principal part of the food consumed by the lower classes in the Mediterranean civilizations. Meat or fish added variety to flavoring and texture. Galen mentioned a lentil and barley soup, which presumably was nourishing to invalids.[21] Apicius gave a recipe for barley soup with lentils and vegetables:

> Soak chickpeas, lentils and peas. Boil crushed grain with these. Drain then add oil and the following chopped greens: leeks, beets, and cabbage. Add dill, mallow and coriander. Pound fennel seeds, oregano, asafoetida, lovage, and blend these with *liquamen*. Pour this mixture over the vegetables and grain, heat and stir. Put chopped cooked cabbage leaves on top.[22]

Peas

Like the bean, the pea was first domesticated in the Near East about 8000 B.C. From there it passed into Egypt, where it was a welcome food. It spread throughout the Mediterranean world and was soon cultivated in northern Europe. It is a highly sustaining protein food and, like the bean, could be dried and stored, but when boiled produces a nourishing soup. Peas were regarded favorably as not causing flatulence. When fresh, peas provide a sugar substitute.

Vetches and Lupines

Both Celts and Romans used vetch as an animal food, but in the wild it would inevitably be found growing with grain crops and was therefore ground with the grain for flour. In Celtic lands it may have been eaten in the form of soup. In Greece and Rome it was eaten in times of scarcity. Lupines were a food and a decorative garden plant. The flat, yellow seeds must be boiled, as they are poisonous when eaten raw. As lupines were eaten in large quantities by the lower classes in Greece, the plant became associated with poverty and was noted for a tendency to cause flatulence. Pliny said that it was eaten by humans and "hoofed quadrupeds ate it as also a cheap fodder crop."[23] In Egypt lupines were sold as a snack delicacy. The seeds have been found in tombs and in the Fifth Dynasty Sun Temple at Abasir.

FUNGI

Mushrooms

Mushrooms have been part of human diet since prehistoric times; they were always gathered from the wild, as cultivation is a modern development. There was a difference in outlook. The Greeks saw them as a subsistence food, probably because Greece is poor in natural fungi; only the wealthy imported them from Italy. The Romans, having a greater variety, enjoyed them enormously. The first century A.D. Roman politician, Seneca, to deny himself, gave up mushrooms as an unnecessary luxury.[24] Both Ovid and Horace (the first-century B.C. Roman poet) mentioned fungi gathering. The best was considered to be *Boletus edulis*. Martial moaned when his host got boletus while he got *fungi suilli* (ordinary cépes).[25] Some species are poisonous: possibly the most famous poisoning was that of Emperor Claudius. He was poisoned by his wife, Agrippina, who seemingly slipped a poisonous mushroom into a dish of his favorite boletus.[26] Pliny, who discussed different varieties, said they were choice eating, but, like other writers, warned against their poisonous properties; he recommended pears as an antidote.[27]

Apicius gave recipes for tree fungi and mushrooms, including one for mushroom stalks, because the caps were the part of the mushroom most prized, and often the stalks were discarded.[28]

Truffles

The Greeks and Romans knew about truffles, although they could not understand how they were buried in the earth. The Greeks thought they were produced by the action of thunderbolts and lightning. This idea may have arisen because they could be found if lightning struck the ground and cracked it open. Pliny mentioned them being imported from Africa, while the second-century A.D. Roman poet, Juvenal, pins this down to Libya. Martial preferred mushrooms. Pliny mentioned the story of the praetorian Licinius Lartius, who, while serving in Spain, bit into a truffle and broke his teeth on a denarius contained within it.[29] Apicius had four recipes for truffles and two sauces. The flavor of the truffle might be overwhelmed if using the following recipe:

> Boil the truffles, put on skewers and grill lightly. Put into a saucepan *liquamen*, virgin olive oil, *caroenum*, wine, ground pepper and honey. Bring to the boil and thicken with a little flour. Prick the truffles so that they may absorb the liquid. Undo from the skewer and when they are saturated, serve. If you wish you can wrap the truffles in a sausage skin, grill and serve.[30]

FRUITS

Apples

Apples originated in Anatolia (Turkey), but a variety of wild apple, probably the crab apple, was found in northern Europe and was known to the Celts. Swiss Iron Age sites have revealed large quantities of crab apple seeds. The Greeks and Romans cultivated apples in orchards and, by means of grafting, produced larger and more succulent fruit. They were an important crop because they could be dried for the winter. Columella recommended they be stored in sawdust.[31] Apples play a part in myths—the golden apple of the Hesperides; the apple presented by Paris, which began the Trojan War; the apples used to prevent Atalanta from winning the race. Suetonius said that Domitian ate such an enormous luncheon that in the evening he could eat only a Martian apple and a small pitcher of wine.[32] Martian apples were named after C. Martius, a friend of Augustus, who was said to be an expert on cooking and gardening. Apples were presented as gifts in Egypt, but most were imported. Some apples were grown in an orchard at the delta palace of Ramses II. Ramses III offered baskets of apples to Hapy, the Nile god of the Inundation, probably because the fruit was a rarity.

Apricots

Apricots originated in the Far East and probably became known to the classical world after Alexander's expedition in the fourth century B.C. Pliny referred to them as Armenian plums because of their scent, but he was confused as to their origin.[33] They seemed to have been a food eaten mainly by the wealthy because of their rarity. They were used in sweet-sour recipes such as this one, provided by Apicius:

> Put in a saucepan oil, *liquamen* and wine. Add chopped shallots and diced shoulder of port, cooked previously. Stew gently. Add pounded pepper, cumin,

dried mint and dill, and moisten with a liquid of honey, *liquamen, passum,* a little vinegar and some of the cooking liquor. Add stoned apricots. Bring to the boil and cook till done. Crumble pastry to thicken. Sprinkle with pepper and serve.[34]

Blackberries, Raspberries, Strawberries, Bilberries, Mulberries, and Elderberries

Berries were found in northern and Mediterranean Europe, and remains have been discovered in prehistoric villages. They are useful sources of sweetness, but must be eaten fresh and therefore were entirely seasonal. Pliny described their different types of flesh and skins.[35] The shoot of wild brambles could be eaten and were pickled in vinegar. Strawberries remained a small fruit; the larger fruits are the product of modern cultivation. Most of these fruits were regarded as laxatives, and the leaves and fruits of elderberries were thought to have medicinal properties.

Carobs

The carob tree has pods and seeds, which are sweet and can be eaten by humans but are an excellent fodder crop, as the pods are rich in protein, starch, and sugar. They are therefore an excellent energy source for working animals and for fattening cattle. The tree grows well in dry soil, although irrigation produces a more prolific crop. In spite of the Greek philosopher Theophrastus stating that the carob was not grown in Egypt, both pods and seeds have been found in tombs, as for example in the Eighteenth Dynasty burials at Deir el-Medina.[36] It has been suggested that the locusts and wild honey that St. John the Baptist ate in the desert (St. Matt. 3:4 AV) and the husks that the prodigal son ate (St. Luke 15:16 AV) were carobs. The latter may be true, but there was no reason why St. John did not eat locusts and wild honey, which would have been a good combination of fat, protein, and sugar. After all, the Hebrews were allowed to eat locusts (Lev. 11:22 AV). The carob trees were grown around the Mediterranean, but the fruit seems to have been rarely used in classical times. The Romans ate carobs green and fresh, and Pliny considered them to be very sweet, but Galen said that they induced constipation.[37]

Cherries

The sour cherry probably arrived in Greece from Anatolia. Pliny said that the cherry was brought to Rome by Lucullus from Pontus after his campaigns in Anatolia (A.D. 74) and gave a precise date (A.D. 47) for its arrival in Britain.[38] He detailed the different types of cherries, noting that they could be dried in the sun and stored in casks like olives. Columella and Palladius gave details of propagation by grafting, probably onto wild cherry trees.[39]

Christ's-Thorn

This tree, sometimes erroneously called the jujube tree, has small, juicy, cherry-sized fruit, which becomes sweeter as it ages. The leaves can also be eaten. At the base of each leaf stalk is a pair of very sharp thorns, and so this plant was said to be that which composed Jesus' crown of thorns. The tree grew wild in Upper Egypt but could be easily cultivated. The fruit was found in tombs from the predynastic era to a Twentieth Dynasty tomb at el-Hibeh. Whole fruits as well as seeds were found in simple burials as well as royal tombs. The flesh was used to make a fruit bread. Fruit, leaves, and the wood were used in medicine, both for internal and external use.

Dates

The date palm provided one of the most useful fruits, as a source of protein and sugar, and was an economic staple for the Egyptians; it was extensively cultivated through history but especially in the Ptolemaic period. The tree can produce a prolific crop, as much as 200 kilograms (440 pounds) of dates on about eight bunches. In Egypt dates were found in the Upper Paleolithic site of el-Khargo, but date palms seem to have been first cultivated in the Middle Kingdom. The date palm was sacred to Ra, the sun god, and was symbolic of life over death. As such it was the emblem of Upper Egypt, and the Saharan oases produced a constant supply of the fruit. This could be eaten fresh, dried and preserved, pressed into cakes, made into a conserve, or used as an ingredient in bread. Pastry cooks used them so often as a sweetener that they were known as "workers in dates." Dates could also be fed to camels and other animals. Date syrup, made by boiling the whole fruit and allowing the liquid to ferment, was added to barley in the Egyptian New Kingdom to flavor beer. It was also added to wine. Beverages could also be made from fermentation of dates. Domestication of dates probably began about 5000 B.C., and this soon became common across Mediterranean regions. Pliny detailed the variety of dates and palm trees and their methods of cultivation; he also mentioned a date wine made from soaking the fruit in water.[40]

Dates also had medicinal uses (for example, in a drink to reduce fever) and were noted for their laxative qualities, especially when eaten to excess. Date kernels were soaked and used as animal feed. The Romans imported the *caryotae*, or Jericho dates, which were noted in Palestine for their flesh and juice, which could be made into date wine. Jericho dates were regarded as supreme among the varieties of dates. Apicius used them in most of his recipes that include dates, especially in sauces, which include those to accompany fowl both large and small, and ostrich, flamingo, and crane:

> Boiled chicken. Prepare the following sauce. Pound pepper, cumin, a little thyme, fennel seed, mint, rue, asafoetida root; moisten with vinegar, add Jericho date and pound this as well. Blend with *liquamen*, oil, honey and wine. Pour over the cooked and dried chicken and serve.[41]

The doum palm, known only in Upper Egypt, produced a shiny, brown fruit eaten locally. This is soaked in modern Egypt to get the fibrous spongy flesh, which, tasting faintly gingery, is used raw and in baking. The tree is easily recognized because of its forked trunk, on each of which are about 40 oval fruits. Both the fruit and cakes made of the fruit were placed in tombs, and the fruit is depicted in the Fourteenth Dynasty Theban tomb of Sennedjem. The dried fruit was used as an astringent. The argun palm is a smaller version of the doum palm, but its dry, purple fruit is tasteless. If, however, it is buried in the ground, it becomes sweeter and tastes of coconut.

Figs

Figs were native to the Near East. Fertilization of trees by the pollinating agent, the caprificatory wasp (fig wasp), was described by Herodotus and Aristotle, and Pliny described the practice of planting wild and cultivated fig trees near each other.[42] Figs are prolific in quantity. The main crop is gathered in autumn, but there can be two more crops during the year. Such a range of varieties was available that figs became a standard feature of diet, especially as they could be preserved by drying to provide a sweet in winter months. Columella detailed the varieties.[43] Figs, like dates, were a rich sweetener, and both fruits were highly regarded as laxatives and as a cure for worms. In Greece and Rome, where they were extremely popular, they were mainly eaten as a dessert. Fig leaves were wrapped around food in cooking, especially around fish. Cheese makers used fig tree sap as rennet. The common fig is depicted on paintings in Egyptian tombs of the Old and Middle

Kingdoms, where model figs were also found, probably because they were regarded as suitable food for the dead. Figs were selected by the goddess Netpe for those who were judged worth of admission to the otherworld.

In Egypt the main variety was the sycamore or wild fig, where the fruit grew in twos and threes from separate stalks. The tree produces fruit all year round. The caprificatory wasp was not present in Egypt, so the tree had to be propagated by means of cuttings. A gall wasp, however, can grow inside the fruit, so to hasten the ripening process before it could develop, the fruit was notched or scraped. It is a prolific crop, because picking the fruit leads to more fruit growing at the same place. The fruit was sacred to the god Hathor and was believed to provide nourishment for the deceased; hence its proliferation in tombs. It was eaten in funerary feasts and by all social groups. The cultivated variety was found in the predynastic necropolis at Saqqara. Fig gathering is portrayed in tomb paintings. In the Twelfth Dynasty tomb of Khnum-hotep at Beni Hassan humans compete with baboons to gather fruit. Baboons, however, are also representative of the god Thoth. Figs were

Detail from a wall painting in a tomb at Thebes. Monkeys were used to pick figs from the trees, but they always ate some of the fruit. Redrawn from Sir John Gardner Wilkinson, *The Manners and Customs of the Ancient Egyptians*, 1837.

also used medicinally, especially for a disease called "blood devourer," which may have been scurvy.

Grapes

Grapes were native to the Near East and southern Europe, but vine growing extended to Britain and Germany in the northern parts of the Roman Empire. Grapes grew wild until the Greeks and Romans cultivated the plants assiduously, developing the skills of viticulture. Pliny detailed the varieties of grapes and said they were uncountable and infinite.[44] They were eaten as a fruit, dried as raisins, and made into wine. As a dessert they were very popular, and it was noted that grapes eaten without pips passed through the stomach more easily, which indicates that varieties of seedless grapes were available. Smoked raisins were popular. People eating raisins that had been kept for a long time were advised to soak them in water both to soften the raisin and make the pips more easily removed. Two types of grapes were cultivated in Egypt, with the best variety growing in the Fayum. Grapes are shown as offerings on paintings in Egyptian tombs. The stela of Sensebek, Twelfth Dynasty, has pictures of offerings of bread, onions, grapes, melons, and lettuces, the essentials of existence. Grapes and dried raisins were found in tombs, for example in that of Tutankhamen.

Jujube

The jujube tree produces a berrylike fruit with a yellowish flesh, similar to a small date, but with a hard, glutinous texture. First grown in India, it spread to the Near East and Africa. It was introduced into Italy in the first century A.D. from Syria. Columella highly recommended it as a crop.[45] Some classical writers dismissed it contemptuously as only food for women and children, believing that as the fruits gave little nourishment and were hard to digest, they were unsuitable for men.

Mandrake

This fruit has a slightly poisonous flesh with a sickly taste. The stones are toxic, but the fruit has a narcotic effect. When mixed with beer, it caused people to become unconscious. Baskets of the fruit are reproduced on tombs of the Eighteenth Dynasty at Thebes. The Egyptians sniffed it and ate small doses of it at banquets to produce hallucinations. It was also believed to have aphrodisiac qualities and to help conception.

Medlars

Medlars were a somewhat rare fruit in the classical era. They were prolific in the Near East and southern Europe, They cannot be eaten raw but must be cooked or left to ripen until almost rotten.

Melons and Watermelons

Melons and watermelons were popular in the classical world, but in an elongated rather than a round form.[46] They were thought to be good for the stomach, but acted as a diuretic and a laxative. They were well known in Egypt, and the Israelites berated Moses, as it was one of the foods they remembered while wandering in the wilderness (Num. 11:5 AV). Apicius used the melon in one recipe, but the taste must have been drowned by the addition of pepper, pennyroyal, honey, *liquamen,* and vinegar, not to mention asafetida.[47] Melon seeds have been found on many sites in Egypt; seeds were a popular snack. It was also a fruit offered to the gods. Watermelons were cultivated in Egypt from 2000 B.C., where they were known as *bedoukhia.* Both flesh and seed were popular. In Greek and Roman cuisine they were doused in vinegar, presumably to give them a "pick-up."[48] When grown in polluted waters, they can be a source of food poisoning, which is why they were thought to cause vomiting.

Peaches

The Greeks knew peaches as "Persian apples." They were probably introduced into Greece as a result of Alexander's expedition. Pliny said they were "introduced lately," meaning in the first century A.D., and that the fruit was difficult to grow.[49]

Pears

Pears spread west from Anatolia, where they grew wild and were cultivated by grafting. The wild pear was found in northern Europe, and some seeds have been found on the Swiss Iron Age sites. Wild pears have been found in the Franchthi Cave in Greece dating to 9000 B.C. The Greeks liked pears, and they were served as a dessert or at a symposium. Pliny, in discussing the variety of pears, said that the best was the *crustumion.*[50] He mentioned a wine made from pears, possibly perry cider, and pear vinegar, and recommended that when pears are boiled with honey, or cooked in wine and water, they are wholesome to the stomach.[51] Dried pears could be kept for the winter or preserved in grape syrup. Galen recommended that they be cut into rings.

Persea

The Egyptians regarded the *Persea* tree as sacred, and the pharaohs were often depicted as being covered with its foliage. The fruit, with a sweet, strongly flavored pulp similar in taste to an apple and two hard stones in the center, was popular in Egypt, probably being introduced from the Near East. The first-century A.D. Greek physician Dioscorides said it is grown in Persia, but was inedible there, and Pliny described the fruit and noted that the tree produced a prolific crop.[52] Dried fruits were found in Egyptian tombs of the third millennium B.C. Faience models of *Persea* and figs were found in a Twelfth Dynasty tomb at Lisht. The fruit was so prized that it was grown in Egyptian temple gardens. An old Egyptian proverb said, "When the *Persea* fruit ripened the Nile would rise; may the *Persea* fruit not fall the night when the waters of the Nile rise and may the wind not blow them off." By the Ptolemaic period in Egypt, the trees were dying, so felling them was prohibited.

Plums

Sloes and plums grew wild in Europe and were gathered for food. Both the Greeks and the Romans cultivated plums, the Greeks cultivating a sweeter variety. Pliny described the different types and also mentioned that damsons from Damascus had been grown in Italy for "a long time."[53] The Egyptian plum, a spiny tree, grew in dry areas, but it could be cultivated in orchards.

Pomegranates

Pomegranates were native to Iran and from there spread to Egypt, the Near East, and Greece, where they became the subject of myth, as for example in the legend of Demeter and Persephone. The Romans took cultivation of the fruit to southern Mediterranean countries. Pliny said there were five kinds of the fruit, from sweet to vinous, and that it was introduced into Italy from Carthage.[54] The Greek physician Hippocrates noted its medicinal properties; boiled juice brought down the heat of a fever.[55] Pomegranates grew well in Egypt, where they were probably introduced from Palestine or Syria. The Egyptians made wine from this fruit. Pomegranates were painted in the tomb of Akhenaton. Models of pomegranates found in tombs of the Middle and New Kingdoms and strings of pomegranates painted on the walls were probably intended as funerary offerings.

Quinces

The quince was often confused with the apple. It arrived in Europe from the Near East, being cultivated from its wild state in Persia. According to Anthimus, it should be eaten cooked. As in many modern recipes, he recommended that the fruit be quartered before being cooked: "Cut the fruit into quarters. Boil in fresh water in an earthenware pot and then eat."

In a second recipe he advised baking them. This could be in an earthenware dish, but Oribasius in a similar method advised wrapping them in dough before putting in the embers: "Bake them for a long time covered with hot ashes."[56]

Columella recommended that they should be preserved in honey:

Put quinces in a vessel filled to the top with the very best and most liquid honey so that the fruits are preserved. The liquid has the flavour of honey water and can be given without danger to sufferers from fever with their meals. It is called *melomeli*.[57]

All classical authors write of the fruit with approval but emphasize that it should not be bruised. Palladius mentioned quince jam, and Oribasius quince syrup and stewed quinces with honey and wine.[58] Quince juice was regarded as having a keeping quality and could be stored after boiling with honey. When left to stand, a thick crust formed on the top. Martial wrote that if a person had quinces put in front of him, he would say, "These honey apples are delicious."[59] Pliny gave the varieties and extolled their medical qualities.[60]

NUTS

Acorns

There were many species of acorn, both sweet and bitter, which could be either gathered wild or cultivated. Pliny said that nuts constitute the wealth of many nations.[61] They have been found on Iron Age sites in Switzerland and Britain. They were a prolific animal food, especially for pigs, and were used as one of the main foods for fattening dormice. The Greek regarded them purely as animal food, but in Spain and Asia Minor they were regarded as a winter food. Acorns were useful because they could be ground into flour and used for bread, especially in times of famine. If acorns were boiled for a long time, mashed, then cooked, this could form a basis for pottage. Strabo said that the people of northern Spain ate acorn bread for almost two-thirds of the year, because it could be stored for a long time.[62]

Almonds

Almonds were collected from trees, which grew wild in the Near East as early as 10,000 B.C., but such a useful nut used both for cooking and in medicines was soon produced in a cultivated form, especially as it could easily be grown from seed. Almond oil was useful in cooking. The Greeks and the Romans loved to include almonds as a dessert, and Apicius used them as flavoring. Pliny detailed the varieties of almonds, praising in particular those of Thasos and Alba.[63] Sweet almonds produced mildly flavored oil, while bitter almonds were used to give flavor to wine, and such a drink was reputed to prevent drunkenness. They were also popular in Egypt, but jars of almonds, found in Tutankhamen's tomb and at Deir el-Medina, were probably imported.

Beechnuts

Beechnuts have been found on Iron Age sites, probably because they can be used as a meal for bread. They also produce a useful oil. The Romans ate them for dessert, noting their sweetness.

Chestnuts

The sweet chestnut reached the west from Anatolia, spreading rapidly after 1200 B.C. Pliny detailed the varieties and said they were best eaten roasted and ground.[64] The best came from Tarentum and the Campania. The Greeks liked to serve them with wine at banquets. Pliny also mentioned chestnut bread being a kind of imitation bread for women when they are completing a fast. Xenophon (an Athenian soldier, fifth–fourth century A.D., who joined the expedition into Asia Minor), who said that when the Greeks plundered the capital of the Mossynoecians they found chestnuts, which could be boiled and baked into bread, thereby providing them with supplies, confirmed this type of bread.[65]

Hazelnuts

Hazelnuts were prolific throughout Europe, and the Celts regarded them as a staple food, gathering the nuts from the wild. The Romans and Greeks cultivated them in plantations.

Pine Nuts

Pliny noted four varieties of pine nuts, mentioning their medicinal properties, and commented that kernels of the *pityis* variety were an excellent remedy for coughs when boiled in honey.[66] Apicius used them frequently in his recipes, especially as an addition to sauces.

Walnuts

Walnut trees were prolific in the Balkans, but the nuts have also been found on Iron Age sites in northern Europe. The trees were cultivated from the wild by the Greeks and Romans, who called the nuts "Persian nuts" and valued them for their culinary and medicinal properties. The nuts were pressed for their oil and were highly regarded as a dessert.

VEGETABLES

Vegetables grew wild in Europe and the Near East from prehistoric times. Northern European tribes gathered them as a welcome addition to diet, but it was the Greeks and Romans who realized the value of a cultivated crop and appreciated their use. Ofellus, Horace's neighbor, knew the simplicity on working days of eating smoked ham shank and greens.[67] In Egypt, although the major part of the land was given to the production of cereals, vegetables were cultivated in gardens and on small plots of land between larger fields. Roman writers treated vegetable growing seriously, emphasizing the low cost of production, the fresh flavor, and the fact that such cultivation gave great pleasure.

Asparagus

Asparagus was found wild in the Mediterranean regions but seemingly was not cultivated in Greece. The Romans realized its commercial value, and Cato gave detailed instructions for its cultivation.[68] He recommended that it be planted in reed beds and covered with straw throughout the winter to survive any frost. Although Pliny said it grew wild for anyone to gather, he noted that of all the cultivated vegetables, asparagus needs the most diligent attention. It was one of the most beneficial foods to the stomach; if cumin was added it would disperse flatulence of the stomach and colon.[69] Both Galen and Hippocrates praised this vegetable.[70]

Cabbages

Cabbages grew wild in northern Europe and were popular in the classical world. The Greeks thought that cabbages sprang from the sweat of Zeus's brow. The Romans promoted their cultivation throughout the Empire, regarding them as having healthy properties. Cato classified them and spelled out their many virtues, stating that they could be eaten raw, cooked, or pickled in vinegar.[71] Oribasius, quoting Mnesitheus of Cyzicus, gave a recipe for what may be considered a kind of vinaigrette coleslaw.

> Cut up the cabbage with a very sharp knife. Wash the pieces and drain off the water. Add sufficient quantity of rue, and coriander; sprinkle with honeyed vinegar and grate on top a small quantity of asafoetida.[72]

It had value as a medicine and eating it was essential to good health, especially for those suffering from gout. If suffering from dysentery, people should eat boiled cabbage sautéed in olive oil. Cato recommended that it should be eaten both before and after a feast to combat drunkenness. Pliny described the different varieties and considered them a luxury.[73] Eating them promoted good digestion; they were an excellent laxative and had numerous medicinal properties. Theophrastus recommended that cabbage should be boiled in *nitron* to improve both flavor and color.[74] Pliny suggested adding a pinch of soda.[75] Juvenal, on the other hand, thought they were the food of the poor.[76]

Celery

Celery grew wild in northern Europe, but began to be cultivated by the Romans, thus becoming widespread. It was often used in hors d'oeuvres, but was a useful product in that it could be added to the preparation of all foods.[77] It was a smaller and a more bitter plant than its modern equivalent. Seeds, leaves, and stems were used for flavoring. As celery was related to parsley, it was wound into a victor's wreath, and thin celery stems were found entwined in Tutankhamen's funeral wreath. Celery was found in the foundation deposits of Hatshepsut's temple at Deir el-Bahari. Its medical properties included an ability to retain urine, which seems somewhat confusing as celery juice was also regarded as being a diuretic. It was applied to wounds and stiff joints.

Fennel

Fennel was native to the Near East and appreciated for its distinctive flavor. The Romans used the shoots as a vegetable and the seeds as flavoring to food; its roots were used in medicine. Pliny noted the use of the seeds of giant fennel in the diet.[78] Cato used fennel seeds as a dressing for olives:

> Bruise olives and throw them into water. Change the water often and when they are well soaked, press out and throw into vinegar; add oil and half a pound of salt to a modius of olives. Make a dressing of fennel and mastic (or pine resin) steeped in vinegar in a separate vessel. If you wish to mix them together they must be served at once. Press them out into an earthenware vessel and take them out with dry hands when you wish to serve them.[79]

Lotus

There were several varieties of lotus in Egypt. These included the pink lotus introduced from India, the white lotus, and the blue lotus. Both roots and the seeds were edible; the seeds and the center of the lotus could be ground for bread. The pink lotus had its seed in a container resembling a wasp's nest, which held up to 30 seeds. Parts of the blue lotus were eaten only in starvation conditions.

Samphire

Samphire, found on seaside rocks, was collected in spring both in the Mediterranean and in northern Europe. It was eaten raw or boiled or, by using brine, could be made into a pickle, which would keep for over a year.

ROOT VEGETABLES

Root vegetables were tougher and more fibrous than their modern equivalents. One way of making them edible was to pulverize them by using a pestle and mortar or to rub them in a large *mortaria*. Vegetables usually thin and wiry in shape, eaten by the Celts, were gathered from the wild, but it was the Greeks and Romans who cultivated them, thereby producing a better crop.

Beets

The modern beetroot is a sixteenth-century propagation. The plant was cultivated in the ancient world mainly for its leaves, which were often used to wrap around other food when it was being cooked, much as vine leaves are used today. The leaves were popular in a salad with lentils and beans. The roots were not popular, as they were regarded as a laxative. Martial condemned them as insipid and a common noon meal for artisans.[80] The shape was more like a bulb than the modern large root. Oribasius, quoting from Galen, said that beet and lentil stew is a good food if salt and *liquamen* were added. He praised this dish as a laxative.[81]

Carrots and Parsnips

Carrots were thin and pale in color and more popular than parsnips. The leaves and roots of both plants were used for medicinal purposes. Remains of wild parsnips have been found on Iron Age sites in Britain and Switzerland. Pliny and Columella both mention wild and culti-vated parsnips; the unopened flowers of the plant were dried and used as herbs. Pliny noted that they were a bitter vegetable even if the woody middle was removed, but this could be tempered with hon-eyed wine. Apicius had three recipes, which may apply either to pars-nips or carrots.[82] One, which requires the vegetable to be served raw with salt, pure oil, and vinegar, must refer to carrots.

Leeks

Leeks were grown in Mesopotamia at the beginning of the second millennium B.C., in the Near East and Mediterranean lands. The Egyptians were so fond of them that the name became used for veg-etables in general. The Hebrews, wandering in their desert exile, fondly remembered them as part of the diet that they had eaten in Egypt (Num. 11:5 AV). They are a labor-intensive crop because they need transplanting, but their constant growth means that they can be available for most of the year. Their flavor is equivalent to that of onions; in fact, Apicius preferred them, for they appear constantly in his recipes. They are a versatile plant: the green tops can be eaten raw in a salad, the white bulb can be cooked as a vegetable, and when chopped both parts can be used as a seasoning. Leeks grew wild in northern Europe, but the Romans introduced the cultivated variety. Pliny mentioned its medicinal qualities, especially as an antidote to a variety of illnesses. He noted that Nero ate them on certain days of the month to improve his singing voice.[83]

Onions, Shallots, and Garlic

Like leeks, onions added flavor to a dish, but were less popular in Greece and Rome. In the wild, they were known to the Celts, but the Romans introduced a domesticated version to northern Europe. They are native to the Near East, where they were cultivated in the third millennium B.C. A variety called *Ascalon* got its name from the excellent onion market in that Palestinian town.[84] Onions store well, so they could be kept through most of the winter. They also had other uses. Columella gave a recipe for pickled onions:

> First dry the onions in the sun, then cool in the shade. Arrange it in a pot with thyme or marjoram strewn underneath, and, after pouring in a liquid consisting of three parts vinegar and one of brine, put a bunch of marjoram on the top, so that the onions may be pressed down. When they have absorbed the liquid, let the vessel be filled up with a similar liquid.[85]

In both Greece and Rome, however, onions seemed to have been regarded more as poor man's food. Apicius made great use of them, but Horace included them in his poor man's diet of onions, pulses, and pancakes. Pliny gave varieties of them, those with the strongest taste coming from Africa, followed by those from Gaul. Because a mature onion is mostly composed of water, they were placed in the moist category of vegetables and had numerous medical properties.[86]

Shallots known as "pearls," a Marsumian variety, were presumably as small as a cocktail onion and similar to the Egyptian variety. The standard lunch of the poorer classes in Egypt was bread, onions, and beer. As onions are compared to sound white teeth, they were presumably of a small variety. They were reputed to be of a mild, excellent quality and flavor, and were eaten raw as well as cooked. On the wall of the Aten Temple at Karnack was a sketch of a workman eating his lunch of bread, cucumber, and an onion. Onions and garlic formed part of the wages of the builders of Khufu's pyramid (2589–2566 B.C.). Onions are depicted growing close to water in Old Kingdom and New Kingdom reliefs. They were found wrapped in bodies of mummies in tombs, often being placed in the armpits or the groin. Priests, however, were forbidden to eat them.

Garlic was important in dishes around the Mediterranean lands, though more popular with the Greeks than with the Romans. The bulbs were smaller than the modern ones. Garlic adds relish to dishes, but anyone eating it has smelly breath and, if they have overindulged, a smelly body. Roman comedy writers, therefore, as might be expected, made fun of garlic eaters. Anthimus emphasized that it was useful for people on a journey, but it should be avoided by anyone with faulty kidneys.[87] Palladius said that smoked garlic was good because it will keep for a year. Apicius used onions but made little use of garlic.[88] Pliny said that the Greek writer Menander recommended eating roasted beetroot with or after eating garlic to neutralize the smell.[89] Galen suggested that garlic could be boiled to remove its bitterness, although this could make it less efficacious.[90]

Garlic was grown extensively in Egypt, and it was one of the foods remembered with longing by the Hebrews in their desert wanderings. Clay models of garlic bulbs were found in predynastic burials at Naqada. Bulbs were often placed in the armpits and groin of mummified bodies. The cloves were smaller than those today, many having 45 cloves to each bulb, which may have made them milder in flavor. Ramson, or wood garlic, was known in northern Europe. It was best eaten raw; when cooked it lost its flavor.

Radishes

The Romans also knew a kind of horseradish, although they had little use for it.[91] The radish, now mainly a salad vegetable, was used for both its roots and leaves, although eating leaves was more from necessity than from choice. Radishes were appreciated in the Mediterranean world, where there were two main varieties. One was akin to the bulbous variety known today; the other was a black, woody variety. They were eaten raw as an aid to digestion or could be boiled for a vegetable.[92] Radishes were cheap to buy and had a medicinal use, being particularly useful for dispersing phlegm, although they could cause flatulence. Horace noted that radishes whetted a jaded appetite.[93] Apicius's recipe would do the trick:

Serve radishes with a pepper sauce made by pounding pepper with *liquamen*.[94]

In Egypt illustrations in tombs show that a long variety of radish and radish oil was used extensively before the introduction of olive oil.

Turnips

Turnips were grown as a standby for winter food. Pliny thought that the turnip's "utility surpasses that of any other plant"; even its leaves could be eaten, although he admitted that its main use was as a fodder crop, and the Greeks and Romans regarded it more as poor man's food.[95] Columella, in particular, thought turnips a filling food for peasants. Classical writers recommended that turnips should be boiled twice, with the first lot of water poured away. The fact that it is a white vegetable meant that Roman cooks could stain it to pass it off as something else. Pliny said that it could be stained in at least six colors, the most popular being purple. Apicius had one recipe for boiled turnips sprinkled with oil and vinegar, but he obviously used the vegetable as a base for flavors:

> Boil the turnips. Drain. Pound together plenty of cumin and somewhat less rue and asafoetida. Add honey, vinegar, *liquamen, defrutum* and a little oil. Bring to the boil and serve with the turnips.[96]

SALAD VEGETABLES

Salad vegetables included lettuce, rocket, endive, and cucumbers. Lettuces were a favorite in Egypt. On wall paintings in the temple of Min at Luxor, they are portrayed as elongated, suggesting something akin to a cos lettuce. They were sacred to the god because the milky sap of the plant was regarded as the semen of his fertility. The Egyptians therefore consumed lettuces as a cure for impotence and to improve fertility; the Romans regarded them as an antiaphrodisiac, but believed that rocket, eaten in large quantities, caused arousal. Pliny gave the following recipe: "pound three leaves of rocket with honey water."[97] Rocket could be counterbalanced by lettuce, which cooled the blood. The Greeks and Romans used them both mainly as hors d'oeuvres,[98] and the Romans introduced them to the Celts, with rocket having a more pleasing flavor. Pliny recommended mixing rocket with honey to remove spots from the face.

Lettuce seeds were used in Egypt as culinary flavorings. Cress was prized for medicinal and aphrodisiac purposes. Pliny liked the Babylonian cress, saying that it sharpened the senses and cleared the vision. Chuba, an Egyptian marsh plant, was, and still is, part of the Egyptian diet. In England it is known as knotgrass. The root has a sweet flavor. Endive was served cooked because of its bitter taste when raw. It was used for both culinary and medicinal purposes. Seeds of cucumbers have been found in excavations, and the snake cucumber, with its curved shape and numerous longitudinal grooves, is illustrated in paintings in the Egyptian tombs of Nakht and Userhet. The Romans ate cucumbers cooked or raw, peeled or with the skin left on. Pliny and Columella described how they could be cultivated under movable frames.

WEEDS

Many plants now regarded as weeds have been found growing on Bronze Age and Iron Age sites in northern Europe in such profusion that it is highly probable that they were used as food supplies. Nettles were boiled before eating to remove the sting, and the water made an antiseptic. The thread in the plant was used to make netting and cloth. Mustard was used as a vegetable when gathered from the wild. Apicius made a patina, which seems to be a puree, of wild herbs, spices, *liquamen,* vinegar, oil, black bryony, mustard plant, and cabbage, which could be added to fish fillets or chicken.[99] Chickweed, rich in copper, added variety to diet. Dandelion, although bitter when eaten on its own, becomes palatable when mixed with other leaves. Marsh thistle, burdock, shepherd's purse, clover, and groundsel can all be made palatable. Yarrow was boiled to make a drink. It is now known by the name "wound healer," as the liquid has antiseptic qualities. Fat hen was certainly eaten from prehistoric times, probably as early as 3000 B.C., and its seeds have been found in the stomachs of bodies buried in bogs in Germany, Britain, and Denmark. When boiled it reduces itself in the same way as spinach. It contains calcium and vitamin B_1. Orache, used as an herb, could be prepared in the same way as spinach and was noted for its medicinal properties. Silverweed, prized for its roots, could be boiled, roasted, or ground for a thick pottage. Sorrel was both a vegetable and a medicinal plant, as it is highly useful as a laxative. Horehound was used to make a drink that was useful to combat a sore throat.

HERBS

A wide variety of herbs was available in the ancient world. Apicius's recipes indicate the use to which they could be put. Many were incorporated into medicines. Herbs grew wild in the Middle East but spread from there by trade or human contact to northern Europe. Herbs traveled well because they could be dried. They are easily grown, but some, such as parsley, may be more difficult to strike. The Greeks used them extensively because fewer spices were available to them. The Romans often preferred to use spices, but continued to cultivate herbs in garden plots ready for immediate use. Apicius used fresh herbs liberally.

Bay

Bay had a use as flavoring and was also intensively used in medicine.[100] Cato placed the leaves under a cake when baking it.[101] It was important wound into a wreath to crown victors in war or athletics. Palladius said that it was used to flavor olive oil.[102]

Basil

Basil was often eaten as a salad vegetable, where it was dressed with olive oil. It was also mixed with *liquamen* as flavoring. Pliny detailed its medicinal properties.[103]

Chervil

Care has to be taken with this herb because in the wild there are a number of poisonous plants with which chervil may be confused. These include fool's parsley and hemlock. Chervil was found in the coffin of a Danish burial dating to 1400 B.C., which indicates knowledge of its properties in northern Europe. It was used in the classical world for binding in a wreath. Pliny indicated its aphrodisiac qualities, especially for older men.[104] A basket of chervil seeds was found in Tutankhamen's tomb.

Dill

Both the fresh leaves and the seeds were used extensively in cooking. Its use spread across the empire because of the fondness that the soldiers had for this herb. The seeds have been found in fort latrines in Germany and Britain. Dill was also used bound into wreaths and in ritual contexts. Its medicinal uses included dill oil, used in ointments.

Hyssop

Hyssop is frequently mentioned in the Bible (e.g., Heb. 9:19 AV) and was native to the Near East and the Mediterranean regions. Used mainly in medicine in Greece and Rome, according to Pliny and Galen, it does not seem to have been used greatly in cooking, although Archestratus (a Sicilian Greek in the fourth century A.D. who wrote a long poem describing food eaten in Mediterranean costal cities) gave a recipe for fish with shredded hyssop and vinegar.[105] It was used as flavoring for wine.

Lovage

Lovage grew wild in the Mediterranean region, but seemingly was unknown to the Greeks. The Romans appreciated it, probably for its intense flavor, and it is one of the most frequently used in Apicius's recipes. The first-century Greek physician Dioscorides said that it was often used instead of pepper. It was used in medicine to cure wind and flatulence.[106]

Mallow

Mallow grew widely in Europe and was used extensively both as an herb and a vegetable by the Celtic tribes; hence it was mainly regarded as a food for the poor, but it had an extensive use in medicine. Poets mocked its laxative qualities.[107] The first-century traveler Lucian said that it was used as a garnish.[108] Apicius considered it a vegetable and, as today, it was probably cooked like spinach.[109] Mallow leaves were used as a soup thickener in Egypt.

Marjoram

Marjoram was used more as an aromatic in perfume than an herb. It was often confused with oregano.

Mint

Several varieties of mint were available to the Celts and the Romans but not to the Greeks. Wild mints were prolific and were used to aid digestion. Chewing mint leaves is noted for freshening the mouth and is also said to suppress hunger. Mint can be infused with honey to make a pleasant drink. For the Greeks, however, the word *menthe* can mean mint but also means shit; in Latin it could mean women's pubic hair. Hence there was problem concerning its use in cooking. Pennyroyal, a variety of mint, was more frequently used, especially as its medicinal use was recommended for women in childbirth.[110] Peppermint leaves were found in wreaths from the Twentieth to the Twenty-sixth Dynasties in Egypt.

Mustard

Mustard was known in prehistoric Europe, where it was used as a salad vegetable, and was used in Greece as early as 2000 B.C. The seeds were mainly used in classical cuisine and medicine.[111] Columella referred to mustard being "brightly coloured."[112] Black mustard seeds were found in Egypt in New Kingdom tombs. Honey mustard or charlock, related to radishes, was found in the wild in the Mediterranean regions. Caesar's troops had to eat it when they were short of food in Dyrrhachium (modern Durres, Albania). It was praised for its medicinal properties.

Myrtle

Myrtle, native to Europe and the Near East, was useful as a resinous herb. A residue of myrtle, emmer, cranberries, and honey, found in Bronze Age and Iron Ages burials in Denmark, is suggested to be a kind of beer. The Greeks and Romans chewed fresh berries to sweeten the breath, according to Pliny, and used the dried berries as a condiment.[113] Palladius noted that myrtle oil was used medicinally and as an aphrodisiac.[114] In Greek legend Myrrha was a favored priestess of Aphrodite, who transformed her into a fragrant evergreen to save her from an ardent suitor. The plant was therefore sacred to Aphrodite and was planted around temples dedicated to the goddess; the leaves and branches were woven into bridal wreaths.

Oregano

Oregano was widely used in cooking, especially in fish dishes, and had numerous medicinal uses.

Parsley

Parsley was used by the Greeks to crown victors at the Isthmian Games and to decorate tombs as it was associated with Archemurus, the Herald of Death. Homer records it as part of food fed to horses. The Greeks cultivated it for its medicinal qualities, but the Romans used it to flavor food. Placed in garlands at banquets, it was believed to discourage intoxication and dissipate strong odors. Chewed raw, it freshened the breath.

Rue

Rue, an herb appreciated by the Romans for its bittersweet flavor, was used frequently by Apicius to flavor his recipes. It was cultivated in gardens, but Pliny said that it was more potent when gathered or "stolen" from the wild.[115]

Sage and Savory

Sage and savory grew wild in the Mediterranean regions and were appreciated for both culinary and medicinal uses. Rubbing leaves of summer savory on a bee sting relieved pain.

Thyme

Thyme was used as a culinary flavoring in Roman dishes. Apicius was particularly fond of it. It was noted for its other uses. Martial sent a friend cakes steeped in "Hybla's thyme-fed honey."[116] Columella mentioned its use as rennet in cheese making, and Pliny discussed its medicinal qualities.[117] An aromatic thyme, a creeping plant, was used in wreaths and for medicinal purposes. The Egyptians used thyme as one of the embalming ingredients.

SPICES

Most spices reached the Mediterranean lands from the Far East, although some, such as mace and nutmeg, were already is use in the ancient world. Some were used for perfumes; others had a religious purpose, especially in festivals as offerings to the gods. Most were used in cooking to add taste and aroma to bland food. Cellulose forms the bulk of spices; it encapsulates the essential oils, which confer aroma and flavor. These oils are released by pounding and grinding—hence the use of the pestle and mortar—and provide a bite and flavor that is released during the cooking process. Spices were believed to aid digestion; hence their use in medicine.

People may, however, become so used to a certain flavor that they consider it to be too mild and want more of it; this particularly applies to spiced foods. People who constantly eat hot, spiced food experience such intense pleasure and well-being that they become addicted to it; the food also stimulates endorphins, the body's natural painkillers. The more the flavoring of the food is boosted by spices, the greater the reaction of the taste buds. These feelings may help to explain the love of spices and the search for new and even more exotic tastes in the Roman Empire.

Asafetida and Silphium

Asafetida is the dried resinlike substance from the rhizomes of fennel-like plants, which grew mainly in Afghanistan and Iran. Alexander's soldiers used it as a digestive when they were forced to eat raw horsemeat for want of other food. It was a costly spice in Rome, and Apicius said it could be made to last indefinitely by storing it in a jar with pine nuts. The crushed pine nuts would be used to flavor the food and then replaced by more nuts. It was often used as a substitute for silphium, which was a more highly regarded spice. Silphium was the resin from the root and stem of a fennel-like plant found in Libya, especially in the kingdom founded by the Greeks at Cyrene in North Africa. As it was not cultivated, it almost became extinct in the first century A.D., and asafetida took its place. It was highly valued, but Pliny, writing in the A.D. 70s, stated that where it grew, tax farmers rented pasturage and stripped it clean by grazing sheep on it because this was more profitable: "Only a single stalk was found within our memory, which was sent to the Emperor Nero."[118] The Romans also greedily devoured both the whole root and stem of silphium. Some was later imported from Syria, but this was of poor quality. It was used in medicine for sore throats. It could be grated and added, together with cheese and vinegar, to roasted birds and cooked fish. It added flavor to sauces and marinades, and in Egypt it was highly regarded for spicing food.

Caraway

Caraway is native to central Europe. It seems to have been rarely used in Greece but was well known to the Romans.

Cardamom

Cardamom was brought to Greece and Rome from India. Pliny said that it was gathered in Arabia and that there were four varieties. It was not greatly used in cooking but was included in some medicines. The price of the best was three denarii a pound.[119]

Cinnamon and Cassia

Cinnamon is finer than cassia, and the ancient world knew the difference. Pliny said that a pound of the cheapest cinnamon was 10 denarii but that a pound of the most expensive could be 1,000 denarii.[120] Both spices came from southeastern India and were extensively used in the ancient world once the trade route to the East had been established. They were valuable as flavorings in food, wine, and oils, and were also used widely in medicine and perfumes. In Egypt cinnamon bark had been tentatively identified as a spice called *ty-sheps*, which seemingly came by trade from Syria and was shipped in the form of peeled bark.

Cloves

Cloves were rare in the classical world, as they grew mainly in the Indonesian islands of Tenate and Tidore. Pliny knew of them but regarded them as being mainly used in perfume.

Coriander

Coriander was in use early in the second millennium B.C., and its use in food and medicine spread widely by trade throughout the Roman Empire. Coriander seeds have been found in Roman military latrines in Germany and Britain and in Egyptian tombs, for example that of Tutankhamen and burials at Deir el-Medina.

Cumin

This spicy seed was well known in the ancient world. Poseidonius (a Greek traveller in the first century B.C.) records its use by the Celts to flavor fish and wine. It was usually ground before use and acted as a cheap flavoring. Apicius was lavish in its use, especially for fish. Ground cumin could be mixed with salt in classical Greece to enhance both appearance and flavor. It was widely used in medicine, being recommended in particular for stomach pains. A basketful of cumin seeds was found in the burial place of Khe, architect to Amenophis, at Deir el-Medina.

Ginger

Ginger came to the classical world from Sri Lanka and was widely used pickled. Dioscorides described it in detail and noted its warming, appetizing, and gently laxative qualities. Pliny said that it grew on farms in Arabia.[121]

Juniper

Juniper trees, which were long-lived, some reputed to live for more than 100 years, grew in the Near East and were later cultivated in Greece and Rome. The strong-flavored berries were dried and used as spices. The Egyptians ground them to be used as a purge in medicine and used the sap of the tree in embalming. Eating too many berries caused nausea, and they acted as a diuretic.

Malabathron

Malabathron was more an aromatic than a spice. The dried leaves were brought to Europe from China to India and then, via the trade routes, to Egypt once the trading route to the East had been established. The leaves were pressed for their oil, which was perfumed for export to Rome, and this was also widely used in Egypt. Martial recommended it to perfume hair; in sleep it would "perfume the pillow."[122]

Pepper

Pepper was vital in cooking. It was known in Greece by the fifth century B.C. as a rare commodity and was probably the long pepper from northeast India. Diphilus of Siphnos (a Greek medical writer of the second century B.C.) is said to have put pepper on scallops in the third century B.C., the first known use of the spice in food. Once the trade route to the Far East had been established, pepper became more abundant. Long pepper is hotter than black pepper and was twice its price—so prized was it that it could be used as a currency. It was vital in cookery, and Apicius used it constantly for both savory and sweet recipes, including one that he described as "spiced wine which keeps forever given to travellers on a journey":

> Put pounded pepper in a jar with skimmed honey and when required for drinking, mix some of the honey with some wine.[123]

Emperor Domitian built special warehouses, *horea piperatoria*, for its storage. Peppercorns, however, do not seem to have been known in Egypt until the Greco-Roman period. When the Goths invaded Rome in A.D. 408, they demanded 3,000 pounds of pepper as tribute money in addition to gold and silver.

Poppy

Although not strictly a spice, poppy seeds were regarded as one in the ancient world. The seeds were gathered from wild poppies as they spread from Sumer about 3000 B.C. to the Mediterranean regions and then to Europe, where they have been found on prehistoric sites. The opium poppy was used in Egypt and the classical world as an analgesic, being linked in its modern use to codeine, morphine, and heroin. If too much was taken it caused lethargy. The corn poppy seeds were pressed for their oil, which is not narcotic. The leaves were used in salads. In Greece and Rome, poppy seeds were mixed with beaten egg and sprinkled on bread before baking.

Saffron

Saffron, the flower stems of the saffron crocus, was native to Turkey. Both the spice and yellow-red dye were used extensively in the Mediterranean regions. One purpose was to make sweet wine more yellow, and the wine was sprayed in the air in the theater. In the *Satyricon*, at Trimalchio's feast this wine squirted out when the guests bit into fruit, and this might be the one described by Apicius in a recipe for "spiced wine surprise."[124] Ovid mentioned it being burned on the sacrificial hearth.[125] Its high cost was accounted for by the fact that 20,000 stigmas of the saffron crocus yield only 125 grams (4 ounces).

Sumac

Sumac was the ground fruit of a tree in the Near East. The Syrians prepared and exported it to the Mediterranean lands, where it was used only in its dried form. It was used in Athens in the fourth century B.C. Pliny stated that it could be sprinkled on meat instead of salt, and with silphium added to it "makes all meat sweeter." He warned that it could be a laxative. Its external medicinal qualities include mixing it with honey as a cure for running sores, for relieving a rough tongue, and for clotting a head wound. When eaten, it "checked excessive menstruation."[126]

MEAT

Cattle, sheep, and goats were kept for their meat, milk, and hides. Oxen and cows were domesticated in the Near East before 7000 B.C. and were seen as working animals, especially oxen, which provided traction. Sheep seem to have been domesticated in southwest Asia in the ninth millennium B.C., and from there domestication spread to the Near East. They were herded in Egypt about 5000 B.C.; domestication of goats had taken place in the previous millennium. All these animals were regarded as suitable animals for sacrifice to the gods. In Egypt it was unlikely that peasants ate much meat and would rely on poultry for their protein. In Greece and Rome fresh meat was more available, especially to people in the towns, where meat was sold in the marketplace. Other animals were eaten, but sparingly, as an acquired taste. The meat of bear, for example, according to Galen, should be boiled twice before being eaten.[127]

All parts of animals were used, especially the blood, which was used for a kind of black pudding. Liver might be regarded as heavy on the digestion, although the Greeks cooked it with milk and honey, but geese were force-fed to provide foie gras, and other glands were regarded

A butcher's shop. On the right stands the butcher chopping up a rack of lamb with his huge cleaver on a three-legged butcher's block. His wife sits on the left, adding up the accounts. From the bar above hang sausages, another rack of lamb, and possibly a large liver. Relief in the Dresden Museum. Courtesy of the author.

as excellent foods. In the Near East the fat tails of sheep were especially prized. Opinion on eating brains was divided, some considering it to be an excellent food, others regarding it as an abomination. Tripe was boiled before being eaten. Aristophanes in his play *The Knights* made fun of the sausage seller who also sold tripe: "While to tripe sellers the Gods grant great glory, unless they chose to sell sausages."[128] Bones were split to obtain the marrow, which was regarded as an easily digestible food. Kidneys were less often eaten, although some were found in Egyptian tombs as food for the deceased. In Egypt the heart was regarded as a source of strength. It could be roasted for a sacrifice to the gods, and the worshipper would share in the feast.

Sausages

Much of the offal, as well as other parts, was minced and placed in casings of intestines to make sausages. These could be eaten fresh or cured with salt or brine to preserve them. They were very popular because as they were soft they could be easy to eat, especially by those who had few or no teeth. Greek playwrights made fun of sausage sellers and those who ate them. Strepsiades in Aristophanes' *The Clouds* forgot to slit a sausage when cooking it so that it burst, burned his face, and spattered blood into his eyes.[129] One of the most famous sausages was a Lucanian from southern Italy, composed of minced pork flavored with pepper, cumin, savory, rue, parsley, and bay leaves. Varro said that soldiers appreciated it when they were on service in Lucania. He also mentioned a *fundolus* (bag sausage) open at one end and a *longavo* (long sausage).[130]

Cattle

In all ancient societies beef was eaten sparingly, partly because there was too much meat to eat once an animal had been slaughtered; pork and poultry were more easily obtained sources of protein. In central Europe the early Celts tamed the wild aurochs as well as hunting it for food. Wild aurochs existed in Egypt but by 1400 B.C. seem to have disappeared, probably because they were absorbed into domestic herds. Short-horned cattle were more easily domesticated, and these provided the main meat supply. These had been brought into Egypt as a result of the military operations of the pharaohs and with Asiatic emigrants. In southern Europe bison were hunted. The water buffalo was brought from southern Asia to eastern Europe and from there came to Italy. They were also found in Egypt. Young animals were killed for their meat, which was prepared by boiling or steaming. It was difficult to preserve meat, so usually it was eaten fresh. In Egypt, Greece, and Rome cattle were butchered, jointed, and sold in the marketplace, but could also be given away to the populace after being sacrificed, providing that the gods got their share. Cows were usually slaughtered when they were old and ceased to breed, but young animals were often castrated because they could be more easily fattened; hence the constant allusions to the fatted calf (e.g., St. Luke 15:23 AV). Joints of meat were presented as presents, the haunch or the leg having the most prestige; in Egypt this was presented in temples to the gods. Beef was served more at the tables of the rich than the poor, who made do with other meat or vegetables.

Dog and Hyena

Dog was eaten only as a subsistence food. There is somewhat scanty evidence for the consumption of both dog and cat in Britain. Galen recommended boiled puppy for invalids.[131] Generally, however, although cats and dogs could be sacrificed or mummified, especially in Egypt, they were kept more as pets than as a food supply. Hyenas were included in the food sacrifices for the dead in Egypt. Tomb illustrations, for example, in two mastabas of Mereruka and Kagemni, show them laid out on their backs with their legs in the air while they were force-fed quantities of flesh and roasted duck. The hyenas may have been trained for hunting, but it is possible that poorer people ate them, as the meat was very sweet. These people also ate hippo meat, if hippos were killed when they ravaged crops. Both meat and skin would be of use.

Dormice

Dormice were domesticated and fattened for eating by the Romans, who regarded them as a great delicacy. At Trimalchio's feast in the *Satyricon* they were served glazed with honey and coated with poppy seeds.[132] Varro gave instructions on creating a dormice warren.[133] A large jar with ledges on the inside that could be used as runs was filled with their favorite food, usually acorns and chestnuts. Penned up and left in the dark, the dormice ate constantly and thus became very fat.

Goat

Goats were also kept for their milk, which made excellent cheese. It was the most common cheese in Greece and was also appreciated by the Romans and the Celts. In Egypt goats were raised primarily for their meat and their skins, as leather. Goat meat can vary in taste and smell during the year and if indulged in too much can cause the eater to give off a rank smell. The young were eaten as suckling kid, but this was part of bravado conspicuous consumption, as goats do not produce prolifically and a kid has little meat on it. Wild goats, especially the Barbary goats in Egypt, were hunted in prehistoric and classical times, their wild haunts being part of the attraction of the chase.

Horse

Horse was eaten only when absolutely necessary, because horses were mainly used for traveling. Barbarian tribes, especially those in the steppe regions of central Europe, drank mares' milk. Horace mentioned the "Concanian [a member of a Spanish tribe] who enjoy drinking horses' blood."[134] The Roman historian Tacitus recounted that some troops of Germanicus, returning from a campaign against the Germans in A.D. 16, were shipwrecked off the coast of Schleswig.

Many died of starvation "except a few who supported themselves on the dead horses washed up on the beach."[135]

Pig

Wild boars were tamed in Egypt about 10,000 B.C. and in Europe about 7000 B.C., but both Celts and Romans regarded hunting the wild boar as a sport. Pigs, domesticated about 7000 B.C., were regarded by the Celts, Greeks, and Romans as the most useful of animals, and pork was probably the meat that people ate the most. Varro asked rhetorically, "Who of our people cultivates a farm without keeping swine?"[136] Everything could be used from a pig except the squeal. Pigs were prolific, producing two litters a year, as many as ten piglets per farrow, and were easy to keep, as they would eat almost anything, even each other. One of their favorite foods is acorns. In the *Satyricon*, Trimalchio, as a joke, asks his guests to see on what delicious acorns his pigs are fed; the slaves reveal baskets of dates.[137] Some pigs were fed on figs, as these were said to produce finely flavored liver, and Galen noted that pigs fed in this manner fattened quickly.[138] The young were particularly appreciated, as suckling pig and the eating or presentation of this was a sign of wealth. Pork has to be well cooked; otherwise it may be indigestible and have worms in the flesh. It is, however, easily preserved, and smoked, salted, or placed in brine would last through the winter. Large smoked hams were especially appreciated in Rome. Pork was boiled or roasted. Loin of pork was appreciated, as was suckling pig.[139] Pork can be turned into sausages, and the pigs provided the casings from their intestines; their lard was used for cooking. Herodotus said that the Egyptians thought swine to be unclean beasts.[140]

Sheep

Sheep were kept for their wool, meat, and milk, which makes excellent cheese. They could be kept on sparser pasturage than cattle and were therefore easier to manage. In Greece and Rome they were killed for sacrifices and thus provided a cheaper source of meat than beef to be distributed to worshippers. Plutarch said that in Egypt priests did not eat mutton because they revered the sheep.[141] Young lambs were a luxury for those who could afford them and were therefore a sign of conspicuous consumption. Wealthy Romans, in particular, appreciated spring lamb.

GAME

Hunting for food and sport was common in the ancient world. For many poorer people it supplemented a vegetable diet, secured protein, and often kept them from starving. There was no prohibition against hunting, as was the case in the medieval and subsequent periods. For wealthier people hunting was a source of pleasure and exercise. The catch could be eaten or given as a gift. Both the Egyptians and the Romans set aside regions where rare animals could be hunted, but not necessarily to obtain food.

Boar

Wild boars were hunted for their meat, which both boiled and roasted was regarded as being very nourishing, and because their cunning tactics provided excellent sport. The legendary boar of Formael in the Irish Fenian cycle was reputed to have killed 50 hounds and 50 warriors in a day. Once captured, boars could be fattened. Varro explained how boars could be kept "with no great trouble."[142]

Deer, Antelope, Ibex, Gazelle, and Oryx

Red, roe, and fallow deer were sought for their food value. Venison was eaten more in northern Europe than in Greece and Italy. The elk was hunted in northern Europe. In North Africa gazelle, antelope, ibex, and oryx were hunted. The ibex, in particular, was far more valuable than just for its meat. Its blood was regarded as a cure for gallstones and its heart was eaten for strength. Bezoar, a concretion found in its stomach, was used to treat fainting, diarrhea, jaundice, and melancholia. The Pharaohs were great huntsmen, although they probably hunted more for sport than catching the animals to eat. But when Amenhotep III (Eighteenth Dynasty) issued a scarab commemorating his single-handed killing of 100 animals in one day, which were probably driven toward him rather than being chased, the amount of animal meat resulting must have been eaten rather than left to rot.

Rabbit and Hare

Rabbits were known in Spain and Italy and were believed not to have reached the northern parts of Europe until after the end of the Roman Empire. Recent archaeological excavations in England, however, have revealed that the rabbit was present and eaten from the first or second century A.D. If Julius Caesar is to be believed, the Celts did not eat hare, but this taboo was certainly not observed in Britain and Gaul, for bones have been found in food debris.[143] Hares were enthusiastically hunted in Greece, where they formed an important part of the diet. Pliny said that rabbits were hunted with ferrets. Cut young from their mothers before birth, they were a great delicacy, especially when served without being gutted.[144] Both rabbits and hares could be domesticated in enclosures (*leporaria*), according to Varro, but the hare gives better value, especially after being hunted.[145] Their meat was regarded an excellent food for those who were suffering from dysentery. The desert hare is depicted in scenes in Egyptian tombs being hunted with spears and bows and arrows.

FOWL

Birds of all kinds were caught or kept for their meat and eggs. Apicius's recipes indicated that most varieties of bird were eaten, although not necessarily as everyday fare. Wild birds were trapped, sometimes as songbirds, sometimes as food, but in times of famine and for the poor were always a source of food. The Celts and the Egyptians depended on fish and fowl for their protein. Many game birds were domesticated. Martial spoke of his friend Fautinus's villa at Baiae. In a dirty poultry yard wandered cackling geese, spangled peacocks, painted partridges, speckled guinea fowl, pheasants, domestic poultry, cockerels, wood pigeons, and turtledoves. Faustinus also captured "greedy thrushes."[146]

Chicken

Chickens were easy to keep, providing meat, eggs, and feathers. They were sacrificed to the gods and used for divination and for the sport of cockfighting. Cocks crowing at dawn were useful timekeepers and the equivalent of an alarm clock (St. Mark 14:30–72 AV). They are mentioned in Greek texts of the fifth century B.C. as awakeners. Chicken is an excellent basis for soup, pâté, and other dishes. Columella gave details for fattening them that seem suspiciously like battery farming.[147] The red jungle fowl has been found in Egypt illustrated on an ostracon of the Nineteenth Dynasty, ca. 1350 B.C. Chicken bones and eggs were found in a Seventeenth Dynasty tomb. These birds may have been imported at this time, but they remained comparatively rare until the late Ptolemaic period, probably being brought from Syria. Illustrative evidence is found in the tomb of Petosiris at Tuna el-Gebel, which dates from the reign of Philip Arrhidacus (323–316 B.C.). Diodorus noted that men who were in charge of poultry and geese did not use the birds for hatching eggs but placed the eggs in large ovens to incubate, a practice that continues in modern Egypt.[148]

Apicius had 15 recipes for chicken. Some were "ethnic," such as his chicken in the Numidian fashion. The addition of Jericho date indicates how Roman cookery was cosmopolitan; Apicius's gourmet tastes indicate that this recipe is intended for wealthy households who could afford this imported product.

> Prepare the chicken in the usual way, boil till almost tender and take out of the water. Sprinkle with asafoetida and pepper and roast. Pound pepper, cumin, coriander seed, asafoetida root, rue, Jericho date and pine kernels. Moisten with vinegar, honey, *liquamen* and oil. Mix well and heat. Add to the chicken, sprinkle with pepper and serve.[149]

Cranes, Herons, and Pelicans

Cranes and herons were used in Egypt as decoys to catch waterbirds. It is not certain if herons were eaten, but cranes certainly were being force-fed. A relief from a Fifth Dynasty mastaba at Saqqara shows a man straddling a crane from behind, prying open its bill and forcing food into it to produce a plump bird. They were kept in flocks in aviaries with poultry. Large numbers of them have been found mummified in tombs. They were hung before use and sprinkled with salt and flour and served with a sauce. In Egypt they were eaten in huge numbers, but although the Romans farmed them, they ate them for their rarity value. The Greek prose writer Plutarch, in a somewhat macabre passage, stated that if the birds' eyes were sewn up, they would then "fatten better making the flesh more appetising."[150] Anthimus said to eat them when there was a craving for them, "for they have dark meat and bring on melancholy humour."[151] But most Romans regarded them as a delicacy and excellent food. Apicius reminded his readers to twist and pull the head so that it came off with the sinews, leaving the meat and bones behind.[152] The Greeks and Romans did not eat pelicans, but the birds and their eggs were a favorite food in Egypt in spite of both having a fishy taste. Other water birds enjoyed were snipe, avocet, and coot. Coots were eviscerated before being prepared as a dish for the table. Like the pelican, the flesh has a fishy flavor.

Ducks

Wild ducks were captured in Greece, but the Romans domesticated them. Columella and Varro showed how they should be kept; Columella recommended that teal is the best for keeping in captivity.[153] These birds were much appreciated in Egypt. Some varieties, such as the pintail and the common sheldrake, are not very palatable, but mallard, first domesticated in Italy, was a popular dish. Pintails in Egypt were trapped in a clap-net and force-fed. Illustrations reveal that they were plucked, left to dry, and cooked on spits. Their necks were wrung and the birds were presented as offerings to the god Aten. Herodotus said that the Egyptians salted them and ate them raw.[154]

Geese

Geese were common throughout Europe and were domesticated very early in Greece. Both Greeks and Romans prized their meat and eggs. Goose eggs "in pastry hoods" were eaten at Trimalchio's feast in the *Satyricon*. Caesar said that the Celts did not eat fowl or geese but reared them for pleasure, but the frequency of bones on habitable sites seems to indicate otherwise. In Europe the main variety was the greylag goose; in Egypt it was the white-fronted goose. Anthimus recommended the breast as the most suitable for eating; the hind parts should be avoided because they burden the stomach.[155] Herodotus said that the "fox goose" was sacred to the god of the Nile.[156] Sacred it may have been, but the priests ate it at religious festivals. Roasted goose was a common dish in the dynastic periods. Remains of bean goose and brant were found among the remains of Tutankhamen's funerary meal, and mummified geese were found in the Eighteenth Dynasty tomb of Tuthmosis IV. The white-fronted goose was a sociable and peaceable bird well suited to domestication that provided excellent meat. The Egyptians used these geese as decoys to attract other wild fowl. Geese were force-fed, usually with bread pellets sweetened with dried figs and wine, to fatten them and to produce foie gras. This was highly regarded in Italy, and Martial noted aggressively, "See how the liver is swollen bigger than a big goose. In wonder you will say, 'Where I ask, did it grow?'"[157]

Guinea Fowl

Guinea fowls had been domesticated in pharaonic Egypt, but were not as popular as other birds, as they were more difficult to keep. They were sacrificed to the goddess Isis. Varro said that in Rome they were "the latest foods to come from the kitchen to the dining room because of the pampered tastes of rich people. On account of their scarcity, they fetch a high price."[158]

Ostrich and Flamingo

The Egyptians bred ostriches on special farms for their feathers and for sport, but they also ate them, as did the Persians. Their fat was used in cooking. Ostrich eggs were prized as being able to feed up to eight people. Few Romans ate them, although Apicius gave a sauce for them, which can also be used for parrot and flamingo.[159] Flamingo was rarely eaten. Its tongue was a great delicacy. Emperor Vitellius (A.D. 69) presented the goddess Minerva with a dish containing peacock brains, pike livers, pheasant brains, and flamingo tongues, which he afterward ate. Galen said ostrich could be eaten but the flesh was tough. Emperor Heliogabalus (A.D. 218–222) served it at banquets, and the usurper Firmus was reported to have eaten an ostrich in a single day. Heliogabalus's exotic tastes also extended to eating nightingales' tongues as a protection against disease.

Peafowl

Peacocks and peahens were domesticated birds kept more for show than for eating. Varro said they should be pastured in flocks in fields and are best fed on barley.[160] If they were to be eaten, it was recommended that they should be hung for four or five days until they gave off a good smell. The Roman orator Quintus Hortensius Hortalus (114–50 B.C.) was said to have been the first to serve them at a meal on his inauguration as aedile. The Romans roasted them, and Apicius said that the most prized rissoles were made from the flesh of peacock "if they are fried so as to make the hard skin tender."[161] Peahens' eggs were noted for their eating qualities.

Pheasant and Partridge

Pheasants are a game bird of Europe and the Near East. They were captured in the wild by the Celts, but both pheasants and partridges were being farmed in Greece at an early date. The pheasant is native to central Asia, from whence it spread through the Caucasus to Europe. The Greeks and Romans farmed both birds under careful conditions.

Their eggs were noted as being suitable for invalids. Partridge breasts were good for those who suffered from dysentery. Pheasants, however, were more of a luxury food and were offered as sacrifices by Caligula, together with guinea fowl and flamingos. Martial made a distinction between pheasants and guinea fowls and birds of the farmyard.[162]

Pigeons and Turtledoves

Pigeons and doves were eaten from the wild but were domesticated in pharaonic Egypt and by the Greeks and Romans, first in the open and then in cotes. They bred well in captivity in pens. Pigeons are found among food offerings in tombs, for example a meal in the Second Dynasty tomb at Saqqara. Their dung was used as a fertilizer for growing fruit and vegetables. Turtledoves were considered more of a luxury than pigeons. Classical writers distinguished between domesticated and wild birds and gave instructions for their safekeeping. Varro regarded keeping them as a profitable source of income.[163] Warnings were given about eating wild pigeons, for they might have eaten hellebore, a poisonous plant; the antidote to this was drinking warm oil and old wine to bring up the poison. Squabs of domestic pigeons were, however, much appreciated and recommended as good eating for sick people.

Quails, Orioles, Figpeckers, and Thrushes

Avifauna in the ancient world were abundant and therefore easily available as food. The Egyptians trapped small birds—usually quail, *Teturnix xeturnix*—in large nets in the twice-yearly migration between Africa and Europe, many being exhausted and therefore easy prey by the time they arrived in Egypt. Quails were found in a Second Dynasty tomb at Saqqara, which dated to ca. 3000 B.C. They were often salted and eaten raw. Quails were trapped in the summer and kept for eating in autumn when they were thought to be at their best. In the *Satyricon*, Trimalchio served them, covered with peahen yoke, in pastry cases shaped like eggs. Other small birds were trapped wild and then prepared for table. Varro gave detailed instruction as to how they may be fattened.[164] Thrushes were regarded as a delicacy in both Greece and Rome, being fattened and sold. One way to make them look fatter when they were sold was to blow into their stomachs. Skewed, covered with honey, and roasted on a spit, they were luxury items. It was while roasting thrushes that Horace's innkeeper almost set his inn roof on fire.[165] Orioles were trapped to protect the fig and date crops, but eating these fruits was also presumed to make their flesh sweet. Figpeckers were a delicacy, being easy to digest.

EGGS

The Egyptians ate eggs of all birds, including those of pelicans, which have a fishy flavor. The Eighteenth Dynasty tomb of Haremhed at Thebes has an illustration of a pelican and a basket of eggs. Eggs were easily obtained and were recommended as a wholesome food, being consumed hard- or soft-boiled, fried, poached, and used as a binding agent in cookery, especially in soufflés and sauces. Eggs were taken from both domesticated and wild birds. Duck eggs were eaten in northern Europe and by the Egyptians, but do not seem to have been appreciated by the Greeks and Romans, who preferred chicken and pheasant eggs. Goose eggs had to be lightly boiled; otherwise they were indigestible. Eggs were used in baking to enrich dough and in Egypt are illustrated in tombs, where they are presented as offerings to deities. They are depicted placed in bowls, layered between leaves, which could help to keep them cool. The Egyptians had devised a way of incubating eggs. They were collected from peasant farmers and given to rearers who followed a traditional procedure to ensure incubation for 26 days.

Anthimus noted approvingly that a person could eat as many eggs as he or she wanted, but that the correct way to prepare eggs was to place them in cold water and cook them over a low flame.[166] The poet Ovid, as might be expected, mentioned their use as an aphrodisiac, and other authors extolled their quality.[167] Pliny commented on medicinal uses and said no other food was so nourishing in sickness without overloading the stomach.[168] Soft eggs were regarded as a remedy for diarrhea, and goose eggs were beneficial in medicine. Hard-boiled eggs were regarded as more substantial food.

Apicius gave a recipe for an egg custard:

> Measure five eggs to a pint of milk or three eggs to half a pint. Beat the eggs with the milk. Strain into a dish and cook very slowly over a fire. When the mixture is set, sprinkle with pepper and serve.[169]

FISH

Fish were a major source of food in the ancient world, although its availability and palatability depended on how far a market was from the river or sea. Dried and salted fish could extend its range of sale.

The Egyptians caught fish in shallow pools at the time of the Nile's inundation. Diodorus commented that the "Nile contains every variety of fish for it supplies the natives not only with abundant subsistence from the fresh fish caught, but also yields an unfailing multitude for salting."[170] Small fish could be made into garum or *allec*. The Romans bred fish in fishponds and knew how to exploit fishing techniques. Ausonius, a Latin poet who lived in Gaul in the fourth century A.D., detailed in his poem *Mosella* the fish obtainable from the River Moselle in Germany. Aelian (a Greek rhetorician who taught in Rome in the third century A.D.) in *The Nature of Animals* remarked that the Danube freezes in winter but fish could still be caught by cutting holes in the ice.[171] The variety of fish available can be deduced from depictions on mosaics, wall paintings, and pottery and from Apicius's chapters headed "Thalassa" (the sea) and "Halieus" (the fisherman).

Bonito, Mackerel, and Tuna

Bonito, mackerel, and tuna were an oily, nutritious, and important part of the diet and could be eaten fresh, smoked, or salted. When caught in bulk, the intestines of mackerel provided one of the main ingredients of *allec*. Mackerel could be salted for consumption in winter, and salted fish was a huge industry at some Mediterranean ports. Intestines of tuna and bonito were also used for garum and *allec,* but the firm, tasty flesh was greatly appreciated. The migratory patterns of these fish were predictable, and fishermen prepared themselves to make huge catches at specified times. Cooks appreciated these fishes to serve at banquets, although when fresh the flesh of bonito and tuna is somewhat chewy. Archestratus provided a recipe:

> Wrap pieces of tunny [tuna] in fig leaves. Season with marjoram but not too much; no cheese and no nonsense; fasten the fish neatly within the fig leaves; tie it with hemp. Place the parcel in hot ashes and note the time so that you do not burn it.[172]

Drying could preserve the oily meat. The best mackerel came from Gades (Cadiz), being exported in barrels to Greece, Italy, and North Africa. Galen thought that the second-best tuna came from Spain, and "the best was the Byzantine."[173]

Flounder, Halibut, Plaice, Sole, and Turbot

The ancient world had a problem in matching names to these individual flat fishes. Xenocrates (who was head of the Athens Academy in the fourth century B.C.) referred to this group of fish as *plateis,* while Pliny called them *plani.*[174] Though often referred to in general terms, they were appreciated for their size and eating quality. Galen implied that their size might be a problem for the cook to fry; baking was recommended.[175] Turbot was particularly prized. Martial complained, when dining with Ponticus (a friend), that he was served brill while Ponticus had turbot.[176] Plaice and sole were regarded as being especially good for the sick, being easily digestible, especially when simply cooked. Apicius provided a recipe for a hot mayonnaise sauce; it is best to cook the soles slightly before adding the sauce:

> Place clean soles in a shallow pan. Add oil, *liquamen* and wine. Pound and grind pepper, lovage, and oregano; mix with some of the fish stock, add beaten raw eggs and work into a smooth mixture. Pour this over the soles and cook gently over a low fire. When the mixture has set, sprinkle with pepper and serve.[177]

Mullet

Species of red and gray mullet were caught in great quantity in the Mediterranean. Gray mullet was also a freshwater species, which traveled up the Nile as far as the first cataract. They were honored at Elephantine as heralds of the flood and messengers of the flood god, Hapy. In the Nile gray mullet was so abundant that it was salted and exported, especially the roe. The fourth-century Greek poet Antiphanes said that the gray mullet was best split down the center, then flattened and sprinkled with salt, vinegar, and crushed stalk of silphium.[178] The Romans farmed both gray and red mullet so that they could be fattened to get a good weight. Red mullet was prolific in the Mediterranean. They were most appreciated in the spring, grilled over a brazier. Pliny said that the fish was the most popular. He had a bizarre recipe for wine in which red mullet had been left to ferment and decompose in wine, although he did say that this might forever put one off drinking wine.[179]

Salmon

Salmon was probably the most appreciated fish in northern Europe. It played a central part in Celtic mythology, such as the tale of Finn mac Cumaill, and was regarded as the source of wisdom. Roman soldiers in northern Europe consumed its flesh avidly, but it was unknown to the Egyptians and the Greeks. Ausonius liked the pink-flaked salmon of the Moselle, and Pliny said that the salmon was appreciated in Aquitania better than any sea fish, but the sixth-century senator Cassiodorus preferred the Rhine salmon.[180]

Sea Bass, Grouper, and Comber

Sea bass could be caught in rivers, especially at the mouth of the Tiber. Juvenal said that it was a regular visitor to the cesspit of the Tiber, that is, the spewing out of the Cloaca Maxima.[181] The grouper was a popular fish in Greece, and the comber, a much smaller fish, according to Pliny, was useful for its medicinal purposes.[182] Sea bass should be cooked whole without being gutted or scaled, and the head of the fish was regarded as a great delicacy.

Shark and Swordfish

Shark was not widely eaten, but Xenocrates in the fourth century B.C. approved of this fish for display at banquets. Swordfish were caught with harpoons.[183] These large fish must have been difficult to catch but obviously were worth the effort. Xenocrates recommended eating a swordfish's tail with mustard.[184] Aelian said that swordfish, with its sharp weapon, attacked ships.[185]

Sturgeon

Sturgeons were eaten for their flesh, not for their caviar. Pliny said that in his time the fish was held in no esteem, but he also mentioned the sturgeon of the River Po, which grew so big that, when they were caught, they had to be pulled out of the water by a team of oxen.[186]

Other Sea Fish

Smaller fish included the wrasse or rockfish, which were regarded as a tender and healthy meal. The parrot wrasse, a fish with rainbow-colored fins, was much admired for table display. Sprats, sardines, whitebait, anchovies, and pilchards were often fried together. Baby squid could be included. Archestratus recommended adding sea-anemone tentacles to this small fry dish.[187] The Romans often used smaller fish, especially anchovies and sprats, as a basis for garum and *allec*.

Eels and Lampreys

Eels were prolific in European rivers and were eagerly sought as a source of food as they were rich in oil. In Greece the best source was said to be Lake Copais (north of Thebes in Boeotia) and the River Strymon in northern Greece, where the eels were reputed to be huge and amazingly fat. Copais is a landlocked lake, and it is difficult to see how the eel, which migrates from the Atlantic to European rivers, could have reached it. One suggestion is that eels might have used the underground river Cephissus. In northern Europe river eels were trapped in basket traps or speared with tridents. The Egyptian eels were rare south of Cairo but could be fished along the coast. As eels live in freshwater, one way of catching them was to muddy the water, but then the eels must be scrupulously cleaned before cooking. They cannot be farmed and must be eaten absolutely fresh or cured or smoked. Galen advised that they should be smelled to ascertain their freshness. One method of cooking was to cut them into chunks and place them on a skewer, basting them constantly with brine.

Apicius had a sauce for eels:

> Pound pepper, Lovage, Syrian sumach, dried mint, rue berries, yolks of boiled egg, mulsum, vinegar, *liquamen* and oil. Mix well and gently heat.[188]

Lampreys were not appreciated so much. Pliny mentioned that they were caught in Gaul, although this may refer to the moray eel, and said that Gaius Hirrius devised ponds where lampreys could flourish.[189] Like eels, it might be dangerous to catch large lampreys, but they were a source of food. The Atlantic species were caught off the coast of Spain and exported from Gades (Cadiz). The Romans farmed them in fishponds and even used them as an instrument of execution. Vedius Pollio is reputed to have punished his slaves by tossing them into a fishpond; Crassus kept one as a pet and cried bitterly when it died.

Freshwater Fish

In Egypt, the Nile had its own plentiful species of fish. They were an important source of protein, although eating of some fish was taboo for religious reasons. In Ptolemaic Egypt salted and pickled fish was exported to Rome. The most important were the gray mullet, the shad, and the catfish, which was believed to guide the solar boat through the dark river of the underworld. Catfish-headed demons are depicted on royal tombs as hauling the solar boat through the dark until it could rise the next morning. In prehistoric Egypt it was the custom to remove catfish heads, dry them, and store them to be eaten elsewhere.

Fish peculiar to the Nile included *mormyridae,* or elephant-snout fish (distinguished by their long, trunklike snout); tiger fish; the *barbus,* a river bream; the Nile perch; and the *Tilapia nilotica,* which was a favorite in Rome.

European freshwater fish included carp, chub, perch, pike, and trout. Carp were caught in European rivers and might also be farmed; the fish is noted for its numerous bones. Chub was similar in appearance and taste to gray mullet and again was suitable for farming, but one problem was that it had to be eaten the day it was caught. The Greeks do not mention trout. It was extensively fished in European rivers, and bones of the fish have been found on Roman sites in Britain, where it was probably eaten boiled or fried. The Romans fished trout for sport and food in the Moselle. Ausonius, who said that its taste was better than that of any other river fish, also described the salmon trout. Pike often inhabit rivers in northern Europe. He despised it as preying on other fish, and said that it was fried in cook shops "rank with its greasy flavour."[190] Sheatfish were common in the Danube, the Main, and the Moselle. The fish was salted for winter eating. Poorer people ate tench and shad, presumably because there was not much flesh on them. The shad, migrating from the sea, was a very bony fish.

CRUSTACEA

Clams, Cockles, Mussels, Scallops, and Whelks

These were less appreciated than oysters. Nevertheless, the best clams were said to be Venus clams from Alexandria, and large scallops came from the Greek Straits of Tarentum. Martial noted that "Ponticus eats oysters fattened in the Lucrine Lake, but sucks a mussel through a hole in its shell."[191] Mussels were best eaten in spring and were regarded as a laxative and a diuretic. Pliny thought drinking water in which they had been boiled caused a person to put on weight.[192] Whelks and cockles had tougher flesh but had the reputation of being an aphrodisiac. Scallops were served with sauces, although eating too many might cause diarrhea.

Crabs, Crayfish, Shrimps, and Lobsters

Most of these were avidly consumed, but consumers were aware that if not fresh they could cause illness. Columella in his detailed instructions on rearing ducks said that they could be fed on river crayfish and any other shelled fish.[193] Pliny preferred small crustaceans to be used for *allec*. Minced prawns and lobsters could be made into fishcakes, and Apicius had a recipe for crayfish rissoles:

> Boil the flesh, chop, and form into balls with *liquamen*, pepper and eggs.[194]

Lobsters were portrayed on tomb reliefs in Egypt, for example that at Deir el-Bahari of Queen Hatshepsut's Punt expedition. Archestratus said that good prawns were available in Macedonia and Ambracia.[195] Martial believed that the best prawns came from the lower reaches of the River Liris in Latium, and Pliny the Younger said he found them near his Laurentan villa.[196]

Cuttlefish, Octopus, and Squid

Cuttlefish were regarded as more of a delicacy than octopus or squid. Their ink was used in sauces as well as in medicine. Columella said ground cuttlefish shell, when blown into the eye three times a day, could cure swellings.[197] The flesh of octopus and squid was beaten to tenderize it. Octopus flesh was regarded as an aphrodisiac.

Oysters

Oysters were the most popular of all the mollusks and were eaten in great quantities in prehistoric and classical times, as evidenced by the huge heaps of shells found on habitable sites. Xenocrates and Pliny listed places where the best oysters could be found.[198] The Romans appear to have cultivated oysters in *ostriaria*. These consisted of ropes with stones on the end to provide anchorage, hanging down from horizontal wooden supports; oysters attached themselves to the ropes. The Romans appreciated British oysters, which were exported to Rome. Some of the best were Brundisian oysters, which were fattened in Lucrine Lake in the Bay of Naples. Oysters are eaten raw or fried. If eaten raw they must be fresh; hence the warnings against food poisoning. Eating large quantities of oysters indicated a person's wealth. Juvenal satirized Nero, who could tell at his first bite from where an oyster had come.[199] Oysters were considered to be an aphrodisiac; hence their popularity. Recent research has indicated that there is some proof for this belief. They are rich in amino acids, especially in spring, which spur on increased levels of testosterone in males and progesterone in females. They have to be eaten raw to be most effective.

Sea Urchins

This spiny, hard-shelled creature was used in the production of *allec* but was also regarded as a delicacy. The shell was ground and used in medicine. Apicius treated them as another produce of the sea.[200] They were boiled and served with a sauce. That they were relatively unknown to the Greeks is indicated by the account of a Spartan soldier who was invited to a banquet, took one, and, not willing to confess his ignorance, stuffed one into his mouth to consume it whole, with predictable consequences. Rather than display any weakness, he declared he would not let it go but would eat no more of its kind.

Snails

Edible snails were found all over Europe. Prehistoric people enjoyed them, but it was the Romans who fattened them for dinner parties using a mixture of emmer and wine. Some writers stated that they should be boiled three times to make them tender, but Apicius fried and roasted them as well as detailing how they should be fattened on milk.[201] Varro noted the different varieties—small white ones from near Reate, big ones from Illyricum, and those of middle size from Africa—and explained how to make a small enclosure (*coclearium*) for them.[202] Pliny said that Fulvius Lippinus was the first to keep and fatten snails (ca. 49 B.C.), on thickened wine and spelt.[203] An interesting discovery in modern times is that snails, especially in hot regions, contain a great deal of fluid in their shells. To anyone living in those regions the meat and the fluid (hemolymph) would provide food and drink, a factor that may account for the popularity of snails.

DAIRY PRODUCTS

Milk

The earliest reference to milk in Egypt seems to be in the first millennium B.C. An illustration on an Eleventh Dynasty sarcophagus of Queen Kahyat shows cows shedding tears for the loss of their milk, which is being taken away from them instead of feeding their calves.

There could be a problem with milk in Mediterranean areas, as it needs to be kept in cool conditions. Pliny implied that cow's milk, although important nutritionally to the Romans, was of greater value in cheese making. His reasoning might be that milk quickly goes sour in a hot country. In the northern areas of the Roman Empire, given the cooler climate, both milk and cheese could be equally important. Fresh milk is readily available to keepers of herds of animals, and milk and cheese were the normal food of shepherds. In the *Odyssey* Odysseus and his men stole milk and cheese from the cave of the Cyclops, Polyphemus, and escaped by tying themselves under the bellies of the sheep as they emerged from the cave.[204] Roman writers, however, discussed the various qualities of animal's milk, but indicated that milk is best taken when mixed with honey, wine, or salt. Cow's milk was the best, followed by horse's milk, camel's milk, goat's milk, and lastly sheep's milk. Goat's milk, however, was recommended when a person had dysentery, as it was thought to be the most nourishing. Curdled milk (*oxygala* or *melca*), probably a kind of yogurt, was acceptable because it was easier to digest. Even so, it was still to be mixed with honey or olive oil. Columella gave instructions on how to make sour milk with seasoning into something resembling flavored yogurt.[205]

Butter

Butter was used mainly in northern Europe. The Romans and the Greeks regarded it as a barbarian food, and the Romans used it for oiling the skin after a bath in a cold area. Like cheese, it could be kept for long periods in a cool climate without going rancid; in southern Europe and in Egypt it was not a practicable commodity. Wooden casks containing a fatty substance given the name "bog butter" have been found in Irish and Scottish bogs. Although some may be adipocere, a waxy material formed from animal fat, some is conceivably butter, and the cask was put in the bog to preserve it. In the Near East and Egypt, clarified butter seems to have been produced that was akin to the ghee used in the Far East today, that is, butter that has been melted until it froths, then strained and allowed to solidify. This eliminates the salt and water and lessens the tendency of butter to burn and discolor. Strabo mentioned something similar as a product of Arabia and Ethiopia, where it was used instead of olive oil.[206]

Cheese

Cheese was popular throughout Europe and the Mediterranean. Two jars from the First Dynasty tomb of Hor-aha contained fatty substances, which have been identified as the remains of soft cheese. Cheese was made from the milk of cows, sheep, goats, and camels. It is a nutritious food with a high energy, protein, and calcium content. It is also high in saturated fat, and disagrees with people who are lactose-intolerant. This fact was known to Hippocrates, who said that some people could eat as much cheese as they liked without any problem, whereas others suffered acutely if they ate even the smallest amount. Columella and other writers give detailed descriptions of cheese making, and discuss the differences between hard (or dry, salty) cheese and soft cheese akin to the modern ricotta. Localities of cheeses are given. The Greeks liked soft cheese from Cythnoso and Nelabrum. In particular demand by the Romans were cheeses from the Apennines and from Sarcina in Umbria, and a Luna variety from the borders of Etruria and Liguria. Smoked cheese came from the Velumbrian district. Roman writers, however, were careful to point out that cheese could cause flatulence and constipation. Pliny noted that animals put to pasture on salty land produced milk, which gave "a far more pleasing quality to cheese."[207] In Egypt a soft cheese was made, which could be mixed with oil or herbs. Cheeses were washed in brine to preserve them, which also reduces the saltiness.

CONDIMENTS

Honey

Honey was the universal sweetener of the ancient world and was used by the Celts as a basis for mead. It was available all year round and had excellent storage qualities. It is an excellent source of energy and is easily digested. Even if the ancient world did not know this, the value and power of honey was realized; hence honey and milk, also a wholly natural food, are frequently mentioned as being offered to gods, and the land of Israel flowed with it. Honey resists bacterial growth; hence its use as a preservative. Columella said that there was no kind of fruit that could not be preserved in honey.[208]

Honey was gathered from the wild, but beekeeping had begun in Egypt in the third millennium B.C. The bee symbolized Lower Egypt and tributes from Upper Egypt included honey. The Theban Eighteenth Dynasty tomb of the vizier Rekhmire showed honey being brought in by tax collectors and being poured into jars of different sizes as if they were for different kinds of honey. In another scene bakers are heating honey and dates to add to or serve with loaves. In Egypt honey could be used in kind to pay taxes and pay wages.

The Greeks and Romans also knew the art of beekeeping. Columella, Varro, and Virgil were eager to share their knowledge.[209] As today, smoking was used to keep bees at a distance when the honey was collected, so that some honey probably had a smoky taste. A relief in a temple at Abusir shows the process, from bees being smoked to subdue them while a man takes the comb to the final product being packed into jars. There were varieties and qualities of honey, the best being that collected from the bees on Mount Hymettus in Attica. Other honeys came from Salamis, Letos, and Hybla. Some, however, were poisonous, such as honeys from Corsica. Diocletian's Price Edict put the best quality of honey at 40 denarii a pint and the second quality at 24 denarii a pint.

Honey was used in cooking, and there are references in early Irish legends of salmon being cooked coated with honey; meat was rubbed with honey and salt and then spit-roasted over a fire. Honey was used in bread making; honey cakes were popular as gifts to both humans and gods. Honey was added to wine to make a sweetened drink called *mulsum,* which the Romans served with the first course of a meal. Dissolved in water and with spices added, it was used to treat a sore throat; mixed with vinegar, it was known as *oxymeli;* and mixed with water, it was known as *hydromeli* or *melikreton.*

Honey had many medicinal qualities. The antibacterial activity in some honey is a hundred times more powerful than in others. The high sugar levels create an environment that cleans a wound and inhibits bacteria. With chronic wounds there is also a malodor for which honey provides an excellent remedy. When certain varieties of honey are diluted, they release hydrogen peroxide, which is an antiseptic, useful in treating burns and ulcers. It is hypertonic and can draw water from bacterial cells, causing them to shrivel and die. This added to its value in the ancient world. There were limitations, as it could not be used on anyone with an allergy to bee stings or pollen.

Liquamen, Garum, *Muria,* and *Allec*

These were most important culinary ingredients in the Roman world acceptable to enhance a flavor, increase salt content, and possibly disguise a tainted taste. Parts of fish normally considered refuse were made into a fish sauce or paste. *Liquamen* (or garum; the names seem to be interchangeable) was a fermented fish sauce made by placing whole fish, preferably mackerel, in troughs and mixing them with salt. Other fish used might be tuna, anchovies, and sprats, and even sea urchins, oysters, and other shellfish. The mixture was left to ferment for up to three months. The reaction, which takes place when the guts of the fish react with salt to produce brine, is an enzymatic proteolysis.

It took place in the open; the sun would hasten the process. The liquid (*liquamen*) would then be drained off ready for sale. *Liquamen* is related to the fish sauces used in the Far East: Filipino *patis*, Vietnamese *nuoc-mam*, and Thai *nam-pla*, although the last tastes more of salt than fish. *Liquamen* could be made in any quantity, providing that the precise ratio of salt to fish was observed and that the product was allowed to mature for the required time. The ratio could be between 5:1 and 1:1. Each production area would have its own distinct taste, which might be due to the addition of wine, herbs, and spices; the length of preparation time; the quantity of salt; and the temperature. The product was used subtly in every kind of dish, savory and sweet. Serving both as a culinary and as a medicinal product, it substituted for salt. Apicius had a recipe for a *patina* of pears:

> Peel, core and stew pears, pound with pepper, cumin, honey, *passum, liquamen* and a little oil. Add beaten eggs to make a thickened *patina* mixture, sprinkle with pepper, and serve.[210]

Muria seems to have been a product akin to garum but not properly fermented. Martial considered it as an inferior product when made of the entrails of fish other than mackerel, mainly tuna.[211] *Allec*, the residue after the liquid is drained off, is akin to the fish paste *blachan* used in Southeast Asia today. It was probably a valuable source of calcium as small bones were included. According to Pliny, *allec* was produced from a variety of fish otherwise too small to be economically useful and was used for a variety of purposes, including cures for burns, ulcers, and pains in the mouth as well as for alleviating dog or crocodile bites. It could be mixed with *mulsum* until it was sweet enough to drink. Other products were *hydrogaron*, where the fish sauce was diluted with water or wine and seasoned with herbs, and *oxygaron*, where the sauce is mixed with vinegar. In Greece *halme* was a salty liquid used for stewing fish or as a dressing for suitable foods. This seems to have been a vegetarian version for it produced from pears.[212]

Olives, Olive Oil, and Other Oils

Olives and olive oil were imported into Egypt, especially in pharaonic times. Olive trees were cultivated in Egypt from the Eighteenth Dynasty. In Egypt, Ramses III was reputed to have tried to plant olive groves near to the temple of the sun god, Ra, at Heliopolis. Strabo said, however, that olive trees grew only at Alexandria and in the Fayum.[213] In pharaonic times olive oil was imported into Egypt in large quantities and more attention was paid to growing olive trees. The Egyptians probably used less olive oil in cooking than the Greeks and Romans because they used rendered animal fat. There were also other oils that were preferred, such as linseed oil and *bak*, an oil obtained from the seeds of the *ben* tree. A sweet oil was extracted from the oil-bearing seeds of the fruit of the *hegelig* tree. Linseed oil and castor oil were also used for lighting and as a cooking medium.

The olive tree was domesticated in the Near East about the fourth millennium B.C. and then spread to the Mediterranean regions. Olive-tree culture was most important to the Greeks and Romans because it was an important source of food and oil. Bread, salt, and olives were the staple food of the peasant class. Cato recommended that they be given windfall olives and mature olives that yielded little oil.[214] Columella, Cato, and Pliny gave detailed instructions about the growing and storage of olives and the production of olive oil, as well as information of the different varieties of olives.[215] Methods of cultivation, harvesting, production, and storage all mattered. The best way of storing olives was by layering them with fennel in jars filled with brine. Olive oil must be stored in the dark and with little or no contact with air. The ideal storage vessel therefore was the amphora.

Cato gave a recipe for a relish or confection of green and mottled olives:

> Remove stones from green, ripe or mottled olives and season as follows. Chop the olive flesh and add oil, vinegar, coriander, cumin, fennel, rue and mint. Cover with oil in an earthen dish and serve when required.[216]

The olive was prized so much that the Greeks and Romans used an olive wreath to honor victorious athletes or triumphant soldiers. The fruit can be very bitter, but this can be alleviated by pressing it between the finger and thumb before eating it; when pressed for olive oil the bitterness is automatically removed. Olive oil was used in cooking, as a marinating medium, as a dressing for salads and vegetables, and for conserving food. It could be used for lighting by the wealthy, sealing wood, and lubrication. It was used in perfumes, in medicine, for oiling clothes, and for ritual practices. The Roman army rubbed it onto limbs in the belief that it made them supple, and also used it to oil joints in their armor. Pliny said that a happy life was one that used wine inside and olive oils outside, but he warned against keeping both olives and olive oil too long. Columella thought that the Posean variety of olive oil lasted for about a year.

Although Poseidonius said that the Celts disliked the taste of olive oil because they were not used to it, the vast quantities of olive oil that the Romans brought to the northern parts of their empire seemingly retrained the Celtic palate.

Salt

Sodium chloride is one of the minerals essential to human and animal life. The Celts at Halstatt mined it to use as a trading commodity. The Celts and the Romans exploited salt mines for rock salt, and the Egyptians had naturally occurring saltpans in the western desert, but the main supply of salt was obtained by evaporating seawater in coastal areas. In the Roman Empire part of a man's pay was made in salt; hence the term *salarium,* or salt money, and the modern term *salary.* In Egypt, salt was an acceptable commodity for bartering. Salt was a necessity in culinary preparation and was the most efficient preservative known at the time. It also ensured that the proper flavor-producing organisms developed in bacon, ham, cheese, and fish products. Salt is a natural drying agent, which draws water out of a product by osmosis. Food could be rubbed with it or put into casks between layers of salt and pressed with stones so that the natural juices flowed out. Only high-quality products and good-quality salt would ensure a decent result, because poor-quality salt will not penetrate quickly enough and the inner part of the product will deteriorate before the salt or brine reaches the center.

The Romans kept salt production under imperial control, organized by a procurator, although extraction and distribution could be leased to private contractors. The salt produced was of a grayish color, so it was often mixed with herbs when placed on the table. Brine mixed with vinegar could be used in preparation of *liquamen,* and the use of this produce often canceled the need for salt. Several different types of salt were known. Herodotus mentioned that in Libya a purple salt was mined. Different types of salt named in lists in Egyptian tombs mention a red salt. Salt producers could have important status. In Egypt, Ramses III granted them special privileges. Salt sprinkled on bread was offered to guests as a sign that they were welcomed, and acceptance of this meant that the guest agreed that no harm would be done to the household. Natron, a crystalline mixture of sodium carbonate (washing soda), sodium bicarbonate (baking soda), and sodium chloride (salt), was not

Salt panning at Roman Middlewich, England. Drawn by Charlotte Fawley. Courtesy of the author.

used in Egypt for cooking but was used extensively in preparing bodies for mummification, as its dehydrating action decreases fatty tissue.

Sugar

Both the Greeks and the Romans had heard of sugar. Dioscorides spoke of a crystallized honey found in India and Arabia that could be crunched in the mouth like salt, and Pliny had heard of something similar, describing it as "a kind of honey which collects in reeds, white like gum and brittle to the teeth."[217] Some sugar was therefore imported, but it was expensive and was mainly used for medicinal purposes, somewhat surprisingly as a laxative.

Vinegar

Vinegar, produced from secondary fermentation of wine, was not used so much as a condiment but was important to preserve food and to use in cooking and in medicine. When mixed with water, it was a popular drink with Roman soldiers on the march for slaking their thirst. Flavored with herbs, it became a drink called *posca*. Mixed with water and known as *oxykraton*, it was a medicine.

BEVERAGES

Beer

If cereals are allowed to ferment, an alcoholic drink can be produced. The most useful cereal for this is barley. Barley, allowed to germinate and produce shoots, develops an enzyme, diastase, that converts starch into fermentable sugars. To encourage this process, the grain is spread out and dried to convert it into malt. Roasting can stop this malting process, after which the crushed malt can be steeped in water to produce a brown sweet liquid called wort. To increase the taste, the wort can be boiled with honey, wormwood, or herbs. One such was costmary, a hardy perennial brought to the northern areas of Europe by the Romans. Its other name is *alecost*, as its main use is in flavoring ale. Beer needs hops to produce the bitter taste, but the beer produced in the ancient world was more like a barley wine or ale. Ale, lacking hops, needs to be brewed more frequently and probably contained more residue than a modern drink. Indeed, Xenophon had noted than in Armenia beer was drunk by pushing a straw beneath the top layer.[218] A funerary stela of the Eighteenth Dynasty from Tell el-Amarna in Egypt shows men drinking through a long straw, bent at an angle to go deep into the jar.

Beer was more appreciated in northern Europe and in Egypt than by the Greeks and Romans. Aristophanes quite bluntly called Egyptian beer a "dark, laxative purgative."[219] But when the empire was extended, the troops often drank the local beer. The Greeks brewed *zythos*, meaning a drink, which is fermented or leavened, a name they originally applied to Egyptian beer brewed from barley. Beer was known in Sumer and Mesopotamia in the third millennium B.C., where it was widely appreciated. In Egypt beer was the drink of the common people, especially workmen, and it was brewed in a variety of strengths. Much of it was made from a deliberate fermentation of barley, but samples of starch granules in ancient Egypt in beer residue reveal a fermented mixture of coarsely ground baked, cooked malt or grain together with unheated and uncooked malt. Egyptians were specific about the origins of beer. Most was produced in Egypt, but there is mention of beer imported from Syria and from Qede. It could be flavored with fruit juices or sweetened with dates. Diodorus said that Egyptian beer "had a bouquet not much inferior to that of wine."[220] A writer of the Nineteenth Dynasty said that every street stank of beer and that beer would send a soul to perdition.[221]

Cider and Perry

Cider was made from sweet apples. A large pit at Doncaster in Britain contained about 1,400 crushed apple pits, which probably were used to make a cider drink. If cider was made, then pears could have been used to make perry. Palladius mentioned cider and cider vinegar.[222]

Mead

Mead is a fermented drink of honey and water, which was drunk widely in northern Europe and was the main drink for the Celts at the great ritual festivals, which implies that mead drinking was a communal act. Mead could be flavored with herbs and spices and in particular wormwood, which was believed to be excellent for the stomach.[223] Aristotle described the process of making it by the Taulantii of Illyria, and Pliny commented on *hydromeli* made in Phrygia.[224]

Posca

Posca was a drink made from the poorest wines, which were often vinegar and mixed with herbs. It was a common drink among the poorer classes and in the Roman army. Some emperors, such as Hadrian, drank it to show they were as one with their troops. This was probably the drink offered to Jesus on the cross (St. Mark 15:36 AV), and therefore this was not intended as an insult but as the usual drink of Roman soldiers.

Water

Both the Greeks and the Romans were aware of the need for clean water. Varro stated that stagnant water bred minute creatures, which were invisible to the eye. They could enter the body through the mouth and nose, causing serious disorders. Athenaeus declared that running water was better than still water and when aerated became better still. Mountain water was healthier to drink than water from the plains because it was mixed with less solid matter. Water was, of course, needed for cooking and cleaning and was mixed with wine. In cooking it was often boiled, which would have helped to sterilize it. Athenaeus said that water that cooked vegetables slowly, such as that with soda and salt, was poor.[225] He had obviously noted the hardening of vegetables by the formation of calcium pectate through heating them in water containing calcium ions. The provision of clean water was therefore essential, and although water was available in streams, rivers, and wells, the Romans increased the supply, bringing fresh water to cities and town by means of aqueducts. The water also supplied bathhouses, which were an essential part of the classical lifestyle; at mineral spas such as Bath in Britain and Wiesbaden in Germany, the waters would have been drunk for health reasons. In Egypt, water was obtained from the Nile and from wells and collected in cisterns. The Greeks and Romans used snow as a cooling agent for wine. This was collected from mountain areas and kept in deep pits to conserve it. Pliny the Younger mentioned the use of snow in foods, and Apicius the use of snow to cool a kind of chicken salad dish:

> Pound together celery seed, dried pennyroyal, dried mint, ginger, fresh coriander, stoned raisins, honey, vinegar, oil and wine to make a dressing. Place in a mould pieces of Picentine bread and arrange in alternating layers chicken meat, goat's sweetbreads, Vestine cheese, pine-kernels, cucumbers and finely chopped dried onions. Pour the dressing over this. Cool in snow and serve.[226]

Wine

In Egypt there was a long tradition of wine making from the time of the First Dynasty, about 3000 B.C. Vineyards in Egypt produced large quantities of grapes, which were turned into wine. The Egyptians drank it in great quantities, as they thought it no disgrace to get drunk at parties and festivals. Residue in vessels found in tombs has been assumed to be either wine or grape juice. Ramses II planted numerous vineyards in northern and southern oases and in the delta region. Foreign slaves tended them. Wines in Egypt were usually named according to their vintages, with details of the village, town, district, and region being recorded, and this included a range from sweet to very dry. The Mareotic, produced in great quantities, was the most esteemed. Athenaeus said that it was remarkable for its sweetness.

Strabo said that Egypt "produced wine in no small quantity."[227] Some wines were so light that they could be drunk by invalids without inconvenience. Another problem was that the wines could go sour in the hot climate. Egyptian wines could be spiced, and there was a suggestion that they might be drunk through straws if a heavy sediment was noticeable. They therefore often sieved their wine, a custom followed by the Romans. The lees were used as a poultice, an enema, and as a bandage.

The Egyptians also had a wine, which Pliny called factitious or artificial wine, extracted from a variety of fruits.[228] Palm wine was common, and Herodotus noted a wine used by Egyptians in the embalming process.[229]

Wine was produced in great quantities and varieties in Greece and throughout the Roman Empire, where vine growing and the subsequent production of wine became widespread. Drinking wine was common among the upper classes and thus attractive to the lower classes. Wine was popular because it was a pleasant drink that produced a feeling of well-being. It was a safe drink because the fermentation process killed microorganisms, but water was often added to wine to prevent drunkenness, which although tolerated in Egypt and by the Celts, and to some extent in Greece and Rome, was frowned upon when taken to excess. Athenaeus recognized 10 stages of drunkenness, quoting a play by Eubulus, now lost, and Aristotle could be scathing about it.[230]

The Greeks usually drank what might be called "pure" wine, a sweet wine, which because of the hot weather and low yields probably reached a potency of 15–16 percent, as opposed to 12–13 percent today. Greek red wines were dark in color and somewhat tannic. Most of the wine probably came from local vineyards and was commonly known by the Athenians as *trikotylos,* equal to a *vin ordinaire.* The Greeks seem to have had no appreciation of particular vintages, and although they recognized the value of aging wines, most wines were drunk young. Some vineyards produced a higher quality, and certain cities specialized in producing one type of wine; the Chians even depicted their particular form of amphora on their coinage. Wine was mixed with perfumes and herbs, used in cookery to give both flavor and sweetness, and was a basis of many medicinal products. It was poured out as a libation to the gods.

The Romans cultivated vines extensively in Italy and throughout the empire. Cato, Columella, and Pliny gave detailed instructions for planting and tending vines and the production of wine. The main production areas were Greece, Italy, Spain, southern Gaul, and North Africa. Even Britain produced some wine. From these areas wine was transported to all parts of the Roman Empire, although many wines were drunk locally, as they could not travel. Wine was usually drunk young, although older wines are mentioned. The source of origin of the various wines may be recognized in the type of amphorae used to export wine. Amphorae were often sealed internally with resin, which gave its taste to the wine. This wine might therefore become an acquired taste or might be used medicinally as an astringent. In Gaul some wines were matured quickly by placing them in the *fumarium,* a warm, smoky room high up in a building. This obviously added a taste to the wine.

The Romans took the economics of wine making seriously, especially regarding the different pressings. The first pressing was the best, but the fourth produced a vinegary wine acceptable only to slaves. Writers mentioned specific wines. Pliny detailed four classes of Roman wine and listed numerous foreign ones, most of which could be tasted in Rome; Horace bemoaned the winter chill while drinking a four-year-old Sabine wine.[231] The Romans liked spiced wine, wine sweetened with honey or even softened with gypsum or lime. *Conditum*—wine and hot water with the addition of honey pepper and spices—was a popular drink in Roman bars. Wine heated with spices was recommended as a drink for intemperance. A hangover is basically an upset stomach, a condition that the Romans probably knew well, so spiced wine could have served as a pick-me-up, a hair-of-the-dog cure.

Wine had a great number of medicinal uses. It could be used as a disinfectant and to purify water. Hippocrates prescribed wine for specific illnesses and diseases.[232] Red wine was good for digestion and white for bladder problems, but wine should not be given for treating nervous diseases, as it can bring on a headache. In *Aphorises* he said that it was better to be full of wine than full of food, but he is probably indicating that it is better to be a drunkard than a glutton.[233]

Must was fresh grape juice that was often drunk in place of wine. Cato said this must be drunk as soon as grapes were pressed, as otherwise it would ferment, but if boiled it becomes more stable:

> If you wish to keep grape juice through the whole year, put grape juice into an amphora, seal the stopper with pitch and sink in the pond. Take it out after thirty days; it will remain sweet the whole year.[234]

Must was used extensively in cookery where it gave an intense flavor. Pliny gave instructions for making it sweeter.[235] *Must* could be reduced to two-thirds of its volume to produce *caroenum*. Reduced even further, the syrup became *sapa*. *Mulsum* was wine mixed with honey to produce a sweetener. *Passum* was wine made from a grape called *apiana*, dried in the sun, and was therefore a kind of raisin wine.

Verjuice in the ancient world was produced from the juice of unripe grapes and used for cooking and for medicinal purposes.

NOTES

1. Ovid, *Fasti,* translated by Sir James Frazer. 2nd ed. revised and edited by G. P. Goold (London: Loeb Classical Library, 1989), 169–172.

2. Cato, *DA* 85.

3. Pliny, *NH* 18.12; Ovid, *Metamorphoses,* translated and notes by D. E. Hill (Warminster, England: Aris and Phillips, 1985), 5.450.

4. Frontinus, *Strategemata,* translated by C. E. Bennett (London: Loeb Classical Library, 1925), 4.1.25, 4.1.27.

5. Oribasius, *Dieting for an Emperor: A Translation of Books 1 and 4 of Oribasius' Medical Compilations* with an introduction and commentary by M. Grant (Leiden: Brill, 1977), 1.13.

6. Pliny, *NH* 18.52–54.

7. Pliny, *NH* 18.149–150.

8. Galen, *AF* 6.514; Pliny, *NH* 18.141.

9. Galen, *AF* 6.525.

10. Anthimus, *OC* 70.

11. Martial, *Epigrams,* 2 vols., translated and edited by W.C.A. Ker, revised edition (Cambridge, Mass.: Loeb Classical Library, 1978), 13.7.

12. Apicius, *The Roman Cookery Book,* translated and edited by B. Flower and B. Rosenbaum (London: Harrop, 1961), 5.6.4.

13. Pliny, *NH* 18.117–12, 22.140–141.

14. Heroditus 2.37; Diodorus Siculus 1.89.

15. Aristophanes, *The Peace* 1136.

16. Martial, *Epigrams* 1.103.

17. Anthimus, *OC* 66.

18. Pliny, *NH* 13.13.

19. Pliny, *NH* 18.12.

20. Anthimus, *OC* 67.

21. Galen, *AF* 6.527–528.

22. Apicius 4.4.2.

23. Pliny, *NH* 18.133–136.

24. Seneca, *Letters* 95.25. Quoted in A. Dalby, *Food in the Ancient World from A–Z* (London: Routledge, 2003), 223.

25. Martial, *Epigrams* 3.60.

26. Suetonius, *The Twelve Caesars,* translated by R. Graves (Harmondsworth: The Penguin Press, 1957), 44.2; Juvenal, *Satires* 5.147; Martial, *Epigrams* 1.20.

27. Pliny, *NH* 22.92.

28. Apicius 7.15.1–6.

29. Pliny, *NH* 19.33–37.

30. Apicius 7.16.1–6.

31. Columella, *RR* 12.47.6.

32. Suetonius, *Domitian* 21.

33. Pliny, *NH* 16.103.

34. Apicius 4.3.6.

35. Pliny, *NH* 15.97–99.

36. Theophrastus, *Historia Plantarum* 2 vols., translated by Sir Arthur Hort (London: Loeb Classical Library, 1916–1926), 4.2.4.

37. Pliny, *NH* 13.59; Galen, *AF* 6.615.

38. Pliny, *NH* 15.102–104.

39. Columella, *RR* 11.2.96; Palladius, *OA* 11.12.4–8.

40. Pliny, *NH* 13.26–52, 14.102.

41. Apicius 6.9.7.

42. Herodotus 1.193; Aristotle, *Historia Animalium,* 3 vols., translated by A. Peck and D.M. Balme. Prepared for publication by A. Gotthelf (Cambridge, Mass.: Loeb Classical Library, 1965, 1970, 1991), 557b. 25–31; Pliny, *NH* 15.81–82.

43. Columella, *RR* 10.414–421.

44. Pliny, *NH* 14.10–53.

45. Columella, *RR* 9.4.3.

46. Pliny, *NH* 15.47.

47. Apicius 3.7.

48. Anthimus, *OC* 58.

49. Pliny, *NH* 15.44.

50. Pliny, *NH* 15.53.

51. Pliny, *NH* 23.115.

52. Dioscorides, *MM* 1.125; Pliny, *NH* 13.60–61.

53. Pliny, *NH* 15.41–44.

54. Pliny, *NH* 13.112–113.

55. Hippocrates, *Epidemics,* vol 2. 4–7, translated and edited by W.D. Smith (Cambridge, Mass.: Loeb Classical Library, 1994), 7.67, 7.80.

56. Anthimus, *OC* 83.

57. Columella, *RR* 12.47.

58. Palladius, *OA* 11.20; Oribasius, *Medical Compilations* 5.20, 4.2.20.

59. Martial, *Epigrams* 13.24.

60. Pliny, *NH* 1.20, 23.100–104.

61. Pliny, *NH* 16.16.

62. Strabo, 3.3.7.

63. Pliny, *NH* 15.90.

64. Pliny, *NH* 15.92–93.

65. Xenophon, *Anabasis*, rev. ed., translated by C. L. Brownson (London: Loeb Classical Library, 1968), 5.4.29.

66. Pliny, *NH* 15.35–36, 23.142–143.

67. Horace and Persius, *Satires*, translated and edited by P. Green (Harmondsworth, England: Penguin Press, 1967), 2.2.116.

68. Cato, *DA* 161.

69. Pliny, *NH* 19.145–151.

70. Galen, *AF* 6.641–644; Hippocrates, vol. 4 *Regimen in Health*, translated by W.H.S. Jones, E.T. Wilkinson, and P. Potter (London: Loeb Classical Library, 1923–1995), 54.

71. Cato, *DA* 157–158.

72. Oribasius, *Medical Compilations* 4.4.

73. Pliny, *NH* 19.136–144.

74. Theophrastus, *Historia Plantarum* 7.4.4, 7.6.1–2; *De Causis Plantarum (On Plant Physiology)*, 3 vols., text and translation by B. Einarson and G.K.K. Link (Cambridge, Mass.: Loeb Classical Library, 1976–1980), 2.5.3.

75. Pliny, *NH* 20.96.

76. Juvenal, *Satires* 1.134.

77. Anthimus 55.

78. Pliny, *NH* 19.175.

79. Cato, *DA* 117.

80. Martial, *Epigrams* 13.13.

81. Oribasius, *Medical Compilations* 4.1.26.

82. Apicius 3.21.

83. Pliny, *NH* 19.108–109, 20.44–49.

84. Strabo 16.2.29.

85. Columella, *RR* 12.10.1.

86. Pliny, *NH* 19.101–107; Oribasius, quoting Galen, *Medical Compilations* 3.34.3; Pliny, *NH* 20.39.

87. Anthimus, *OC* 61.

88. Palladius, *OA* 12.6.

89. Pliny, *NH* 19.114.

90. Galen, *AF* 19.496.

91. Pliny, *NH* 19.82.

92. Galen, *AF* 6.654.

93. Horace, *Satires* 2.2.8–9.

94. Apicius 3.14.

95. Pliny, *NH* 18.126–132.

96. Apicius 3.13.1.

97. Pliny, *NH* 20.126.

98. Horace, *Satires* 2.8.8.

99. Apicius 4.2.7.

100. Pliny, *NH* 23.152–158.

101. Cato, *DA* 8.121.

102. Palladius, *OA* 12.22.

103. Pliny, *NH* 20.119.

104. Pliny, *NH* 22.80.

105. Pliny, *NH* 14.109; Galen, *SF* 12.149; Archestratus, *Hedypatheia (The Life of Luxury),* translation with introduction and commentary by J. Wilkins and S. Hill (Totnes, England: Prospect Books, 1994), 22.

106. Dioscorides, *MM* 3.51.

107. Pliny, *NH* 20.222–228; Martial 10.48.7.

108. Lucian, "On Satirical Posts in Great Houses," in *Lucian,* vol. 3, translated by B.O. Foster, F. Gardner Moore, and M.D. Macloed (8 vols.) (London: Loeb Classical Library, 1913–1961), 26.

109. Apicius 3.8.

110. Pliny, *NH* 20.152–155.

111. Pliny, *NH* 20.236–240.

112. Columella, *RR* 12.57.

113. Pliny, *NH* 23.159.

114. Palladius, *OA* 2.17–18.

115. Pliny, *NH* 19.123.

116. Martial, *Epigrams* 5.39.

117. Columella, *RR* 7.8.7; Pliny, *NH* 20.245–246.

118. Pliny, *NH* 19.39.

119. Pliny, *NH* 12.50.

120. Pliny, *NH* 12.91.

121. Dioscorides, *MM* 2.160; Pliny, *NH* 12.28.

122. Martial, *Epigrams* 14.146.

123. Apicius, 1.2.

124. Petronius, *The Satyricon and the Fragments,* translated and edited by J.F. Sullivan (Harmondsworth, England: Penguin Press, 1965), 60; Apicius, 1.1.

125. Ovid, *Fasti,* translated by Sir James Frazer. Revised by G.P. Goold (London: Loeb Classical Library, 1989), 1.76.

126. Pliny, *NH* 13.55, 24.91–93.

127. Galen, *AF* 6.664.

128. Aristophanes, *The Knights* 143–122.

129. Aristophanes, *The Clouds* 409.

130. Varro, *De Lingua Latina,* 2 vols., translated and edited by R.G. Kent (London: Loeb Classical Library, 1938), 5.111.

131. Galen, *AF* 6.664.

132. Petronius, *Satyricon* 31.

133. Varro, *RR* 3.15.

134. Horace, *Odes,* translated by N. Rudd (Harmondsworth, England: Penguin Press, 1973), 3.4.34.

135. Tacitus, *Annals* 2.24.

136. Varro, *RR* 2.4.3.

137. Petronius, *Satyricon* 40.

138. Galen, *AF* 6.679.

139. Anthimus, *OC* 9–10.

140. Herodotus 2.47.

141. Plutarch, "De Iside et Osiride," in *Moralia,* vol. 5, translated and edited by E. C. Babbitt et al. (15 vols.) (London: Loeb Classical Library, 1928–1969), 5.352.4–5.

142. Varro, *RR* 3.13.1–3.

143. Caesar, *De Bello Gallico* 5.12.

144. Pliny, *NH* 8.217–218.

145. Varro, *RR* 3.12.4–7.

146. Martial, *Epigrams* 3.58.

147. Columella, *RR* 8.7.

148. Diodorus 1.74.

149. Apicius 6.9.1–15.

150. Plutarch, "De Esu Carnium (On the Eating of Flesh)," in *Moralia,* vol. 12, 997a.

151. Anthimus, *OC* 27.

152. Apicius 6.2.2.

153. Columella, *RR* 8.15; Varro, *RR* 3.5.15, 3.11.

154. Herodotus 2.77.

155. Anthimus, *OC* 22.

156. Herodotus 2.72.

157. Pliny, *NH* 10.52; Martial, *Epigrams* 13.58.

158. Varro, *RR* 3.9.18.

159. Apicius, 6.1.

160. Varro, *RR* 3.6.2.

161. Apicius, 2.2.6.

162. Martial, *Epigrams* 13.45.

163. Varro, *RR* 3.7.

164. Varro, *RR* 3.5.2.

165. Horace, *Satires* 1.5.71–73.

166. Anthimus, *OC* 35.

167. Ovid, *Ars Amatoria (The Art of Love),* translated by J. H. Mozley, 2nd ed. rev. and edited by G. P. Goold (Cambridge, Mass.: Loeb Classical Library, 1984), 2.423.

168. Pliny, *NH* 29.39–49.

169. Apicius, 7.13.7.

170. Diodorus, 1.36.

171. Aelian, *On the Characteristics of Animals,* 3 vols., translated by A. F. Scholfield (Cambridge, Mass.: Loeb Classical Library, 1958–1959), 14.26.

172. Athenaeus, *D* 278b, referring to Archestratus.

173. Galen, *AF* 6.728.

174. Xenocrates, "On Food from the Waters," text in *Oribasii Collectionum Medicarum Reliquae,* edited by J. Raeder (Leipzig: Teubner, 1928–1933), 2; Pliny, *NH* 9.72.

175. Galen, *AF* 6.724–725.

176. Martial, *Epigrams* 3.60.

177. Apicius, 4.2.28.

178. Antiphanes, 216.

179. Pliny, *NH* 9.64–67.

180. Ausonius, *Mosella,* 2 vols., translated by H.G.E. White (London: Loeb Classical Library, 1919), 97–105; Pliny, *NH* 9.68; Cassiodorus, *Variae,* translated with notes by S.J.B. Barnish. Translated texts for historians, 12 (Liverpool, England: Liverpool University Press, 1992), 12.4.

181. Juvenal, *Satires* 5.104–106.

182. Pliny, *NH* 32.107.

183. Oppian, *Halieutica (On Fishing),* text, translation, and commentary by A.W. Mair (London: Loeb Classical Library, 1928), 2.4.62–469.

184. Xenocrates, *On Food from the Waters* 19.

185. Aelian, *On the Nature of Animals* 1423.

186. Pliny, *NH* 9.60, 9.44.

187. Archestratus, *Hedupathia* 9.

188. Apicius, 10.4.2.

189. Pliny, *NH* 9.73, 76, 171–172.

190. Ausonius, *Mosella* 115–140.

191. Martial, *Epigrams* 3.60.

192. Pliny, *NH* 32.111.

193. Columella, *RR* 8.15.6.

194. Apicius, 9.1.4.

195. Archestratus, *Hedupathia* 25.

196. Martial, *Epigrams* 13.83; Pliny the Younger, *Letters* 2.17.

197. Columella, *RR* 6.17.7.

198. Xenocrates, *On Food from the Waters* 95–96; Pliny, *NH* 32.59–65.

199. Juvenal, *Satires* 4.139–142.

200. Apicius, 9.8.1–5.

201. Apicius, 7.18.1–4.

202. Varro, *RR* 3.14.

203. Pliny, *NH* 9.173–174.

204. Homer, *The Odyssey,* 2 vols., translated by A. Murray (Cambridge, Mass.: Loeb Classical Library, 1960–1966), 9.230–234.

205. Columella, *RR* 12.8.

206. Strabo, 16.4.24, 17.2.2.

207. Pliny, *NH* 31.88.

208. Columella, *RR* 12.10.5.

209. Columella, *RR* 9.2–16; Varro, *RR* 3.16; Virgil, *Georgics,* 4 vols., translated by H. Ruston Fairclough (London: Loeb Classical Library, 1932), bk. 4.

210. Apicius 4.2.35.

211. Martial, *Epigrams* 13.103.

212. Palladius, *OA* 3.35.12.

213. Strabo, 17.1.35.

214. Cato, *DA* 58.

215. Columella, *RR* 5.8–9; 12.52–59; Cato, *DA* 6.18–19; Pliny, *NH* 15.1–24.

216. Cato, *DA* 119.

217. Dioscorides, *Euporista,* 3 vols., text in M. Wellman, ed., *Pedanii Dioscuridis Anazarbei de Mareria Medica libri quinque* (Berlin: Weidmann, 1907–1914), 2.112; Pliny, *NH* 12.32.

218. Xenophon, *Anabasis* 4.5.26–27.

219. Aristophanes, "Thesmorphoriazusae," in *Plays,* 4 vols., translated by J. Henderson (Cambridge, Mass.: Loeb Classical Library, 1998–2002), 857.

220. Diodorus Siculus, *Bibliotheca Historia,* 12 vols., translated by C. H. Oldfather (London: Loeb Classical Library, 1933–1963), 1.34.10.

221. Quoted in H. Wilson, *Egyptian Food and Drink* (Buckinghamshire, England: Shire Publications, 2001), 19.

222. Palladius, *OA* 3.5.19.

223. Celsus, *De Medicina (On Medicine),* 3 vols., translated by W. G. Spencer (London: Loeb Classical Library, 1935–1938), 2.24.3, 2.31.

224. Pliny, *NH* 14.113.

225. Athenaeus, *D* 122e–125a.

226. Pliny the Younger, *Letters* 1.15; Apicius, 4.1.2.

227. Strabo, 17.1.35.

228. Pliny, *NH* 14.16.

229. Herodotus, 2.86. In modern times palm wine is made by making an incision in the tree below the base of the upper branches. The sap, which tastes like a new light wine, is collected in a jar. When fermented this liquid has a powerful effect. The action, however, can kill the tree and therefore can only be done where palm trees grow abundantly.

230. Aristotle, *Problems,* 2 vols., translated by W. S. Hett (Cambridge, Mass.: Loeb Classical Library, 1926), 871a.1–878a.27, 953a.32–953b.25.

231. Pliny, *NH* 14.54–87; Horace, *Odes* 19.7–8.

232. Hippocrates, *Regimen for Acute Diseases,* text and translation in W. H. S. Jones et al. (London: Loeb Classical Library, 1923), 62.

233. Hippocrates, *The Aphorisms of Hippocrates,* with an interlineal and analytical interpretation on the principles of the Hamilton System by J. W. Underwood (London: printed for the author by J. B. Souter, 1831), 2.11.

234. Cato, *DA* 120.

235. Pliny, *NH* 18.318.

CHAPTER 3

FOOD PREPARATION AND THE FOOD PROFESSIONS

PROCEDURES, EQUIPMENT, AND UTENSILS

Both the preparation and the eating of food can be considered a social arrangement, but the higher the status of the family in the ancient world, the more the eating of food would be removed from its preparation. Food could be eaten raw, being gathered from the wild, but meat and fish need to be cooked to bring out their full flavor. Many vegetables become softer and more palatable after cooking. The correct preparation of food was therefore essential. Two requirements were necessary—fuel and water. Fuel was readily available, either from abundant woodlands or, in the case of Egypt, in the form of dried animal dung. Wood can be converted into charcoal, and both this and dried dung burn slowly, giving off a steady heat. Charcoal is produced by piling up wood, covering the heap with turf, setting fire to the interior, and damping the turf so that the whole burns very slowly. Charcoal burning was a skilled profession. The Romans and Egyptians sometimes used coal, obtained from surface workings.

Women and slaves probably did most of the cooking in households. The Egyptians had servants attached to households who cooked for the households and often remained devoted to them for their lifetimes. It is less clear who did the cooking in Celtic households, but it was presumably done by the women. The Greeks and Romans had a slave society, where slave society served a household for a lifetime, although they were often freed on the death of the master of the household. For an important occasion professional cooks were hired from the marketplace, where they waited in the expectation of employment.

Roasting and Boiling

Roasting is probably the easiest way of cooking meat. Meat can be spit-roasted over an open fire, placed in a container on the fire, or placed in an oven. The Celtic method was to spit-roast over an open fire on a hearth in the middle of the house, where a bar was set between two andirons. A joint would be spiked on the bar, and this could be easily turned. The Egyptians thrust a bar lengthways through a bird or a fish and a servant held this over a fire. In one tomb illustration a servant is shown waving a fan over a bird, either to keep away flies or to act as a bellows. The flesh would be torn off and eaten with fingers as the parts were done. More sophisticated households eased off the flesh from a fish and rolled it into fillets. It would be difficult to catch any fat or juices, which would fall onto the fire, causing it to burn more brightly and thus give off more heat. The Greeks and Romans used spit-roasting for small game, fish, and pieces of meat, but preferred to roast their meat and fish in iron pans or clay pots, which were placed directly on the fire or on a gridiron set over glowing charcoal. Charcoal was preferred, as it created less smoke than wood and the smoke had to escape through a hole in the roof. The Greeks placed terra-cotta cooking pots over a clay brazier. This method could also be used for frying or stewing.

One problem with cooking over direct heat was that if the fire was not carefully watched it could set the house on fire. The Roman poet Horace recounted that when he was dining on thrushes that were being spit-roasted at an inn at Beneventum, sparks set the ceiling alight, leading to panic among guests and slaves, some rescuing their dinners, other trying to put out the flames.[1] Emperor Augustus created a corps of *vigiles,* or firefighting watchmen, who policed Rome checking on such fires, and this practical arrangement was promoted in other cities and towns in the Roman Empire. Hence the kitchen was often placed away from the house where the fire could be banked up overnight to save rekindling in the morning. Pliny pointed out the inconvenience of going around to a neighbor for hot coals or flint and tinder if the fire had gone out. Many Roman houses had a *lararium,* a small shrine, in the kitchen, referring both to the sacred flame, which cooked the food, and in the hope that the household gods (*lares*) who protected the house would keep the flame under control.

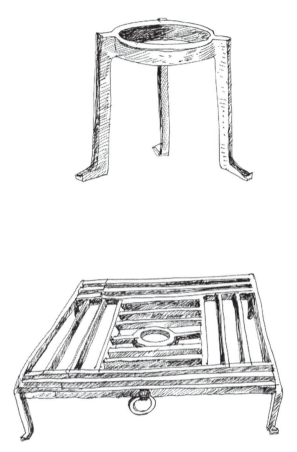

Gridiron and tripod. Drawn by Charlotte Fawley. Courtesy of the author.

The Egyptians cooked mainly in the open air, in a courtyard roofed with matting, or on the upper floor of a house, so that cooking smells were kept away from living quarters. The hearth had a back wall against which the embers could be piled, and the pan or pot was set into this, thus allowing for slow cooking. The Greeks cooked on hearths in courtyards or in houses. Pots were pushed toward the fire by a half-cylindrical shield with a handle on the outside and tabs or pointed ends on the inside to grip the pot. The pots were turned around toward the glowing coals as required to allow the food to cook evenly.

Boiling or stewing was done in small pots placed near the fire or in cauldrons suspended over a fire by chains attached to a beam or hung from a tripod formed by three poles joined at the apex. Meat was probably boiled first, with the vegetables added later. A basic peasant dish was pottage made from grains, beans, or lentils. A large cauldron could easily hold a pig, which was a desired dish of the Celts. Apicius advised that cranes should be boiled in a "large saucepan."[2] A cauldron would be ideal. When the bird had been parboiled, it could be jointed and put into smaller saucepan with herbs. A sauce and vegetables were added later. The Egyptians used cauldrons or large straight-sided pots supported on stones, or a tripod set over a pan of glowing charcoal. A servant regulated the heat, blowing on it with bellows worked by his feet. Poaching, by which food is simmered gently over a fire, was done by the Romans in low earthenware dishes or iron pans. These were set on iron trivets or gridirons. A square pan with rounded indentations in it, found in the House of Panza at Pompeii, may be an egg poacher. Braising was also known. Apicius ordered pork to be cooked by browning meat in its own fat over a glowing brazier and then smothering the meat with a sauce.[3] Pots for braising in Egypt had a lip that curved inward, thus reducing liquid loss through evaporation. In Greece lidded pots were set on braziers with holes or slits in them to provide a draft.

The Celts used a method known as potboiling. The *fulachta fiadh,* or cooking pits, comprised stone or wood-lined troughs filled with water. This was tested by experimental archaeology in Ireland at Ballyvourney (Cork County). Stones were heated and placed in a stone-lined trough of 454.6 liters (100 gallons) of water, gradually bringing it to a boil in 35 minutes. A leg of mutton, wrapped in straw to prevent it getting dirty, was put in and cooked to perfection, allowing 20 minutes to the pound, plus 25 minutes more.

Fricassée, where vegetables and meat are cooked in a sauce, was a well-tried method. Crumbled pastry or bread was added to thicken the mixture. Several recipes of Apicius have a sauce added after the meat has been cooked, thus making a form of ragout.

Baking

In Egypt peasants would bake bread very simply, by placing dough in hot embers and brushing off the ash with a whip before eating it. More professional households had domed bake ovens made of molded clay with a flat baking floor. A fire was lit beneath this to heat the oven. Some ovens were even simpler, being merely a flat stone placed on three upright ones with a fire beneath. Other ovens were box-shaped, with holes on the top on which cooking pans were placed. Low braziers were used to bake flat buns; these braziers could presumably be used for cooking other foods.

A scene in the tomb of Ramses III at Thebes shows two men holding onto long sticks to keep themselves upright, kneading dough in a large bowl with their feet. This is taken in jars to the pastry cook, who makes it into a variety of shapes—one seems to be in the shape of a reclining cow—to be fried on a flattened metal pan over a fire or baked on the outside of a dome oven from which flames burst out at the top. When cooked these were removed with two pointed sticks. Another scene in the Eighteenth Dynasty tomb of Rekhmire illustrates cooks working in the kitchen sifting flour, mixing the dough, and dipping into a large jar of honey to provide sweetening. Others drop the mixture into pans to fry the cake, and then pile them up, ready to be eaten.

Bakery models found in the early Twelfth Dynasty tomb of Meket-Rē at Thebes show the complete process, from grinding the grain to it being taken to the kitchen. One model shows a granary with a broad walk of three storage bins, each with a doorway below for removal of

From a painting in the tomb of Ramses III at Thebes. The sequence starts from the top left, where two men are kneading the dough with their feet. Redrawn from Sir John Gardner Wilkinson, *The Manners and Customs of the Ancient Egyptians*, 1837.

the grain. The grain is put into sacks and taken to be ground or pounded on saddle querns. Another model reveals the kitchen where the dough is mixed in vats, then put into vessels to be taken to workers, who knead it further on tables before patting it into a variety of shapes. The bread is then put into square ovens or set on low braziers. When cooked, the bread is placed into baskets for distribution.

In Greece and Rome baking could be done by means of a base with a dome-shaped cover. In Rome this was called a *testu* or a *cibanus;* in Greece it was a *kibanos.* The heated coals or charcoal were placed inside, the cover was placed over them and left until the inside of the oven was warm enough, and then the cover was lifted and the fuel swept out. This method could also be used on a hardened floor. The food was put inside and the hot fuel was placed around the cover to retain the heat. Oribasius said that when the cakes were taken out, they might be put into hot honey so that the honey was absorbed through them.[4] The Greeks used the pot with a brazier beneath as an oven. A variation on this was an oval-shaped vessel open to one side and standing on a base; a fire was kindled beneath it to bake the food.

The Greeks also had a kind of grill with a handle for hanging when not in use. The grill would be placed directly over the coals or across the top of the brazier or in a flat-bottomed pan that would contain the coals and could be fanned to increase or retain the heat. The Greeks and Romans baked in clay or iron ovens. One from a country house near Pompeii had a rectangular base with a half-circular vault made by reusing a broken *dolia.* Professional bakers had large ovens in which meat or bread could be cooked by the dry-heat method—that is, burning charcoal or other fuel in an oven to raise the temperature, then clearing out the fuel to put the food in and sealing the oven to let the food cook in the retained heat. Such ovens were freestanding or set into a wall. A shovel-like implement similar to the modern baker's peel removed the bread. Sextus Patulcus Felix, a baker in Herculaneum, had a huge rotund oven in a sooty two-vaulted room. To ensure good luck, he placed two large phalli over the oven door, and to double the luck, he placed two ceramic phalli in the dough room. His luck ran out in A.D. 79 when Herculaneum was destroyed in the eruption of Mount Vesuvius.[5]

Preserving

Several methods were used to preserve food. Pickling was done in brine or vinegar or by putting such food as fish into barrels between layers of salt. Cheese was placed in brine to preserve it; a recommended ratio was two parts vinegar to one part brine. Fermented fish sauce was produced in open vats, where the fish or their guts were allowed to rot in the sun. Meat and fruit could be preserved by smearing or covering them with honey. Fruits could be preserved in concentrated wine, *mulsum*, and *sapa*, which were also used to marinate meat. Liquids were reduced to make concentrated stock, which could be added to food as a condiment. Smoking was used to preserve meat for the winter. In Celtic houses, hams attached to beams would be smoked naturally in the smoky atmosphere. Smoking was also done more professionally as a business in the Roman Empire, and smoked cheese was highly regarded. One area in Rome, the Velabran on the west side of the Palatine, was famous for producing these, and Martial spoke approvingly of the Trebulan cheeses in the country of the Sabines, "tamed by a moderate fire."[6] Drying food, especially beans, peas, and lentils, allowed these products to be stored safely for the winter.

Professional and Kitchen Equipment

The Egyptians and the better-off Romans had permanent kitchens; the Greeks in the earlier period, before the fourth century B.C., set up a kitchen where it was convenient. Hence much of their equipment, as indicated, was portable. They used a hearth set on the floor of a house or in the courtyard, but the Romans had a raised platform set against a wall, with an edge to hold in the hot charcoal that was kept burning day and night. This reached waist height, so that cooking could be done while standing. The top of a hearth in the House of the Vetii at Pompeii had charcoal spread all along it, providing glowing coals to heat the pots in which the food was cooking. As they were cooking a fish stew, the cooks had to flee when the ashes of the erupting Mount Vesuvius rained down on them. The charcoal may have given some of the food a smoky flavor. A hole in the front of the hearth provided an aperture in which to keep the fuel and the cooking pots. Not all houses had this type of hearth. In Pompeii only 40 percent of poor homes were fitted with this stable hearth, compared with 66 percent of the well-off and 93 percent of the very wealthy homes.

The fuel and water required for cooking had to be brought to the kitchen. Fuel could be stacked near the cooking area, but water had to be fetched. This was the work of women or slaves. Basins, two-handled jugs, and pitchers were the most obvious containers. Scenes on Athenian vases of the fifth century B.C. show women collecting water in small jugs and tipping it into large *hydria*. Some Roman houses skillfully tapped water from aqueducts or leats. The water table in Europe was much nearer the surface than it is now, so that water could often be obtained from wells. Otherwise a nearby spring or river would suffice. The Greeks and Romans also built fountains in their courtyard houses. The Romans developed sewage systems in towns and cities to dispose of wastewater. Elsewhere, dirty water was just dumped or thrown back into a stream or river. In Egypt and elsewhere in the Middle East, such as Masada and Armegeddon, large cisterns in courtyards contained water, which was taken from wells or the Nile. Professional water carriers also supplied water, carrying it in two pots, each slung from one end of a pole carried across the shoulders. One humorous scene on an ostracon from the Fourteenth Dynasty shows a monkey carrying water in this way, while another balances on the first one's shoulder picking fruit off trees. Sometimes water had to be carried great distances. Towns were often built on the top of hills or on the ruins of a previous village to make defense easier, but this led to problems with water supply. The wells, which served the workmen's village at Tell el-Amarna, were 1,400 meters (4,593 feet) from the village. The water was collected and tipped into pots placed near the wall of the town.

Pottery vessels were used as containers for collecting, storing, and cooking. Pots were easily replaced if broken or unusable because they had become fouled. Large quantities of broken pottery found on sites show how easily pots were discarded. A wide range of vessels was available—bowls, jugs, lidded vessels, and storage bins. The Romans had huge storage vessels called *dolia,* which were sunk into the ground; some had a capacity of 900 liters (198 gallons). Greek storage bowl-shaped bins, made first of clay and by the fourth century B.C. of terra-cotta, had a tight-fitting lid to keep out insects. These had wide bases so that they could not be tipped over easily and two strong handlers for lifting. Smaller vessels sunk into kitchen floors were used as waste containers. Narrow-necked jugs sealed with clay or a wooden bung held wine or oil. Other pottery utensils were cheese strainers, colanders, and mixing bowls. *Mortaria* were large bowls with a gritted surface on which food could be rubbed to pulverize it. A lip on the side allowed liquids to be poured off.

In Greece the terra-cotta *chytra* was used to heat water. This was also a saucepan in which meat and soup could also be made. The main cooking vessel for the Celts was the cauldron, but iron pans were also used. The Greeks and Romans developed a range of pans similar to modern ones because they had comparable functions. These included the Greek *teganon* and Roman *sartago* (frying pans), which sometimes had a folding handle; the *patera* (hemispherical-shaped pan); the *patella* (round shallow pan); and the *patina* (deep pan). These often had elaborately designed handles. They were placed directly in the ashes or on top of a trivet or gridiron. The fourth-century physician Oribasius had a recipe for making pancakes that differs little from the method used today:

> Pancakes are prepared by putting olive oil into a frying pan, which is placed over a smokeless fire. Onto the heated olive oil is poured meal mixed with hot water. As the mixture is fried briskly in the olive oil, it sets and thickens like soft cheese. At which point those preparing it turn it over at once, causing the upper surface to be bottom, so that it is in context with the frying pan.[7]

He did add that the pancake is turned two or three times in this manner and that some people mixed the meal with honey or with salt, making a kind of cake.

Some pans were made of lead or had a lead coating, a dangerous practice because lead is toxic and accumulates in human bones. Skeletons containing lead have been found in Roman cemeteries in Britain. Iron pans can add traces of iron to food cooked in them, but these trace elements can combat anemia.

The Romans also had baking trays, a utensil similar to a bain-marie, and water heaters. An elaborate *thermospodium* found at Pompeii had a square box resting on four decorative legs. This held hot water or charcoal, which heated a barrel-shaped urn. One valve, disguised as a mask, was a safety value for the heated water. Another, on the side, could be used to extract the hot water. In Greece the heating device was a barrel cooker. This was a terra-cotta flat dish on which a barrel was placed, and the fuel was placed beneath it. A small hole in the bottom ensured a draft. Mostly, however, less sophisticated means were used to heat water, with pots placed on braziers.

Other kitchen utensils were wood, bronze, and iron ladles, cleavers, flesh-hooks, graters, and a variety of knives. In the late Celtic Iron Age flints were still used to cut or skin meat. A crescent-shaped knife blade with two rings for a wooden handle fixed on its back found on a Coptic site in Egypt may have been a Roman knife used for chopping or mincing meat. But Egyptian knives often had a turned-up point at the end. This was to prevent the knife from snagging, especially as an animal was being skinned, and to allow the user to get a better grip for slicing and chopping. Some Egyptian knives had a serrated edge to give a better cut. Egyptian ladles were sometimes hinged in the center of the handle, with a bar behind to hold them rigid when they were being used.

The Romans had balances and steelyards. The balances had two scale pans dangling from chains, one at each end of a rod. The steelyard is still used in many countries. The principle is that of an asymmetrical balance in which a weight placed at a distance from the fulcrum will balance a greater weight placed close to the fulcrum on the opposite side. The load to be weighed is either hung from a hook or placed in a pan and the counterweight is moved along until it is in equilibrium with the load. Weights were often elaborately made: heads of divinities or animals were popular. Roman weights were in the form of *librae* (pound), *unciae* (ounces), or *scripuli* (scruples). These, however, were mainly used when food was bought because a good cook would rely on taste, smell, and his own measurements—a handful of this, a pinch of that ingredient.

One of the most useful utensils was the quern, or rubbing stone. In Egypt wealthy households had their own separate granaries and bakeries where wheat could be pounded into flour, and dough mixed on platforms and baked in ovens. Poorer Egyptians pounded or ground grain in homes, as did the Celts. Pounding with the pestle usually produced cracked or crushed grain. Pestles and mortars were also used to pound herbs and pulverize vegetables. In Greece, when actions had to be coordinated, such as when pounding grain, this was done to the sound of a flute. Pliny said that pounding was such a hard task that it was best to fix an iron cap to the head of the pestle. A better method was to use the saddle quern, where an oval stone was rolled over the grain. This method was used in Egypt in early times, and was the only means of producing flour in the Greek classical period. An improvement was the rotary quern, developed in the late Celtic Iron Age and used in the later Egyptian period and by the Greeks and Romans. One stone acted as a base. The other, attached by a spindle, rotated on the top by means of a handle fixed onto the side or to the top. Grain was poured through a hole in the top stone and ground between the two stones. Querns were set on the ground or placed at waist height. Kneeling over the quern was perhaps the best method, as more pressure could be exerted.

At least two grindings were necessary. If bread wheat was used, the first yielded a flour known to the Romans as *siligo*, which had to be carefully sieved. A second grinding produced top-grade flour known as *flos* or pollen. Plato (a Greek philosopher) mentioned that a pollen sieve was probably used to produce finer flour. Even so, it would be difficult to remove all bran, and classical literature mentions flour producing very dark bread. The flour produced might have grit in it, which could leave the bread eater with ground-down teeth, so flour was sieved through a fine linen or woolen bolting cloths, the most useful being that with an operating hole of half a millimeter. The grain had also to be sieved to remove seeds, and weed-seed-removing sieves were used early in Greece. Flour bins were needed for storage and troughs to mix and prove dough. Wooden troughs could be ruinous to a baker's hands because there was the risk of splinters getting under nails. Bran also caused wounds, which could become septic.

Households could buy flour from professional millers. Little is known of professional milling in Greece, but the Romans invented the donkey mill. This consisted of an hourglass-shaped hopper (*catillus*) supported by a spindle above a cone-shaped base (*meta*). The hopper would be turned by means of a wooden framework inserted into the *meta*, either by slaves or by donkeys. Horses past their prime were used if they were blinkered. The hero of Apuleius's *Metamorphoses* (*The Golden Ass*), who was accidentally turned into an ass, portrayed them pacing around, necks chafed by ropes, ribs broken, and hooves flattened.[8] The grain would be poured into the conical space in the top half of the mill and ground as it passed between the upper and lower millstone; the resulting flour was collected around the circular base. The windmill was not invented until the medieval period, but the Romans invented water mills that achieved greater rates of production. The best-surviving example is that at Barbegal, near Arles in southern France.

Meal was kept in storage bins, well fitted to keep out insects. In Egypt and Greece they were made of terra-cotta or clay. Other containers for food were baskets, leather sacks, and jars. The Egyptians used ash to deter insects. On predynastic sites in the Fayum granary, pits contained wood ash mixed with grain, possibly to deter insects or to sterilize the pit. The Celts also used pits, often lined with basketwork, to store grain. In Egypt reed baskets were used for storage. Oval, round, and bottled-shaped ones were found in Tutankhamen's tomb. Some had patterns on them formed by interweaving grasses with date and doum palm leaves. Flat ones could be partitioned to hold fruit or seeds in each compartment. The tomb also contained wooden boxes sealed with resin, many filled with joints of meat.

Wine was transported in amphorae, which had first been used in Greece. These were a most convenient form of transportation, and as

Mule working a mill drawn from a graffito on a house on the Palatine Hill in Rome and now in the Museo Capitolino, Rome. The accompanying inscription reads: "Work my little donkey as I have worked and you shall be rewarded for it." Courtesy of the author.

the shapes altered from province to province and throughout the centuries, it is relatively easy for archaeologists to discover the origin and date of amphorae. The amphora might be ungainly, but it was easily portable horizontally or vertically in wicker or straw packing. The spike on the base was an aid to lifting and also enabled it to be stuck in the ground. The thin, long neck prevented evaporation of liquids. Amphorae could be stacked horizontally in storehouses or in cellars. When empty they were often broken in half and placed in a kitchen, where they acted as a urinal or a refuse container. The jars could be sealed with pottery bungs or with cork secured by mortar. Two men could carry an amphora slung from a pole with ropes through the handles or one man could carry it on his shoulder. The usual capacity was 25–30 liters (5.5–6.6 gallons), which would give a weight of 25–30 kilograms (55–66 pounds). A shipload of filled amphorae could weigh up to 350 tons, and the unloading would require much hard labor and great skill. The shipload of wine carried in amphorae in the Madrague de Giens shipwreck was calculated to be 6,000 amphorae, each holding 24 liters (5.2 gallons), giving a possible total of 144,000 liters (31,680 gallons). The Egyptians also used vessels for wine with pointed bottoms to catch the residue. Like the amphorae, they had to be placed in the earth, on a stand, or suspended from cords. In Tutankhamen's tomb they seem to have been sealed with mud but with a hole to allow the escape of carbon monoxide during fermentation. One had burst with the force of the gas because there was no hole.

As amphorae could be permeable, they were often coated inside with pitch, which tainted the wine or the oil. A more convenient form of container was the barrel. It was lighter, more easily transportable by rolling, and better for storage and aging. The wine contained within need not have come from one source. It could have been shipped to a center, blended, and then transferred to the barrels. Barrels were used in Gaul, as indicated by the reliefs in the Rheinisches Landesmuseum in Trier, which show barrels laid crosswise across high-prowed ships. Pliny said that people in the Alps stored wine in wooden containers and bound them with hoops.[9] He also said that the Gauls did not use yew for transporting wine, for this was poisonous.[10] Strabo commented that the Illyrians bought wine in northern Italy and stored it in wooden jars and that the Cisalpine Gauls stored their wines in barrels larger than houses.[11] This need not be an exaggeration, as remains of barrels that once held 1,000 liters (220 gallons) have been found. When the barrels had been emptied, they often provided excellent linings for wells and cesspits. Glass vessels were also used to transport wine, packed in straw for safety. These provided excellent storage containers in the kitchen.

Dining Room Utensils

The poor in the ancient world did not have a separate dining area and usually made use of wooden and crudely designed pottery vessels. Celtic society ate in round houses and gathered around the central

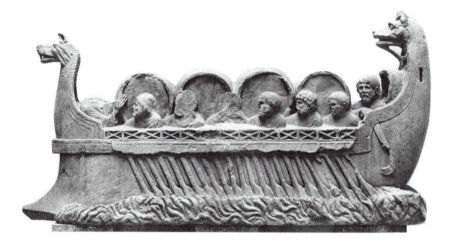

Tombstone relief in the Rheinishes Landesmuseum, Trier, of a Roman bireme with ram and 22 oars on each side carrying a cargo of wine barrels. The deceased was indicating that he had supplied wine to the army, as the labor needed to row such a vessel would have been expensive in relation to the cost of the cargo. Courtesy of the author.

hearth, where feasting could take place, but a dining area was essential to the Egyptian, Greek, or Roman higher society, and these households would expect elaborate utensils. The Celts and the Egyptians used their fingers, although the Egyptians also used spoons of metal, ivory, wood, and bone, often elaborately decorated, when soup or other liquids were consumed. For the Greeks and Romans, the main eating implements were a knife and a spoon; the fork did not make its appearance until the sixteenth century. The Romans had a small spoon (*cocleare*), with a pointed handle convenient for eating eggs or for prizing snails and shellfish from their shells. For the Greeks the flat slabs of *maza* (barley flour cakes) provided a plate, although wooden bowls and terra-cotta platters could be used. Much of the food was pounded or mashed to make it easily digestible or convenient for a mouth that had few or no teeth. The second-century A.D. Greek geographer, Pausanias, however, described the Celts, who held their feasts in their huge roundhouses, as biting meat off the joints in a polite but leonine fashion.

The Celts had drinking horns and tankards. The Greeks had special drinking cups for the symposium, which were filled from the krater in which wine and water were mixed before being distributed to the guests. These could be of pottery, bronze, silver, or gold. Athenaeus gave a list of these.[12] The Greek drinking vessels were usually of terra-cotta. The Laconian *kôthôn* was suitable for military use, as the blurred glass, according to Plutarch, hid the filthy water that a soldier had to drink; in addition, the mud in the liquid was caught and held by the inner rim of the goblet. Thus the water reached the mouth in a slightly purer state.[13] This seemingly implies that the water served to soldiers was brought from a river or stream and not from a well where the water might have been expected to be purer. Decorative bronze and silver jugs, skillets for sieving wine, and silver and bronze bowls would have been in use in the Roman period. Wine could be poured through ice and snow put into a *colum nivarium* to cool the drink.

As drink played a large part in dining, it is not surprising that special vessels were used for drinking. Pliny compared the excellence of Sorrento earthenware cups with those from Asti and Pollentia, and Seguntum in Spain, as well as the *nobilitas* of the red Samian ware of Arretium.[14] Martial mentioned crystal cups, murrine or porcelain cups suitable for Falernian wine, and a *nimbus vitrious* or glass sprinkler, which may have been intended for water or wine.[15] Murrine cups and vases were carved from fluorspar wheels, and to prevent breakage when being carved, had to be impregnated with resin, which could give an attractive flavor to wine. They first reached Rome as booty after the defeat of Mithradate in 6 B.C.

In Egypt drinking vessels were of gold, silver, glass, porcelain, and alabaster. Some were plain, others were decorated; some had handles. Many were made from red-fired Nile silt clay and white-to-greenish marl clays. These provided cheap drinking cups. Alabaster ones could be beaker-shaped with a round base, so that they had to be held in the hand, or when empty turned upside down to indicate that no more wine was required. Saucer shapes were of glazed pottery, with a lotus or fish represented on the upper surface. When a liquid was poured in, the lotus or fish appeared to be in its natural element. Glass vessels appeared in the Eighteenth Dynasty, but were not popular because of the high cost of firing kilns. When the Romans took over Egypt, molded and blown-glass vessels became more common.

Highly decorative silver pieces were displayed as part of conspicuous consumption. The Mildenhall Treasure, for example, a fourth-century set of silverware found in England but imported from the eastern area of the empire, adorned the house of a rich man, possibly used at the table but more likely being displayed on a side table as an indication of the householder's wealth. An inventory on one of the

Vindolanda writing tablets found on Hadrian's Wall in England has some of the contents of the *praetorium* (commandant's house) in the fort. The list included *scutulae* (dishes or plates), *paropsides* (side plates), *acetabula* (vinegar bowls), *ovaria* (eggcups) *calices* (cups), *trullae* (bowls), and *panaria* (breadbaskets). All had been kept in a chest for safekeeping. A wall painting in the tomb of Vestorius Priscus at Pompeii shows a display of silverware on a table, which includes cups like those at Mildenhall. Silverware was displayed on a special stand (*abacus* or *mensa vasaria*), which was considered standard in a wealthy Roman household. This may have been a custom adopted from the Etruscans. Etruscan paintings indicate that such displays were commonplace. The fact that Vestorius Priscus displayed his wealth implies that his status in life was intended to follow him in death. His possessions indicate a display of silverware, which any wealthy Roman family was expected to have as a normal possession.

Roman tableware included a variety of serving dishes and smaller vessels, including side dishes for appetizers and for serving sauces, plates, platters and pottery beakers decorated with barbotine, red-glazed Samian ware produced first in Arezzo in Italy and imitated elsewhere, and glassware from a variety of sources. The most prized glassware was colorless and transparent, almost resembling rock crystal. Items would be both cast and molded. Some of the finest came from the Trier district in Germany, where the outer part of the glass had been pared away to leave a net of glass as an outer frame. In the late third and fourth centuries, pewter vessels became fashionable in the Roman Empire. Several hoards of them have been found in Europe, hidden by owners when trouble threatened in a forlorn attempt to save them for future use.

PROFESSIONALS

Cooks

Cookery in the early ancient world was not necessarily a skilled profession. In Egypt cooks in wealthy households were males. In tomb paintings they are seen boiling, frying, and roasting meat; stirring cauldrons; and baking. In Greece male servants did much of the work in wealthy households, but Aristotle commented that the poor, having no slaves, must use their wives and children as servants.[16] By the late period in classical Athens, however, cooks who were freedmen had set themselves up as freelancers being hired out for dinner parties or to help with sacrifices. Once hired, they tried to assume dominance over any domestic slaves in a household, because they had made it their job to know the exact method of choosing and sacrificing an animal and to prepare the meal, ritual or otherwise, that could follow it. Nevertheless, they had to keep on good terms with the household slaves they might despise, because the slaves knew the routine of the household, the master's preferences, and, on a basic level, where cooking implements were kept. A wary, healthy tolerance resulted. The master probably sent a slave who would stand no nonsense into the marketplace to hire the cook. This was how the cook was hired in the Roman comic author Plautus's play *Pseudolus*. Hired cooks had the right to keep any food that was not used and sell it for their own profit. Cooks could be figures of fun in both Greece and Rome, as indicated in the plays of Aristophanes and Plautus, and there was often a tense rivalry between a professional cook and a household slave cook. From the fourth century B.C. onward, Greek cooks took themselves seriously, comparing their work to that of music and poetry.

In late republican and early imperial Rome, cooks were slaves. According to the Roman historian Livy, many cooks had made their way to Rome from Greece or Asia Minor. He indicated that cooks had made a first appearance in Rome in 189 B.C., the specific date being linked to cooks brought to Rome as booty after Gnaeus Manlius Vulso's campaign in Galatia. Before that, they had been "the most worthless of slaves."[17] Later they seem to have set themselves up as a profession and formed guilds. One guild is mentioned on an inscription found at Praeneste dedicated to the goddess Fortuna Primigenia. Another at Rome mentions a scribe to the cooks (*scriba cocorum*). Cooks knew their worth, and if they were freedmen could earn a wage and set their own standards. Martial grumbled that a cook must not have the palate of a slave—he ought to possess the taste of his master. Both he and Livy before him implied that cooks were becoming more pretentious and that cookery had taken on the form of art, but the first-century politician Seneca satirized a man whom he called a "professor of the science of the cook shop" and excluded such cooks from the liberal arts, which were pursued by intellectuals.[18] The Roman orator Cicero also displayed his contempt for cooks. He placed cookery among the sordid food trades, which cater to sensual pleasures and thus are not a profession becoming to a gentleman.[19] Plautus made his cooks figures of fun, claiming that they were able to rejuvenate the aged with their dishes.[20]

Cooks might not be trusted. When accused of pilfering, Plautus's cook remarked in amicable tones, "Can it be that you expect us to find a cook without a kite's or eagle's claws?" It is perhaps not surprising that the cook's patron goddess was Laverna, goddess of thieves. Plautus also warned against cooks who overspiced food: "When they season dinners, they serve that fodder with more fodder. They serve them sorrel, cabbage, beets, spinach flavoured with coriander, fennel, garlic, parsley, pour on a pound of asafoetida, grate in murderous mustard which makes the grater's eyes ooze out before they have it grated. When these chaps season the dinners, they use for seasoning no seasoning but screech owls which eat out the intestines of the guests alive."[21] They had to be versatile. The Roman satirist, Petronius, in his novel *The Satyricon,* makes a cook devise a fish from the paunch of a pig, a wood pigeon from fat bacon, a turtle dove from a ham, and a fowl from a knucklebone. Martial said that the cook, Caecilius, could serve pumpkins for every course in the meal, making them taste like some other food.[22]

Some cooks had to be extravagant. According to Plutarch, Philoton, a physician of Amphissa, when in Alexandria was taken to view the preparation of a feast for Antony and Cleopatra. Eight wild boars were being roasted. Philoton wondered how many people were dining. The cook laughed and said there were only 12 people but he always had to have everything prepared beforehand to perfection and ready at any moment when Antony should choose to dine.[23]

The Greeks took cookery seriously, for they seem to have had schools of cookery, although the evidence for this is mainly to be found in plays and satires. Athenaeus gave the names of some cooks; others appeared in a play by the third-century B.C. Greek poet Euphron, who had a cook say that he has had many pupils. One, Agis of Rhodes, was the only one who could bake fish to perfection. Nereus of Chios excellently boiled conger eels. Chariades from Athens made "an egg mosaic with white sauce,"[24] Lamprias produced the first black broth, Aphthonetus produced excellent cooked sausages, Euthynus made lentil soup, and Ariston cooked gilthead fish for clubs. A poem by a Greek, Sosipater, in the third century B.C. mentioned a cook, who, together with Boidion and Chariades, followed and preserved the teaching of Sicon. Heracleides of Syracuse wrote a book on the art of cookery.[25] Euphron also mentioned a cook who said he was a pupil of Soterides, royal chef to Nicomedes I, King of Bithynia. This man seems to have been genuine, as does Chariades of Athens, and it is possible that as the other names are specific, they might have been actual persons.

Another genuine cook was Mithaecus, who is mentioned by Plato as the author of a book on Sicilian cookery, and also by Aristophanes. The Sophist and lecturer, Maximus of Tyre, said that he was from Syracuse and was as great in cookery as Pheidias was in sculpture. He went to Sparta to show off his art in cookery and the balancing and varying of flavors, stating that by the application of fire he was able to make all kinds of foodstuffs. He was quickly disabused of promoting his hope of a distinguished reputation. The Spartans told him that their tradition wanted a diet that was nourishing rather than artificially enhanced and that they wished their bodies to be unpampered and pure. Mithaecus promptly went elsewhere in Greece, where his talents were more appreciated. One recipe for cooking wrasse survives him:

> Cut the head off the ribbonfish. Wash it and cut into slices. Pour cheese and oil over it and cook.[26]

Mithaecus was mentioned as an expert together with Thearion, who either invented an oven for the mass production of bread or brought one to Athens. Aristophanes also mentioned him. Sarambus is given credit as a dealer in excellent wine. All, stated Socrates, care for people in a physical way.

Athenaeus mentioned Glaucus of Locri, who may have been another Greek cook.[27] He is credited with inventing a sauce called *hypósphagma*, consisting of fried blood, silphium, honey, milk, cheese, and aromatic herbs for serving over meat. The term also means cuttlefish ink, but whether this was an actual sauce or merely a list of ingredients cannot be determined. Another cook mentioned by Athenaeus was by Hegesippus of Tarentum, who in the fourth century B.C. gave a list of ingredients for *kándaulos,* a dish seemingly brought to Athens from the Lydians, who had invented it in the previous century, consisting of fried or boiled meat, grated bread, Phrygian cheese, dill, and rich broth. Hegesippus is also mentioned elsewhere in connection with cake making.

Athenaeus's discussions included a comment by Alexis, who said he had a cook who gave him specially prepared salt fish. Apart from the silphium, it could be a simple method attractive to any modern cook:

> I must wash it well. Then I will sprinkle seasoning in a casserole, place the slice in it, pour over a little white wine, stir it in oil and stew it until it is soft as marrow, covering it generously with a garnish of silphium.[28]

Some cooks had dishes named after them. Athenaeus named a gourmet called Philoxenus, who gave his name to small cakes called *philoxeneioi.* Apicius gave personal names to several recipes: a *patella* of Lucretius and a fricassée of Terentius, who may be identified with a man called Tarentinos mentioned in the *Geoponica,* a manual in Greek on farming compiled in the tenth century A.D. from Greek and Latin texts. A chicken dish "à la Varius" may refer to Emperor Varius Heliogabalus (A.D. 218–222), who was reputed to have invented dishes; as such this must be a later interpolation into the original cookery book. Another chicken recipe "à la Fronto" probably referred to an author of agricultural writing mentioned in the *Geoponica.* A *conchicla* of Commodus, however, may have been named after the emperor and not devised by him.

Apicius himself is a problem, as the recipe book that has survived may be the work of three men rather than one. The first Apicius lived in the late first century B.C., being mentioned by Poseidonius for his love of luxury. The second, M. Gavius Apicius, was a renowned gourmet living during the reign of Emperor Tiberius (A.D. 14–37). He lived at Minturnae in the Campania. His fastidious tastes are revealed by the story that, when hearing there were large shrimps to be found in Libya, he sailed there, tasted them, and, completely unimpressed, sailed back to Italy without bothering to go ashore. He is best known for his manner of death. He spent 60 million sesterces on food and feasting. Finding that he had only 10 million sesterces left, according to Seneca, this he could not endure, as he would be "living in extreme stavation," and as the last draft of all, quaffed poison Martial commented: "You never did anything, Apicius, more gluttonous."[29] Not only his cookery book achieved fame, however, for other writers referred to some of his methods by the style "Apician." The third Apicius, according to Athenaeus, lived in the reign of Emperor Trajan (A.D. 98–117) and is best known for his advice on transporting oysters.

The second Apicius is thought to have written two books, one a general recipe book and another on sauces. The work that bears the name of Apicius is neither of these. Rather, it is a collection of recipes apparently compiled in the fourth or early fifth century from both the second-century Apicius's books, together with snippets from elsewhere (such as a book of household hints by Apuleius, some of whose work has survived in the *Geoponica*), and certain medical writings from Marcellus, a physician from Side in Asia Minor living at the time of Emperor Nero (A.D. 37–68). The two earliest manuscripts, one held in the Vatican and the other in the New York Academy of Medicine, both date to the ninth century A.D.[30]

Fragments of other cookery books have survived, some in references by classical writers. The Greek philosopher Chrysippus of Tyana, who seems to have lived in Italy during the second or first century B.C., wrote a book in Greek on bread and cake making. Paxamus, a Greek writer, wrote two books, one on cookery, the other on farming. They are mentioned by Athenaeus, although neither book has survived.[31] Paxamus is also mentioned in the *Geoponica*. Other cookery books mentioned by Athenaeus include *On Cookery*, by Simus, and two by Iatrocles, *On Cakes* and *On Bread Making*.[32] Athenaeus himself gave recipes, and others are to be found in writers such as Cato, Varro, and Columella, who are dealing with other topics and are basically concerned with farming methods and agriculture. Dietary writers such as Anthimus and authors of medical textbooks such as Galen and Oribasius also include recipes.

Few recipes, even those of Apicius, note any quantities or measurement. This is to be expected, as good cooks rely on their own experience when cooking and rarely measure out any ingredients. The other authors are often just referring to recipes, as if reminding their readers of them. Cato is perhaps unusual in that he does give quantities, as for example in his cakes.[33]

DINING ESTABLISHMENTS

Many people liked to eat at another person's expense or to dine with them for social or privileged reasons. The person giving the meal also enjoyed a feeling of superiority, possibly one of patronage or with an eye to ensuring fidelity. Eating together also cemented a bond; retainers pledged loyalty and the guest accepted hospitality and will not harm the household during his stay. It is a form of understood ritual. In Homer's *Odyssey*, for example, the communal meal was a simple one, consisting of bread, meat, and wine, but its traditions are well understood, as is that of welcoming and feeding a guest.[34] Sometimes an unexpected reward is the result, as when the poverty-stricken Baucis and Philemon entertained the disguised gods Jupiter and Mercury.[35]

In Petronius's *Satyricon*, Trimalchio's feast was also a tale of an exhibition of power, this time one satirizing Trimalchio, a vulgar, pretentious freeman probably based on people Petronius had seen in Rome. The guests at the feast were willing to be humiliated for the splendors set before them by a man presuming to be their patron. Both Greeks and Romans acted as patrons to men who were willing to

Bakers' shops were situated in every Roman town and supplied their customers with a large variety of breads. Reproduced from a nineteenth-century drawing. Courtesy of the author.

serve them on the hope that they would gain advantage thereby, and this gave them a chance to dine at their patron's table. In Egypt the large number of priests, attendants, and servants dined at the temple's expense, often on food given by a worshipping public.

Some free eating was unwelcome. Suetonius remarked that Emperor Vitellius caused alarm because "he invited himself out to private banquets at all hours, and this never cost his reluctant hosts less than 4,000 gold pieces each." He would also snatch pieces of meat and cake off sacred altars or take hot cuts from meat in cook shops whenever he felt like it to satisfy his voracious appetite.[36] Emperor Augustus, on the other hand, gave frequent dinner parties, paying strict attention, Suetonius said approvingly, to social precedence and personal character. The three-course, sometimes six-course, meal was a cheerful one, especially as Augustus would take pains to make a shy guest join in the general conversation.[37]

Hospitality was necessary because there were few inns in country areas and those there were might have a dubious reputation. Travelers often had to rely on friends or acquaintance for a night's lodging. The poet Horace, accompanying Maecenas on a diplomatic mission in 38 B.C. on the *Via Appia,* did this. Murena lent the party his house at Formiae, Capito lent his kitchen, and Cocceius allowed them to stay at his well-stocked farm, which, somewhat ironically, overlooked the inns of Caudium. It was on this journey while he was staying at the inn at Beneventum that the landlord almost burned down the inn while spit-roasting some thrushes. Travelers might bring their own food and supplies or buy food at an inn for the landlord to cook. Bread, wine, and water were useful commodities. It was then that travelers needed Apicius's spiced honey wine, "which keeps for ever given to people on a journey," although it would seem that the honey and the wine should be kept separately, then mixed when a drink was needed.[38]

Bars, Taverns, and Inns

Bars and taverns for eating supplemented street vendors who sold hot or cold food and provided what could be considered cheap, low-grade fast food. Their cries, according to Seneca, disturbed honest people in their houses. In Greece, taverns (*kapēleion*) were both shops, where food and drink were bought to be taken away, and taverns, which allowed eating and drinking on the premises. Their main drink was wine and their foods fish, sausages, pastries, and cakes. They also gave out torches to light the drinker's way home at night. It is not certain how many there were in Athens; Aristotle ascribed to Diogenes the Cynic the phrase "messes are the refectories of Attica." This was a sarcastic phrase intended to indicate the frequency and degeneracy of taverns in Athens as opposed to the more dignified messes of the Spartans.[39] There was some prejudice against them, as they were thought to be seducing young men from their duties, but as in Rome they not only provided meeting places for the poor and the lonely, but meeting places for the higher strata to meet the lower. It reflected the democracy of most of the Greek states. In Egypt Strabo mentioned rooms or hostels alongside the canal at Canobus where men and women drank and ate together.[40] Athenaeus mentioned cooked-meat shops in Alexandria, where people met to buy and eat.[41] Beer houses in Egypt always provided customers with plenty of drink, so that drunkenness was common. Singers, dancers, prostitutes, and gaming were provided for entertainment.

The Romans developed a variety of eating and drinking establishments, but the names applied to them might be used indiscriminately. A *taberna* could refer to both a shop and a bar. These were often single rooms with a masonry counter, within which were large *dolia*. These were not treated with pitch to make them porous but would have held dry foods, such as grains, legumes, fruit, and nuts. Some of these were found in excavations at Herculaneum. Beets and chickpeas were also found. Service rooms behind taverns held kitchens and latrines. Taverns were placed on street corners to attract trade, as many pubs do in England today. Scenes at Pompeii show diners seated, others standing while drinking, and men playing dice. Bars hang from the ceiling holding hams, sausages, vegetables, and other food. Juvenal sneered at the consul Lateranus for frequenting all-night taverns, where a shameless barmaid lies in wait when he should be preparing to defend the borders of the empire upon the Rhine or the Danube.[42] Sidonius Apollinaris, a fifth-century A.D. Latin poet, who in A.D. 486 became bishop of Clermont-Ferrand, mentioned taking refuge in a dingy tavern in Gaul where the smoke from the kitchen made him choke. With eyes watering, he saw steam from cooking pots mingling with the smoke from hot frying pans, where hot sausages were sizzling, flavored with thyme and juniper berries.[43]

A *caupona* referred to a hotel where travelers stayed the night in shared rooms or even shared beds, but also to a place that sold drinks and fast food, while a *thermopolia* was a bar where quick snacks and drinks were served. Many of these were found to have lined the streets of Pompeii. Cicero in his speech "Against Piso" described his opponent leaving lunch in a *caupona* with a hood pulled over his head and his breath reeking with fumes from eating in a stinking bar. A *popina* had stools where drinkers could sit and was a drinking and eating establishment with a somewhat dubious reputation as the haunt of thieves, drunks, and prostitutes. The excavators of the *vicus* of Housesteads Fort on Hadrian's Wall in England investigated a building thought to have been a *popina*. Two bodies were found under the floor, which raises the possibility of foul play.

An *uncta popina* is what in Britain might be called a greasy spoon café, and *immundae popinae* (foul bars) probably refers to the smoky atmosphere caused by the brazier, used for heating as well as cooking,

Left half of a sarcophagus depicting a buyer at a wine shop. The missing right half probably depicted a bakery. Dijon Museum, France. Courtesy of the author.

as well as the smell of stale food. These places were the equivalent of fast-food establishments, and regulations were made regarding the sale of cooked meat. In Pompeii many of the *popinae* were next to bathing establishments so that customers could get snacks and return to their social activities without wasting time. Outside one survived a painted menu—chicken, fish, ham, and peacock.

All these places were regarded with suspicion because they were places for gambling, political discussions, and competitive drinking, and also centers for popular communal activities. Because they sold food and drink, people could stay in them for as long as they wished, provided food or drink were on the table. They were therefore essential social bases for the urban poor, who lacked spaces in which to meet. They were also neutral terrain and so attracted young men from the patrician class who sought adventure and reacted against the constraints of their class. But they could also be haunts of immoral behavior, providing places for clandestine meetings. Deviants and outsiders could mix with the respectable working class and encourage loose talk, which might lead to precipitate action. Yet such talk could also be a safety valve, gossip picked up—hot air but no action.

The authorities still kept an eye on these places, as they could house meetings of guilds (*collegia*) and were thus social meeting points for freedmen and slaves. Emperor Trajan wrote to Pliny the Younger about a firemen's guild at Nicomedia, noting that "if people assemble for a common purpose whatever name we give them and for whatever reason they soon turn into a political club."[44] The emperor was only too aware that this club could meet in a tavern and therefore had to be under surveillance. Previously Augustus had dissolved all the guilds except ancient and legitimate ones. Claudius went further, "and seeing that there was no use forbidding the populace to do certain things unless their daily life should be reformed, he abolished the taverns where they were wont to gather and drink and ordered that no boiled meat or hot water should be sold."[45] Obviously to control the taverns was to control the guilds, which was the primary purpose.

It is, however, not clear if this applied to all taverns or only to those in which the guilds met—if these could be identified. Tiberius had already restricted the amount of food sold in fast-food establishments, even banning bread and cakes. Caligula had taxed all food sold in any part of the city, and Nero restricted food sold in taverns to green vegetables and dried beans, a somewhat vicious move, since dressed as a slave he spent a great deal of his time in taverns. Vespasian, who was

Amphorae displayed in racks in a wine shop at Herculaneum reconstructed as found in situ during excavations. Courtesy of the author.

one of the most level-headed of emperors, even forbade anything to be sold in taverns except pulses. These laws may not have been for political reasons; some food has moral connotations. Prohibitions on eating meat ordered by those who could afford abundant meat and made against those who could not afford it was a rebuke for the plebeians, who had moved away from the ideal meal of pulses and vegetables. The restrictions seemed also a sign of social control. If patricians could go without meat, so could the plebeians. Horace commented that he liked to stroll in the city to view the circus and the forum free from ambition and then go home to dine on peas, leeks, and fritters, but this satire has political overtones.[46]

These laws seem draconian, but it is not clear how far they could be enforced or obeyed in their entirety. It was impossible to police all the establishments in Rome and other cities in what is now Italy, and the regulations were probably ignored in other parts of the empire. Popular culture and leisure were setting their own rules, opposing what seemed to be a patrician moral control. Considering also that some of the patrician class met in taverns, the rules also smacked of hypocrisy.

Inns provided sleeping accommodation for travelers and stabling for horses. They also provided extras in the form of dancing girls and prostitutes. The barmaid, who was often a prostitute, chatted up the visitors. Excavations of inns at Pompeii indicate that the food provided included grains, chickens, dried and smoked fruits, vegetables, nuts, sausages, cheese, and fruit. Dry foods were placed in huge *dolia,* set into counters. At Herculaneum some survive with the remains of chickpeas and beets. Bread, presumably, would be collected daily, fresh from bakeries. Wine was delivered by cart in huge wineskins, *dolia,* or large amphorae, and was then decanted into amphorae stored in cellars. Some inns at Pompeii seem to have produced their own wine. A small vineyard by the side of the "Inn of Euxinus" near the amphitheater would have helped the innkeeper to supply his customers. Customers could drink at the small bar at the main entrance or in more relaxed fashion in a large open area to the rear. Two large *dolia* found on the site each had a capacity of 454 liters (100 gallons). This was more than a small vineyard would produce, but the owner also bought wine from elsewhere. Wine amphorae found on the site were labeled with the innkeeper's address: *Pompeis ad amphitheatr Euxino coponi.*

Shop counter at Herculaneum showing how the *dolia* were built into it. Courtesy of the author.

It is not surprising that inns regarded as gambling dens and associated with sexual license were also under surveillance and governed by law, probably because, as today, guests were suspicious that they might be cheated. Innkeepers had to put up a menu giving the price of food and drink and the price of a night's lodging. They had also to carefully reckon up what the guest had spent. This applied throughout the empire, for the Greek historian Polybius, writing in the second century B.C., said that in Gaul fixed prices, half an *as* or a quarter of an *obol*, were an all-inclusive price for a day's stay.[47] An inscription (now lost) found at Antipolis (modern Antibes) reads, "Traveller, please come in. A bronze tablet will tell you all you need to know."[48] Perhaps not all. Galen, when comparing pork with human flesh, accuses innkeepers of substituting the latter for the former.[49] In Greek mythology Procrustes kept an inn where, until Theseus killed him, he forced travelers to lie in a bed too short for them and then cut off whichever limb overlapped. Inns in Greece had a bad reputation. In Aristophanes' play *The Frogs*, Dionysus asked Hercules the way to Hades, demanding "the best harbours, bakers' shops, brothels, snack bars, lodging houses, fountains, roads, towns, put-up places, and the landladies who have the fewest bugs on the premises."[50]

A *stabula* was the equivalent of a modern motel, which fed travelers and housed horses. One at Pompeii had a broad passage wide enough to admit carts. Kitchens, latrines, and bedrooms surrounded a central court, and the upper stories had bedrooms or a dormitory. The stables and accommodation for the carts are at the rear of the building. Throughout the Roman provinces, extremely safe lodgings with decent food were provided by *mansiones*, or stopping places placed along important roads where travelers could stay for the night. Some were placed in enclosures so that wagons could pull in for greater protection, and if these enclosures were next to forts, they were under the control of the army and therefore very reliable places to stay.

One at Wall (*Letocetum*) on the busy road Watling Street was a key staging post where important persons and couriers on the imperial post system (*cursus publicus*) could stay on the route to Roman forts and towns in Wales and to the northwest of Britain. As early as the late first century A.D. a large guesthouse had been constructed with bedrooms, offices, an overseer's suite, a dining room, and a kitchen. Nearby was a huge bathhouse where the weary travelers, and possibly townspeople from the nearby area, could relax. The importance of such a site was shown by the fact that both buildings were rebuilt several times for the next two centuries. Recent excavations at Neuss in

Germany have discovered the remains of a modern motel situated on the road from Xanten to Cologne, with a forecourt, chariot repair workshop, restaurant, stable, and two-story sleeping accommodation for about thirty travelers. It would seem that the modern motorway service station has ancient antecedents.

NOTES

1. Horace, *Satires* 1.5.71–76.
2. Apicius, 6.2.2–3.
3. Apicius, 7.10.
4. Oribasius, *Medical Compilations* 1.7.
5. Joseph Jay Deiss, *Herculaneum: Italy's Buried Treasure* (London: Thames and Hudson, 1985), 125.
6. Martial, *Epigrams* 13.33.
7. Oribasius, *Medical Compilations* 1.7.
8. Apuleius, *Metamorphoses (The Golden Ass)*, 2 vols., translated and edited by J.A. Hanson (London: Loeb Classical Library, 1989), 9.13.
9. Pliny, *NH* 14.132.
10. Pliny, *NH* 16.50.
11. Strabo, 5.1.8, 5.1.12.
12. Athenaeus, *D* 459a–505e.
13. Plutarch, "Lycurgus," in *Parallel Lives*, vol. 1, translated by B. Perrin (11 vols.) (London: Loeb Classical Library, 1914–1926), 9.5.
14. Pliny, *NH* 35.160.
15. Martial, *Epigrams* 14.111–113.
16. Aristotle, *Politics* 1323a.4.
17. Livy, *Ab Urbe Condita (History)*, 14 vols., translated by B.O. Foster, F. Gardner, E.T. Sager, and A.C. Schlesinger (London: Loeb Classical Library, 1914–1959), 39.6.
18. Seneca, "De Consolatione ad Helviam," in *Epistulae Moralae*, translated by J.W. Basore (London: Loeb Classical Library, 1928–1935), 10.9.
19. Cicero, *De Officiis* 1.42.150.
20. Plautus, *Pseudolus*, translated by P. Nixon (London: Loeb Classical Library, 1922), 791–895.
21. Plautus, *Pseudolus* 809–820.
22. Martial, *Epigrams* 11.31.
23. Plutarch, "Anthony," in *Parallel Lives*, vol. 9, 28.
24. Athenaeus, *D* 378e.
25. Heracleides of Syracuse is mentioned twice by Athenaeus in *D* 58a and 105c.
26. Maximus of Tyre, *The Philosophical Orations*, translated with introduction and notes by M.B. Tripp (Oxford: Clarendon Press, 1997), 15.1.17.1.

27. Athenaeus, *D* 324a.

28. Athenaeus, *D* 117d.

29. Martial, *Epigrams* 3.22.

30. Athenaeus, *D* 168d; Seneca, "De Consolatione ad Helviam," in *The Annals of Imperial Rome,* translated by M. Grant (Harmondsworth, England: Penguin Press, 1992), 10.8–10; Tacitus, *Annals* 4.1.2; Juvenal, *Satires* 4.23; Pliny, *NH* 9.30, 9.66, 10.133, 19.137. The best translation of Apicius is by Barbara Flower and Elisabeth Rosenbaum. This is translated directly from Latin to English. Other authors have translated Apicius or used his recipes giving quantities, and modern interpretations of the recipes include the following: John Edwards, *The Roman Cookery of Apicius: Translated and Adapted for the Modern Kitchen* (London: Rider, 1984); Ilaria Gozzini Giacosa, *A Taste of Ancient Rome* (Chicago: University of Chicago Press, 1992); Joseph Dommers Vehling, *Apicius: Cookery and Dining in Ancient Rome* (New York: Dover, 1977).

31. Athenaeus, *D* 647c.

32. Athenaeus, *D* 164c, 647c, and 646a.

33. Cato, *DA* 75–80.

34. Homer, *Odyssey* 1.109–160.

35. Ovid, *Metamorphoses* 8.621–724.

36. Suetonius, *Vitellius* 13.2.

37. Suetonius, *Augustus* 74.1.

38. Apicius, 1.1.2.

39. Aristotle, *The "Art" of Rhetoric,* translated by J. H. Freese (Cambridge, Mass.: Loeb Classical Library, 1926), 3.19.4.

40. Strabo, 17.1.16–17.

41. Athenaeus, *D* 94c.

42. Juvenal, *Satires* 8.148–170.

43. Sidonius Apollinaris, quoted in Andrew Dalby, *Empire of Pleasures: Luxury and Indulgence in the Roman Empire* (New York: Routledge, 2000), 83.

44. Pliny the Younger, *Letters* 10.34.

45. Dio Cassius, *Roman History,* 12 vols., translated by E. Cary (London: Loeb Classical Library, 1933–1963), 60.6.6–7.

46. Horace, *Satires* 1.6.111–115.

47. Polybius, *Historiae (Histories),* 6 vols., translated by W. R. Paton (Cambridge, Mass.: Loeb Classical Library, 1922–1927), 2.15.5.

48. *CIL,* vol. 12, 5732.

49. Galen, *AF* 6.663.

50. Aristophanes, *The Frogs* 108–115.

CHAPTER 4

FOOD BY CIVILIZATION

Although the subject of food in this chapter may be considered by area, it is best dealt with by reference to the four civilizations of the Egyptians, Greeks, Romans, and Celts. Only the Egyptians had a compact area that may be considered a country. The Celts formed a civilization that spread across Europe. Greek civilization was formed from many city-states, ultimately becoming part of the Roman Empire. The Romans, inhabiting a small state in the Italian peninsula, ultimately came by means of conquest, treaties, and client kingdoms to form a civilization that spread from the Atlantic to Asia Minor and from North Africa to northern Europe.

Much of the surviving evidence concerns the wealthier part of the population. Writers were more interested in Celtic chieftains, Roman senators, and Egyptian pharaohs than in the poorer population. Provision of food on a grand scale could be considered a form of conspicuous consumption, an expression of power and evidence of wealth. Sometimes food is held up to ridicule, as in Petronius's satire of Trimalchio's feast in the *Satyricon*. The paintings and contents of Egyptian tombs and the archaeological evidence from the graves of Celtic chieftains reveal the wealth of royalty and aristocracy, but they also indicate the religious aspect of food as sustenance for the journey to the afterlife and the continuance of life beyond the grave.

It was the relentless expansion of the Roman Empire that brought or spread new or improved agricultural techniques and crops to much of Europe. This in turn led to improved technical inventions, but there was a limit to what people would accept or need. The four civilizations dealt with in this book had ample manpower, much of it in the form of slavery. Therefore there was no problem in producing, serving, or cooking food. There was also an element of conservatism, in that a civilization will cling to its own customs and either resent being forced to adopt new ones or ignore outside pressures. Admittedly, the relentless promotion of Romanization led to many adopting Roman ways. Tacitus noted, for example, that the Britons were led to those amenities that would make life agreeable, and this included Romanized ways of dining and appreciation of improved foods.[1] New fashions, including those concerned with dining habit and food, have an irresistible effect on people who wish to raise their status. But this might affect only a small section of society. Most of the poorer classes kept to their own way of living, which might be interpreted as a way of surviving.

THE EGYPTIANS

The Nile was Egypt's great blessing. The inundation of the Nile allowed the Egyptians living in part of the African desert zone, in intense heat, aridity, and strong winds, to be supported by an ecology that produced a civilization lasting for more than 3,000 years and through 31 dynasties until it fell before the advancing Roman empire. As Diodorus commented, "the marshes produce crops of every kind of plant. In the marshes tubers of every flavour grow on stalks supplying abundance sufficient to render the poor and the sick amongst the inhabitants self-sustenance. For not only do they afford a varied diet, ready at hand and abundant for all who need it but they also furnish other things which contribute to the necessities of life."[2]

Egyptian civilization probably began about 3100 B.C., following a predynastic period from 5500 B.C. during which time hunter-gatherers settled in agricultural villages and animals and people migrated into the region from western Asia. This society also moved toward a class-centered society ruled by a living god, personified in a king. Burial of the dead in imposing mastabas or mud-brick tombs, accompanied by well-crafted grave goods in a variety of materials, testified to a belief in an afterlife.

During this time, as revealed by evidence from sites in the Fayum region, the population supported itself first by hunting the many wild species that lived in and around the Nile. These included wild fowl, fish, pigs, cattle, antelope, and gazelle. As the population began to establish agricultural communities, the wild pigs and wild cattle were domesticated. Hunting became more of a sport for the wealthy than a means of obtaining food, although poorer people continued to hunt game and wild fowl, and to snare fish to augment their mainly cereal and leguminous diet. Cattle, sheep, and goats were more useful to the poor for their milk, cheese, and butter than for their meat.

Agricultural communities grew grains as well as legumes, and these became the major crops in the Nile valley. They provided the two main staples of Egyptian life—bread and beer. Grain was used as a currency, something with which to barter or to pay taxes and wages. The main grain cultivated in Egypt until the fourth century B.C. was emmer; barley was also grown and was probably the grain of the poor. Production of these grains throughout Egyptian history was the main agricultural activity and provided the basic diet of bread for the Egyptians. The dough was left overnight to sour and then baked into round, triangular, oval, and other shapes. Some loaves were cone-shaped, made of slices placed vertically and used for presenting to the dead. Others had an indentation in the middle, which could hold beans or other vegetables. Some dough was kept back to form a sourdough starter for the next day's baking. Crushed grain, mixed with oil, could be baked into a form of oatcake. Grain was also used to make pottage or thicken soup or added to pulses, for lentils, peas, and fenugreek were also common at this time, and were the most important pulses until fava beans were introduced in the Fifth Dynasty.

Honey or dates might be used to sweeten the bread, but once Egypt became divided into more social groupings, honey became a more precious commodity available mainly to the wealthy. Dates were cultivated and used as a sweetener and also to produce a sugary drink. They and the sycamore fig became an essential part of the diet of the lower classes. Other sources of food were lotus and aquatic plant seeds, which could be eaten raw or ground into flour. Roots and stems were also edible. Melons, watermelons, and chufa, or yellow nutgrass, were grown.

Bread was also used to make the other staple, beer, which was part of the daily ration given to soldiers and workers. The god Osiris was reputed to have brought beer to Egypt, as he found the territory less suitable for the vine. The making of beer was women's work. The Egyptians soon were producing several types of beer; black beer was considered the best. There were two ways of making beer. Leavened loaves, usually made of barley and lightly baked so that they would not kill the yeast, were crumbled or crushed and mixed with water to form a mash, which was then allowed to ferment in the warm climate, changing sugars into alcohol. The brewing process produced a thick, mushy product, which was strained into jars. The second method was to soak grain in water for a day, roll it out, soak it again, and then crush and tread on it in a large vat with the yeast added. This was again filtered and might be mixed with spices, mandrake, and other flavors. Large conical vats at the predynastic site of Abydos were surrounded by a large amount of ash and charcoal, indicating that they were heated to speed up the action. In the later dynasties, dates and date syrup may have been added to provide a source of sugar.

Barley could also be dampened and allowed to stand until it germinated. During this process the enzymes released converted the mush into starch and some of the starch to sugar. This was then ground while still damp and as malt was added to the fermenting loaves. The alcohol content was probably about six to eight percent, producing a liquid more like barley ale than beer. The Egyptians calculated the strength of the beer according to how many measures of liquid was made from one *hekat* (4.54 liters) of barley—the smaller the measure, the stronger the beer.

Wine seems also to have been drunk at this early period. Grape seeds found on the predynastic site of el-Omari, south of Cairo, dating to the fourth millennium B.C., may indicate dried grapes, grapes for eating, or grapes from wine making. The presence of wine jars almost certainly indicates that they were from wine making. The technique of wine making probably came to Egypt from Palestine, and once this had been established, the rulers of Egypt lost no time in establishing the production of this welcome drink.

During the predynastic period Egypt divided into two areas, one centered on Hierakonpolis in southern or Upper Egypt and the other on Buro in northern or Lower Egypt, effectively the delta of the Nile. Both areas had a hunting, fishing, and agricultural economy with a gradually increasing reliance on agriculture, supplemented by trade from outside the regions. Eventually, according to traditional histories, a chieftain-king from Upper Egypt with the name or title of either Menes or Narmer united Upper and Lower Egypt. A green worked slate called the Palette of Narmer shows the king as a tall figure. On one side of the palette he wears the white crown of Upper Egypt and the other the red crown of Lower Egypt. The capital of Upper Egypt was at Thinis, a city close to the sacred burial place of Abydos. Gradually the capital was moved to the more convenient Memphis on the geographical frontier between Upper and Lower Egypt.

Narmer began the series of dynasties of Egyptian history. By the end of the Eighth Dynasty, about 2686 B.C., the basic fabric of Egyptian culture had been established. The king, an absolute ruler regarded as semidivine, reigned from his capital of Memphis. A powerful bureaucracy headed by two viziers, one for the northern and one for the southern area, helped him. The country was divided into regions, each under the control of a governor, but these were often moved from post to post to forestall their office becoming hereditary. Burial in tombs had become increasingly important, especially at Abydos and later at Saqqara, just outside Memphis. There, subsidiary tombs surrounded royal tombs for individuals, some at first sacrificed deliberately to serve the king in the next world, and some later to have the same honors provided for them in the afterlife. It was these tombs, both royal and individual, that, as they became more elaborate, were to provide modern archaeologists with much evidence for the ancient Egyptian way of life, death, and the afterlife.

The Third to the Sixth Dynasties (2686–2181 B.C.) constitute the Old Kingdom, a period of stability under strong kings. No serious threat came from outside the kingdom, and trading expeditions went as far as Lebanon and Nubia. The pharaohs strengthened their authority, submitting everyone to the worship of the sun god, Ra. Taxation and records were in the hands of an efficient bureaucracy, and a huge labor force was directed toward a monumental building program, including that of the pyramids. The first pyramid was the stepped one of the pharaoh Djoser at Saqqara, a departure from the mud-brick tomb. This led to the first true pyramid structure, of the pharaoh Humi at Meidum, but it was Khufu or Cheops who built on a megalomaniac scale. One of his creations, the Great Pyramid, was the first of the seven wonders of the ancient world (and the only one that survives). Nearby still stands the Sphinx, a human-headed, lion-bodied creature.

During the Old Kingdom the Egyptians tried to domesticate other wild animals to increase the food supply. These included the antelope, the oryx, and the hyena. Scenes on tomb paintings show hyenas being force-fed, but it is uncertain whether they were eaten or being trained for hunting. Flocks of sheep and goats and herds of cattle increased, but the by-products of milk, butter, and cheese were the most prized. Pigs appear rarely in tomb painting, which led to Egyptologists accepting Herodotus's report that pork was a taboo meat in Egypt. This may have been for religious reasons, but pork can go bad very quickly. At the workmen's village of Tell el-Amarna, pork was packed in pottery jars in what seems to have been a well-organized operation. A list in the temple of Ramses III mentions pigs as offering to the god Nefertum.

The wealthy consumed beef from castrated bulls or oxen. Oxen were fattened and therefore more economical. The second most important meat was mutton, closely followed by kid. Sheep and goats were easier to rear than cattle, and they provided the poor with dairy produce. Sheep were also important because fat, stored in their rump, was needed for cooking and as a base for medicinal products.

The main meat, however, came from the numerous water birds in the Nile valley and the doves and pigeons kept in cotes. These were often dried and salted. Another source of food came from capturing the numerous birds that passed through Egypt twice a year on their migratory route between Europe and central and southern Africa. Egypt was a wintering area for these migrating birds, which were often exhausted after their long flight. This made them easy to trap, thus providing an abundant source of food.

Mice and hedgehogs were eaten; mice bones have been found in the stomachs of humans, and in tomb paintings, hedgehogs are shown being offered as food. When wrapped in clay and baked in a fire, the clay could be removed, taking with it the spires and leaving tender cooked flesh behind. Fish also provided much-needed protein, most being caught by net, harpoon, or simple angling. The image of a fish was used in the word *bwt*, which meant impure or taboo, and priests were forbidden to eat fish. But fish was an important part of the diet and was often used as payment for wages. Workmen at the tomb of Ramses II were supplied with fish, seemingly each having four a month. Eggs were also welcome, and jars filled with duck eggs have been found in New Kingdom tombs. The Egyptians hunted ostriches for sport, but ostrich eggs were prized, as they could feed up to six people. The shells were carefully preserved so that they could be ornamented and used as vessels.

Bread still constituted a main part of the diet, being baked by servants or wives at home. Larger, more commercial bakeries did not appear until the New Kingdom, when bread was produced flavored with sesame, aniseed, and fruits. Most Egyptian relied on bread, fruit, and vegetables for the main diet, and fruit and vegetable were more readily available than meat. Fruits indigenous to Egypt included the cordia or Egyptian plum. Both these and Christ's-thorn were found in tombs of the period. Vegetables were grown in plots attached to houses and settlements. Pulses—beans, peas, lentils, and chickpeas—were the most popular.

Wages were often paid in food. This could be given monthly—one and a half sacks of grain to make bread, half a sack of barley to make beer, and vegetables in season. Pyramid building, which included not only the pyramid but also a temple complex, a causeway to the pyramid, and surrounding smaller buildings and tombs, provided a huge industry and a livelihood for many people.

According to Herodotus, the workers who built the pyramids lived almost exclusively on bread, onions, and beer. The workmen building the pyramid of Khufu (Cheops) in the Fourth Dynasty were given radishes, onions, and garlic. Radishes were prized for their seeds, as these could be pressed for oil. Garlic was especially popular, as its smell could be imparted to other foods and it was thought to repel disease. Garlic has been found in tombs, and tomb paintings also show a tall lettuce resembling a cos lettuce. It is possible that an elongated, curved object depicted in tomb painting and models as part of grave goods may be cucumbers, but this has been suggested to be the chate non-sweet melon.

Water plants such as rhizomes of water lilies and lotuses are also edible, as is the lower stem of the papyrus. Pulses still continued to form one of the basic foods. The most prolific fruit was the date, eaten fresh, dried, or cooked and used as flavoring and a sweetener. Sycamore figs, the common fig, the *Persea*, grapes, and the doum palm cultivated in Upper Egypt for its nuts added variety to the diet. Some paintings of fig trees show that monkeys were used to gather the fruit from the highest branches. Christ's-thorn had been eaten since predynastic times, and the flesh could be used in bread making. Carobs were used for sweetening.

Wine was now produced in large quantities. Representations of vineyards in tomb paintings show two kinds of viticulture. The vines may be shown trailing along the ground or trained upward, sometimes over a pergola or bower. Paintings in the tomb of Metjen, supervisor of the estates of Snefru, buried at Saqqara ca. 2550 B.C., show his vineyards, probably based on his career in the Nile delta. Depictions of grape harvesting are common on tomb paintings. They show tools—pruning hooks, knives, and baskets—similar to those used today. The grapes were picked by hand and put into baskets, from where they were tipped into low clay, wood, or stone vats to be treaded on by slaves. The juice trickled into a collecting trough, and the crushed pulp (the marc) was placed into a sack of light yellow matting and twisted by two men or even a team of men with poles at the end of the sack. They twisted the sack, and when it could be twisted no further a man placed himself

From a wall painting in a tomb at Thebes. Men twist a bag containing the mass
to extract the wine. A man pushes the poles apart, thus increasing the twist to
ensure that the last drops are obtained. Redrawn from Sir John Gardner Wilkinson, *The Manners and Customs of the Ancient Egyptians,* 1837.

between the sticks and pushed them apart so that the pressure made
the juice pour into bowls placed beneath. The grape juice was poured
into jars and left for primary fermentation, after which it was poured
into other jars for secondary fermentation. These were sealed with
cloth, mud, or leather; even an upturned bowl was placed on the top.
As the wine continued to ferment, a small hole was made in the seal to
prevent the jars from breaking.

In the middle years of the Old Kingdom, Egypt became more prosperous, trading widely with its neighbors, but in the reign of Pepi II
bad harvests and revolts by the provincial governors caused the central
government to collapse into chaos, leading to what has been called the
First Intermediate Period, the Seventh to the Eleventh Dynasties
(2181–2060 B.C.). Eventually Mentuhotep II (2055–1795 B.C.)
restored calm and inaugurated the Middle Kingdom of the Twelfth
and Thirteenth Dynasties (2060–1650 B.C.). During this period
Egypt's prosperity was restored, with long-distance trade being
resumed and large-scale public works undertaken. This period of stability was helped by the long reigns of eight pharaohs. Their tombs,
however, were smaller, being built of small stones or bricks but with
elaborate interior rooms and passages, probably to foil tomb raiders.
Administration of the country was improved, with mayors being
appointed to govern major cities. Advancement in agriculture was

indicated by the increased use of artificial pollination to achieve better quality of fruit. Vegetable gardens were encouraged and more vine-yards planted. Land unsuitable for grain growing in the delta and the Fayum was developed as orchards. Even so, the last ruler of this dynasty, Khendjer, failed to keep control of the country, and his reign ended in chaos, ushering in the Second Intermediate Period, the Fourteenth to the Seventeenth Dynasties (1650–1570 B.C.).

This hiatus allowed the northern part of the Nile valley to be occu-pied by the Hyksos, an Asiatic people. The Hyksos, whose name means "rulers of foreign lands," were probably migrant workers who brought with them a new military technology, the horse-drawn war chariot. They captured Memphis but eventually were driven out, leading to the establishment of the New Kingdom, the Eighteenth to the Twentieth Dynasties (1570–1070 B.C.).

The invasion of the Hyksos led to a more aggressive policy on the part of the New Kingdom pharaohs. This period is one of the best-documented in Egyptian history. The evidence reveals a period of political stability, great prosperity, and considerable advance in art, architecture, and literature. Close control was kept by a competent administration, at the head of which remained the pharaoh, still an absolute ruler, who was head of the army, the religion, and the judi-ciary. Although most administrators were members of the aristocracy, advancement to important posts could be by merit, which ensured that administration remained competent and efficient. The capital, which had been moved in the Second Intermediate Period to Itchtowy, was moved back to Memphis, thus ensuring continuity. Thebes became a metropolitan and religious center devoted to the worship of the god Amun, a cult closely connected with the pharaoh. The god's temple at Karnak was extended and new festivals in his honor were promoted. New buildings were erected to his worship. All this led to a huge increase in the maintenance of religious places, with tremendous amounts of food and drink being offered to the god. Many of the wages of temple workers were paid in this way. A document from the Twentieth Dynasty refers to holdings of the god Amun in the north of Egypt consisting of 35,000 men raising cattle, goats, and fowl and 8,700 men employed in agriculture for the service of the god.

One ruler in this dynasty was Queen Hatshepsut (1473–1458 B.C.), who seems to be one of the first female monarchs in history. Much of her wealth was spent on temples, and it was in her reign that an expe-dition was sent to the land of Punt, a country on the east coast of Africa, variously identified as Somalia, southern Sudan, and Ethiopia.

It was regarded as the source of exotic products and the basis for trading missions. This expedition was vividly recorded in art. Once the queen's reign was over, however, her name was obliterated, either in revenge by her successor or because she was a woman.

In the New Kingdom the diet was widened even further. There seem to have been at least 40 types of bread, cakes, and biscuits having different shapes and ingredients, and these were eaten with a variety of vegetables. Dough was baked in a variety of shapes, long and round, but also in figures of animals, women, and penises. These must have been intended for presentation in the tomb. One estimate of loaves in the New Kingdom suggests that workmen were provided with 10 loaves a day. These might only be small ones. If an estimated 1,575 men were needed to build a pyramid, this would mean that 15,750 loaves would be needed, together with a supply of other food and a backup of cooks, water carriers, and kitchen hands.

Celery was eaten raw or cooked, especially in stews, and leeks became frequent. The variety of food at this time was mentioned by the Hebrews, who bemoaned their lot while wandering in the desert after the Exodus: "we remember the fish which we did eat in Egypt freely: the cucumbers and the melons and the leeks and the onions and the garlic" (Num. 11:5 AV). Increased trade and contact with other areas through warfare led to the introduction of new foods. Pomegranates, apricots, apples, and almonds were imported, the first two soon being grown in Egypt; possibly apple and pomegranate trees were also planted. Date trees were particularly important. The list of trees inscribed on the tomb of the scribe Ani of the Eighteenth Dynasty included 170 date palms. Numerous spices and herbs were available for flavoring dishes. Some olive trees were cultivated so that raw and pick-led olives could be eaten, but they were not pressed for oil. Cooking oil came from lettuce, the castor oil plant, flax, radish and sesame seeds, and the safflower; and ben oil from the seeds of the tree. Animal fats were also used in cooking.

Meat came from birds, which were hunted with throwing sticks. Men are depicted standing on papyrus rafts moving in shallow waters. Birds were used as decoys, and some scenes show a pet cat, who had probably been trained to act as a retriever. The poor also were able to increase their protein intake by eating roasted or boiled wild fowl, as there seems to have been no proscription against hunting these. They would also be able to eat the many varieties of fish caught in the Nile. Mullets were kept in fishponds at the Nile delta and trans-ported to Upper Egypt. Fishing scenes were common in tombs, and eggs were consumed in vast quantities as well as being preserved in tombs.

By now beer was being produced in industrial breweries. At least four types of beer are known—iron beer, sweet beer, dark beer, and light beer. Beer was also imported. One is mentioned as coming from Qede in Asia Minor. Diodorus Siculus mentions a beer called *zythos*, "the bouquet of which is not much inferior to that of wine."[3] By now the Egyptians were obtaining a form of yeast in liquid barm form from the breweries to produce a lighter form of bread.

Wine, usually red wine, was produced in large quantities, because the color of wine was determined by the amount of the skin of red grapes left in the marc. Shesmu, the wine-press god, was depicted as pressing human heads in a wine press. Obviously this was symbolic of red wine, regarded as akin to blood. Wine was drunk more by the upper than the lower classes, as it cost 5 to 10 times as much as beer. Vineyards were located in royal and temple gardens in the Nile delta region and southward to the Fayum. At least 15 vineyards are known in the delta region. Amenhotep III (ca. 1417–1379 B.C.) is reputed to have planted a vineyard at Luxor, which produced wine of good quality. Ramses III (ca. 1198–1160 B.C.) ordered vineyards to be planted in oases. One tomb at Thebes of the New Kingdom shows a servant chasing away birds with sling stones from trained vines. Paintings in tombs may not necessarily mean that the owner had a vineyard, merely that he expected to enjoy wine in the afterlife.

The jars were carefully labeled with the name of the vineyard, the village or town of origin, the name of the owner, the name of the chief winemaker, the year of the vintage, and the year of the reigning pharaoh. Twenty-three of the jars of wine found in Tutankhamen's tomb were filled in the fourth, fifth, and ninth year (1345, 1344, and 1346 B.C.) of his reign. Some were labeled "wine of high quality"; two were labeled "sweet wine," and that wine could be left to mature. One jar, of Canaanite origin, had an elongated body, wide shoulders, and a rounded base. It is noted that 66 percent of the wine came from the "domain of Aten," 5 percent from the "Amun temples," and the rest from other vineyards.[4] His tomb also contained a basket of dessert grapes and an alabaster jar of grape juice. Other pharaohs had jars of wine placed in their tombs, but later jars painted on the walls and written lists symbolically indicated wine.

On tomb paintings the jars are usually shown leaning against each other, but on one, from the tomb of the official Nebamum, dating to the reign of Amunhotep II, the jars stand upright in wooden racks.

Wall painting scene from a tomb at Thebes depicting a servant treading grapes and pouring wine into jars, which are stacked up in the storeroom. Redrawn from Sir John Gardner Wilkinson, *The Manners and Customs of the Ancient Egyptians*, 1837.

They were also used to transport other products such as dried pulses, grain, honey, and liquids. Wineskins made from goats, sheep, and camels were also used, mainly from young animals because they had a softer skin. New wine, which might be still fermenting, had to be put into new skins, as otherwise the skin would burst, an example that Jesus was to use in his teaching (St. Luke 5:37–38 AV). By now there was a wide variety of wine available, mainly from vineyards in Lower Egypt and some of the oases. Temples also had vineyards, and the wine produced was probably used in religious ceremonies. Wine was also made from dates and pomegranates, and a fiery liquor was made from figs. Some tomb paintings show wine jars draped with lotus flowers. Blue lotus petals have a narcotic quality, and these may have been added to the wine.

During the New Kingdom, Egypt pursued an aggressive policy against the Palestinians, the Sudanese, and the Libyans, but the pharaohs preferred to exact pledges of loyalty and fealty and to undertake trade negotiations rather than occupy more territory. In the reign of Amunhotep IV (1352–1336 B.C.), the pharaoh dedicated himself to the worship of Aten, changing his name to Akhenaton. The capital was moved to Tell el-Amarna, where an entirely new city was built. The workmen building the city were paid in grain, fish, vegetables, and water, with bonuses of salt, natron, sesame oil, and meat. Worship of other gods was forbidden. New taxes were placed on towns and villages for the upkeep of the new city and its temples. Other temples were allowed to fall into ruin. Amunhotep's creations did not long outlast his reign, for within seven years the administrative center was moved back to Thebes, and the old cults together with their temples were restored.

The New Kingdom ended with the reigns of several pharaohs named Ramses, who from 1295 B.C. struggled against a challenge from the Hittites and the so-called People from the Sea, a confederation of people from the Aegean and the eastern Mediterranean. Much of the long reign of Ramses II (1279–1213 B.C.) was devoted to thwarting these attacks, but the People from the Sea eventually defeated the Hittites, and this allowed the Assyrians to become the dominant power in the Near East.

In domestic policy, these pharaohs transferred the administration to a new city of Pi-Ramses in the eastern Delta, but without neglecting the cult of Amun at Thebes. The temple and the ritual of worship were extended, with more taxes being extracted for building and ceremonies, for the cult of Amun was the cult of the pharaoh. By now it was estimated that almost one-third of the land in Egypt was held by temples and one-fifth of the population worked for them. At first the workmen at Deir el-Medina, the settlement site for those who built the royal tombs in the Valley of the Kings, ate rather well. They were paid in grain and beer but had additional food—lettuces, cucumbers, garlic, salted fish, and some meat from the temple stockyards. Confectioners were employed to make honey cakes. Later, however, these food allocations were not paid, resulting in a series of strikes. The price of grain increased, which caused riots, and steady decline set in, bringing the New Kingdom to an end.

The Third Intermediate Period, the Twenty-first to the Twenty-fifth Dynasties (1070–656 B.C.), was a time of state decentralization. The administrative center was moved to Thebes, but the lack of money was shown by the fact that temples were rebuilt largely of reused stone from the Ramses monuments of Pi-Ramses. The pharaohs ruled from Tanis while the high priests continued to administer the temple at Thebes. Upper and Lower Egypt split. Battle between rival dynasties eventually led to the Nubian king Piye invading the lower Nile valley in 747 B.C. and reuniting the land under the Nubian kings of the Twenty-fifth Dynasty. By then Nubia was Egyptian in culture and religion. The Nubians worshipped Amun, practiced Egyptian burial rites, used hieroglyphics, and buried their kings in pyramids in the fashion of the pharaohs. When, however, the Assyrians sacked Thebes in 646 B.C., the last Nubian king fled south to Napata. Nubian culture continued, but direct rule of Egypt ended. Eventually Egypt was reunited under the rule of Psammethicus I (664–610 B.C.).

The later dynasties, 26–31 (656–332 B.C.), covered a period of revived achievement. Temples were restored and embellished with art and sculpture, many portraying domestic scenes. Food and drink again poured into temples as offerings. Foreign settlers were encouraged, bringing new crafts and commercial skills. The first Egyptian navy was founded, and a canal was begun to link the Nile to the Red Sea. The Egyptians were unable to keep Greek culture from influencing Egypt, and twice (525–404 B.C. and 343–332 B.C.) were subject to the growing Persian empire. Egypt became a Persian province governed by a satrap and the Persian kings took on the trappings on pharaonic power. Darius I completed the canal and gave Egypt commercial independence, but Egypt hankered after political independence, which came when Alexander of Macedon defeated the Persians in 332 B.C., driving them out of Asia Minor and conquering the eastern Mediterranean seaboard.

Alexander attempted to assume the legitimacy of the Egyptian pharaoh, visiting the celebrated oracle of Amun at the oasis of Siwa where, he stated, the god recognized him as his son. He was crowned at Memphis, restored the temple, and founded a new city at Alexandria, which became a great Egyptian port. Alexander stayed in Egypt only six months, but his death meant that the country soon began to be integrated into the Greek culture of the Mediterranean. An indirect result of his conquests meant that more foodstuffs seem to have begun to be imported into the country, together with significant improvements to agriculture. A network of radial canals at the el-Lahun barrage increased the cultivated area.

Egypt had now entered the Ptolemaic period (332–30 B.C.) under Ptolemy I, who founded a dynasty, which was served by a Greek-speaking aristocracy. Under Ptolemy II the first lighthouse was built on the island of Pharos and a library founded at Alexandria. This, with its agora, gymnasium, and other Greek features, showed how far Egypt was becoming Hellenized. Temples, however, were still dedicated to Egyptian deities, even if some, such as the hybrid deity Seraphis, were to merge Egyptian and Greek ideas.

During the Ptolemaic period the range of food available expanded enormously, mainly due to the trading links with the Roman Empire and the introduction of new foods from Roman sources. Chickens were not indigenous to ancient Egypt but were a jungle bird introduced from Southeast Asia, and although there is a drawing of a chicken on a small ostracon at Thebes, no chicken bones have been dated before the Greco-Roman period. Chickens then become prolific, as if the Egyptians realized the value of this easily obtainable food supply. New vegetables introduced included turnips, broccoli, and kale; radishes, cucumber, and celery appear to have been cultivated as opposed to the Egyptian wild varieties; legumes now included chickpeas. Nuts included walnuts, pine nuts, and pistachios. Fruit trees introduced included the pear, quince, plum, and peach. Although spices and herbs had been grown or imported into Egypt for a long time, the Romans did introduce peppercorns into the country after trade with India was expanded. Garlic growing on a huge scale was introduced and continued throughout the Greco-Roman period, concentrating on certain areas of the Fayum. Large apiaries were situated in the Fayum, increasing the yield of honey.

Until now barley and emmer were the main grains. Now wheat (*Triticum durum*) was introduced and quickly supplanted the other grains. This was probably due to the Greeks who flooded into Egypt in the wake of Alexander. They believed in intense cultivation of the land, and their attempts to get two crops a year appear to have succeeded. The introduction of the rotary quern made for easier grinding of wheat, thus producing finer flour.

Egyptian wines were now exported to Rome, and Egypt received some wines from the producing areas of the Roman Empire. Athenaeus described a white wine produced in Egypt as being of excellent quality, pleasant, fragrant, and not likely to go to the head.[5] Most wines now came from the delta and were standard for drinking. Wine was now mixed together; one Theban tomb shows two men filling jars by means of siphons. More olive trees were planted, and olive oil was now available as an additional cooking fat, and the oil could also be used for other purposes, such as lighting and lubrication.

Egypt was soon to face another power. Throughout the first century B.C. Rome was becoming the dominant Mediterranean power, and when Ptolemy XII (80–51 B.C.) was driven out by a popular revolt, he appealed to Rome to help him recover his throne. His daughter Cleopatra (51–30 B.C.) played an even more dangerous game, marrying her younger brother Ptolemy XIII and encouraging Roman interest. Rome's conflicts extended into Egypt when the Roman general Pompey fled to Egypt after losing the Battle of Pharsalia, only to be beheaded by order of the queen. Julius Caesar followed to support Cleopatra and to have a son by her. After his assassination in 44 B.C., Mark Antony and Caesar's nephew Octavian ruled the Roman world between them. Although married to Octavian's sister, Antony fell under the spell of Cleopatra, and by 36 B.C. was openly enamored of her. Octavian quickly moved against Egypt. At the Battle of Actium (31 B.C.), Cleopatra withdrew her ships, allowing Octavian to enter Alexandria. The enamored couple committed suicide, bringing the reign of the Ptolomies to an end.

In 27 B.C. Octavian, now Augustus, retained Egypt as his personal property, and as such it was bequeathed to his successors. For the rest of the Roman Empire it became the Roman granary, supplying Rome with its bounty. Egypt had a Roman emperor portrayed as a pharaoh, but its culture became even more of a hybrid, easily adapting Egyptian, Greek, and Roman elements until the entry of Christian and Muslim cultures inaugurated radical new values.

THE GREEKS

The Greeks, who in time came to be called the Hellenes, can be defined as the people who spoke the language known as Greek. The earliest archaeological finds in Greece are from Thessalian sites dating from 50,000 and 30,000 B.C. Animal bones, which seem to be cut and boiled, include bear, red deer, wild ox, wild pig, and hare. Until 10,000 B.C. a foraging population occupied sites sporadically. One site, Franchthi Cave, occupied about 11,000 B.C., had a huge concentration of snail shells, as though this was a major part of the diet. Animal bones include wild pig, hare, and red deer. The bones were split to extract the marrow and had burn marks on them, indicating that they had been roasted. Fish bones included those of tuna, which could be eaten fresh, dried, or salted. Other food eaten seems to have been wild almond nuts, which need to be roasted to be edible, and lentisk, a relative of the pistachio. Fruits included the wild pear. Species of lentils and barley seem to have been cultivated; the grains were crushed or cracked to be made into dough and baked on a fire.

In the eighth-century Homeric Age, cereals, essentially wheat and barley, formed the basis of the diet. Later Plato emphasized that a healthy lifestyle entailed men making themselves flour from wheat and barley, kneading the dough, and cooking it on a griddle to produce fines loaves and buns. Athenaeus, looking back to a golden age, said that the Homeric heroes practiced frugality and self-sufficiency, linked with having an excellent cereal and meat diet, which nourished body and soul. Each hero had his own cup and therefore could control his drinking in moderation.[6]

By 6000 B.C. settled communities were cultivating peas and beans and domesticating sheep, goats, and cattle, which allowed food products to be expanded with the addition of cheese, butter, and milk. Emmer and einkorn were soon joined by *Triticum turgidum,* an ancestor of durum wheat. Barley and millet were also grown. Barley meal was mixed with water to provide a kind of porridge to which herbs, especially mint and thyme, were added. Lentils, peas, and wheat grains could be boiled to make pottage or baked into a kind of loaf or cake. This type of food continued to be a major source of the peasant diet. After 4000 B.C. the chickpea seemed to have been introduced from the Near East. Later the broad bean made an appearance. Late Bronze Age excavations in Crete yielded peas, beans, vetch, and chickpeas. Fish, shellfish, and wild birds as well as pig, deer, ibex, and hare provided protein. Wild fruits and nuts were collected, and some, such as the fig, were being cultivated. Sweetening was provided by honey, although later date syrup and dried figs were used. Vegetables seem to have been gathered from the wild—mustard, mallow, sorrel, and nightshade. Coriander was useful, for its seeds can be used as a spice and its leaves as an herb. Other herbs identified in the prehistoric Aegean region include pennyroyal, mint, and safflower, the latter used as a substitute for saffron.

Ancient Greece was a collection of sovereign states in the classical Aegean where elites ruled over lower classes, who cultivated areas of land, from a collection of buildings clustered around a fortified point. The earliest historic period was that of the Mycenaean culture, dating to the sixteenth century B.C. and taking its title from Mycenae. This culture had an aristocratic ruling class, skilled craftsmen, and an elaborate administrative system. The evidence for this culture was found in the shaft graves excavated by the German archaeologist Heinrich Schliemann in the nineteenth century. Later, beehive tombs, the most impressive of these being the so-called Treasury of Atreus, replaced shaft graves. Schliemann decreed that the rich graves that he had discovered proved Homer's story of the Trojan War, but later excavations have suggested that this war, if such a story were true, was likely to have taken placed about 1200–1150 B.C. The Mycenaeans also conquered the Minoan civilization of Crete about 1450 B.C. The Minoans lived in sophisticated elegance in comfortable palaces with decoration including superb frescoes showing plants and animals in their natural surrounding. A black steatite rhyton shaped like an ostrich egg found in the villa of Hagia Triada (ca. 1550 B.C.) shows details of what appears to be gathering an olive harvest accompanied by singing and drinking. Huge storage jars in the palace of Knossos have an average capacity of 181 liters (40 gallons) and were used to preserve grain, dried vegetables, wine, oil, and honey.

The Mycenaean culture was a Bronze Age civilization that lasted until about 1100 B.C., when it was completely destroyed. Sites were plundered, attacked, and burned in an endless series of wars. The citadels of Mycenae, Pylos, and Thebes were destroyed in 1150 B.C., probably by a Dorian invasion from the north. From then until about 950 B.C. there was a very slow recovery, with a gradual return to a more civilized way of life. This can be seen in the development of pottery, with its geometrical motifs, and the development of a writing system, which merged the Greek language with the consonantal Phoenician language. It was during this time that Homer wrote the *Iliad* and the *Odyssey*, basing these poems on a mighty Mycenaean historic past.

This, however, was an aristocratic society, and in the seventh century B.C. it was challenged by the common people (the *demos*). These were mainly agriculturalists who could trace their origins to the first farming communities in the early Neolithic period. These early farmers laid the basis of Greek agriculture, growing cereal crops and legumes and making systematic use of the olive and the vine. Possibly many farmers raised their crops in fields situated around small-village communities and practiced small-scale stock rearing.

The conventional date for the beginning of Greece as a country is 776 B.C., the date of the first Olympic Games. During this time, two important movements occurred—the rise of the city-states and the colonization of part of the Peloponnese. The struggle between the aristocracy and the *demos* led to the rise of the polis, or the city-state. These were individually governed units having their own law codes, armies, and aims. Outside these areas still remained tribal groups such as the Macedonians and the Thessalians. There was still a large amount of territory unoccupied, and these enabled the Greeks to send out colonists, necessary because in the eighth century B.C. there was an enormous increase in population. Chalkis, Eretria, Corinth, and Megara all sent out groups, mainly to southern Italy and Asia Minor, one of the largest being sent to Kumai (Cumai), just south of Naples, and taking with them the benefit of the grape and the olive. Athens alone seems to have sent out no colonists, presumably because it had enough land to satisfy its population. Sparta solved its problem by annexing its neighbors, especially Messenia, one of the most fertile regions in Greece, and turning their inhabitants into slaves or helots. It was to rely on these people to produce the food necessary to continue its military might.

In the Archaic Age (ca. 630–480 B.C.) Athens suffered droughts and famines, which led to lawlessness. The lawgiver Solon, who also tried to prevent famine by forbidding the export of corn and agricultural products, put down the outbreaks. To conserve flour he decreed that wheaten bread should be served only on feast days. Olive oil could be exported because there was a surplus, and this provided an income. Solon created an assembly of 400 citizens, which met on a regular basis, and a court of appeal. He also took the radical step of canceling all debts and abolished the crippling state of *hectemorage*, which meant the handing over of one-sixth of the produce of a person's land on penalty of the family being enslaved. Markers had been placed on the land to indicate this humiliation. Solon uprooted the markers, thus, as he said, "freeing the black earth." The result of this reform was the development of a self-conscious city elite, which managed to survive the following rule of the tyrants who rose to power by allying with a group of the *demos*.

These controlled many Greek states for several generations. Their rule was unconstitutional, but the reaction against them consolidated the adoption of a democratic way of life. Sparta alone did not succumb to tyranny probably, because of the tight control over its people.

In the second half of the sixth century B.C., the Persians attacked Greece. The Persian Wars, from 499–480 B.C., although at first disastrous for the Greeks, eventually led to the final defeat of the Persian navy at Salamis and the army at Plataea. These defeats gave Greece a new self-confidence and a despising of the barbarians, as the Persians were now known. This was the classical period of Greek culture when, under the leadership of Athens, a Greek confederacy was formed called the Delian League. One hundred and fifty members paid an annual tribute to a common fund. Athens thus became an imperial power almost by default, having its central base on the island of Delos, where the common council met.

Athens, however, suffered from a feeling of overconfidence, which was dented by the defeat of an expedition sent in 450 B.C. to help the Egyptians against the Persians, and by problems with gaining tribute money. This led to the First Peloponnesian War, but the politician

Pericles diplomatically intervened in 446 B.C. with a policy that was to last 30 years. The pact increasingly divided the Greeks into those who acknowledged Athenian supremacy in the Aegean and those who acknowledged Spartan supremacy on land and it was increasingly difficult for any state to ignore this polarity. It did, however, usher in the Periclean Age, when Athens began work on the Parthenon and produced works of art and architecture that were to influence history.

Pericles ensured that the population of Athens secured sufficient food. Wheat bread (*artos*) and flat barley griddle cakes (*maza*) could be easily obtained from the many city bakers. Poorer people subsisted almost entire on *maza,* and these flat breads often served as plates, similar to the bread trenchers of the medieval period. Athenian white bread was highly praised, although Athenaeus said that in the past men preferred *maza.*[7] The prevalence of white bread in Athens was due to the Athenians being able to import wheat on a scale that other cities could not equal. The result was that bakers produced a large variety of bread and pastries. Some wealthy households had their own specialized bakers. Cappadocian bakers were considered the best. Phoenician bakers would provide leavened bread as they worked with yeast or a yeast substitute. Breads produced in the shape of animals or human figures were used in sacrificial rituals. This variety of bread, however, ensured that people had a staple with which to accompany an *opson,* a relish intended to make the bread palatable—a little olive oil, onions, sheep or goat's milk cheese, eggs, fish (perhaps smoked or pickled in brine), or, more rarely, tiny pieces of meat. Not all of these would be eaten at one meal, but Pericles insisted that they should be available if required. Beans, peas, and lentils were often pulverized into a puree (*etnos*), which was a filling dish. Cheese, garlic, olives, and onions were also part of the diet, especially in the army.

Vegetables, especially cabbages, carrots, artichokes, chicory, onions, and garlic, were the main diet. Some, such as beets and turnips, were grown more for their leaves than for their roots. Fruit included grapes, figs, pomegranates, medlars, quinces, apples, and pears. Nuts were gathered from the wild. Meat was available, but apart from pork, especially suckling pig, it was expensive and a luxury. Cows' milk was not appreciated. Sheep and goat's milk was used for cheese and butter. One product, *trachanas,* made of boiled milk and coarsely ground millet, laid out in sheets to be dried in the sun and then stored in tightly sealed jars, was probably part of the diet. Most people expected to eat meat only at religious festivals when the meat of slaughtered animals would be distributed.

Fish was relatively cheap, so bread and fish would form part of a staple diet for the Athenians. Some fish, such as mackerel, sturgeon, and mullet, were imported from the Black Sea. The Athenians despised small fish and salted fish, preferring to eat larger fish, such as turbot and bream. Not all fish was cheap. Eels from Lake Copais provided a more expensive dish; meals that included this delicacy were an example of conspicuous consumption. Shellfish was obtainable in abundance from the coastal regions.

The Periclean peace could not last, and the Second, or Great, Peloponnesian War began in 431 B.C. when Sparta invaded Athenian territory. Pericles drew the Athenians into the citadel of Athens, allowing the Spartans to devastate the surrounding countryside. Plague broke out in the citadel, and Pericles was one of its victims. Sparta finally defeated Athens in 404 B.C., but, mindful of its importance, did not destroy the city.

Sparta, however, found itself faced by another enemy. Philip II became King of Macedon in 359 B.C. He quickly saw that the Persian Wars had weakened the grip of both Athens and Sparta on the Greek city-states and accepted an invitation from the Thessalians to come to their aid over control of the sanctuary of Delphi. He found himself in opposition to Athens, and defeated it in 33 B.C. at Chaironeia in central Greece. He also did not destroy Athens, preferring to create a federation with himself at its head so that he could lead an expedition to defeat the revived Persian empire. Before this could happen, Philip was murdered in 336 B.C.

His son, Alexander, then aged 20, took over the Persian throne and intended to finish what his father had begun. He moved swiftly to defeat the Persians in three great victories. After the third, in 331 B.C., the Persian king, Darius, was murdered, leaving Alexander to press on with expeditions to Bactria and India. Here his troops refused to go any farther. Alexander died in Babylon in 323 B.C., leaving an empire stretching from the Adriatic in the west to the Ganges in the east. In 12 years he had extended the boundaries of the Greek world far beyond what anyone could have imagined. He had destroyed the Persian empire, burned the great city of Persepolis, and founded at least 70 cities named after him, although only one, in Egypt, was to become his main legacy.

Alexander had spread Greek culture throughout his empire. In many areas it was superficial, and local customs continued to exist. His death left a vacuum, and his generals fought among themselves to establish their own territorial rights. Eventually three kingdoms were created.

Macedonia was formed in the north under the Antigonid dynasty. Egypt in the south was ruled by the Ptolomies, and Turkey, central Asia, Babylonia, and Syria in the east were ruled by the Seleucids. These were, however, to face a more tenacious enemy. By 280 B.C. Roman armies were expanding into Greece, several advances being the result of an appeal by a king or chieftain for help against an enemy, which only led to them succumbing to Rome.

In 280 B.C. Tarentum in southern Italy appealed to Pyrrhos, king of Epirus in northern Greece, for help against the Romans. Tarentum was defeated, and the Romans came into contact with the Greek civilization in southern Italy. This made them turn their attention to Greece. By 146 B.C. Macedonia was firmly under Roman rule. Steady advancement to the east saw the Seleucid dynasty becoming vassals of Rome, and Ptolemaic Egypt became what amounted to a Roman province in 31 B.C. on the death of Cleopatra. Rome allowed no rivals, so many Greek cities lost their autonomy, but in the end Greece was to conquer Rome, as her culture became the dominant part of Roman artistic life and political thinking. Horace put it neatly when he said, "Conquered Greece conquered its savage victor."[8]

During the historic period of Greek history the food eaten would obviously vary from area to area, but there seems to be certain common foods and food products. When meat was eaten it came from sheep, goats, and pigs. Goats provided cheese and milk, and their meat was only good at certain times of the year because of its rank smell at other times. Its flesh was regarded as being very nourishing, and Athenaeus recounted the story of the Theban athlete who lived almost entirely on goat's flesh but was a source of amusement to his companions, who balked at the smell of his sweat.[9] Young goats or kids were a luxury dish, as the killing of these meant a loss of a mature goat, which would produce milk and cheese. Suckling pig was appreciated, as was lamb, but these were also luxury items. Athenaeus said goat's meat was for slaves but wild boar meat should be kept for oneself and a friend.[10]

Beef was more of a rarity because oxen were sacrificial animals. After the sacrifice the meat could be distributed to the worshippers. More exotic fare came in the eating of dogs and asses. Hippocrates recommended roast dog in some diets, and Galen said that dogs were commonly eaten "amongst some people."[11] Whether this was a regular occurrence or done in times of famine is not certain. Varro and Galen also noted that some people ate the flesh of asses, and Apuleius thought that his hero in *The Golden Ass* was going to be slaughtered, with his guts going to the dogs and the rest of him providing meat for slaves.[12] As with the Romans, both ass's flesh and horseflesh was only eaten in cases of need. This type of meat could be eaten in the form of sausages, of which the Greeks were inordinately fond. Other animals mentioned in Greek texts as being edible included moles, weasles, and badgers. Hedgehogs, whose flesh tastes something like chicken, were popular; a badger's flesh is more like pork.

Meat was also obtained by hunting. Animals included hares, wild boars, wild goats, deer, and birds. On rare occasions even bears and lion were eaten. Galen said that pieces of bear should be boiled twice.[13] Athenaeus suggested that hares should be roasted on a spit and sprinkled with salt.[14] Sauce or cheese may be put over it, but not too much, and oil should be used sparingly. Birds were best served spit-roasted with cheese and oil sprinkled over them, perhaps eaten more as a snack than a full meal. The bird market at Athens supplied small birds of every variety, including thrushes, blackbirds, chaffinches, sparrows, and larks. It would appear that very few birds were safe from the culinary attentions of the Greeks. More acceptable today would be the eating of game birds, such as grouse, mallards, pigeons, and pheasants, and domesticated fowls and geese. The eggs of these birds were also appreciated, either hard- or soft-boiled. Both yolks and whites were used in preparing dishes.

Another highly valued food was fish and shellfish. All types of fish were eaten, including tuna, gray mullet, conger eel, dogfish, angel shark, bream, and swordfish. Even cuttlefish could make a good meal. The annual migration of tuna provided ample opportunities for catching large quantities of this fish, and it was eaten fresh and salted. Mackerel also was salted and smoked. Sometimes sturgeon was available, but as this was obtained from the Black Sea, it was more of a delicacy than a regular meal. Some of the smallest fish were served as a fry called *aphye*. This could include squid and crabs. Oysters were particularly prized, and as with the Romans were eaten in great quantities. The fish sauce, which was so prized by the Romans, seems to have been devised in Bithynia, as a profitable way of making use of small fish that might otherwise have been discarded. From there it spread to Greece, but it was the Romans who made use of it in so many of their dishes, as indicated by the recipes of Apicius.

A minor cereal in Greece was millet. The major cereals were einkorn, emmer, and barley, the latter being both the two-row and six-row variety. Durum wheat was imported into Greece by the Phoenicians. All these grains could be used to thicken stews, make a pottage, or, more often, ground into flour. From the flour a large variety of breads and cakes were made. By now competition in quality and styles of bread were stimulated by market conditions. White bread was the most appreciated, followed by bread made from fine barley flour. Much of the bread was unleavened, producing flat breads, although *nitron* could be used as a raising agent. Bread made in Athens was particularly varied and appreciated. This was possible because Athens was able to import wheat on a scale beyond that of other cities. In households dough was put under a pot on which hot ashes were piled, thus causing the dough to rise.

Other basic foods, especially for the poorer elements of society, were pulses. Many were gathered from the wild before being cultivated, such as vetch, peas, and lupines. Beans, lentils, peas, and chickpeas were useful because they could be dried and stored as well as being used fresh. Chickpeas, if roasted or very young, could be eaten as a dessert. Classical writers commented on the fact that they could cause flatulence, but balanced this against their value as a food. Beans and peas could be added to meat stews; lentils, in particular, were used to make a filling stew or could be served on their own.

Fruits were well known in Greece. Homer in the *Odyssey* described an orchard that contained trees bearing pomegranates, pears, apples, sweet figs, and luxuriant olives.[15] Fruits were regarded more as appetizers than used in dessert, although myrtle berries were an exception. Together with nuts they were regarded with pleasure at the end of a symposium. Apples may have been brought from Anatolia or Iraq, although wild and presumably small and sour apples were known in Greece. Other fruits included two varieties of quinces, the wild and cultivated plum, cherries, watermelon and muskmelon (probably imported from western Asia), and a variety of berries. Dried figs were imported from Anatolia, and their leaves were used as a wrapping for meat dishes. Dried dates were imported, and Xenophon implied that smaller ones were given to the servants while the larger and more fleshy ones were reserved for their masters.[16] Medlars were eaten when they were so ripe that they were almost rotting. Nuts included almonds, walnuts, hazelnuts, and sweet chestnuts. Two lesser-known nuts were lentisk nuts, which were also chewed to cleanse the breath, and terebinth nuts. Both the trees had tender shoots that could be pickled before being eaten. Pine nuts were prolific both as a dessert and in cooking.

Vegetables and salad vegetables included beets, cabbage, cress, lettuce, leeks, carrots, onions, celery, cucumber, and spinach. A wild form of asparagus was available. Herbs could enhance cooking of dishes. Thyme, dill, sage, basil, mint, rue, and hyssop were gathered from the wild or cultivated in gardens. Mushrooms and nettles were available in the wild. Only the poor used some foods. These included fat hen, fennel, wild chervil, wild spinach, hoary mustard, and nightshade. As can be deduced, these were gathered rather than cultivated. Athenaeus recommended a concoction of wild plants and herbs pounded together.[17]

Beekeeping was a major occupation in Greece. The main sweetener and preservative was honey, and certain types of honey were prized. Beekeeping was an admired skill, and the Greeks knew how the flowers and other plants from which the bees gathered pollen could flavor honey. Attic honey was flavored by thyme, but the most admired honey was that from Mount Hymettus, and this was supplied to markets throughout Greece, often in the form of honeycombs. In Athens it was eaten smeared on flat cakes. Mead could be produced by the fermentation of diluted honey, and this was produced in Lydia.

Dairy products were rare apart from cheese. Milk drinking was seen as a feature of the barbarians (the Greeks referred sneeringly to the Thracians as "butter-eaters") but could be allowed to shepherds and peasants who kept sheep, goats, and cattle. Milk became sour very quickly and hence was difficult to transport to towns. *Oxygala*, a form of yogurt, was eaten and sometimes mixed with honey. Cheese, a nutritious product, was probably made from sheep and goat's milk, and eaten throughout Greece with honey, figs, and olives. It could also be incorporated into bread baking. Greeks and Romans disliked milk products, which could be partly explained by the climatic fact that there was a line beyond which olive trees could not be grown. The southern European regions relied on olives and their oil for cooking and other purposes, whereas the northern areas were compelled to rely on milk products for their fats.

Wild olive trees were known in Greece from Neolithic times, but the first cultivated olives, with the intention of pressing olive oil, were grown in Crete. Olive trees were prized because the goddess Athena was reputed to have raised an olive tree on the Acropolis in a contest with the god Poseidon for dominance of the land. Olive trees were grown through the whole of Greece and olive oil was used as a cooking medium, for basting and frying and as a marinade. Other uses were as a fuel and a cosmetic. On its own it was a dip for bread.

Wine was equally important. Grape pips were known from 4500 B.C., but this may indicate dried or fresh fruit and may not be connected with viticulture. Cultivation of vines appears to have been started about 2000 B.C. at Mytos in Crete, when pips and skins indicate wine making. Evidence of wine-lees (sediment) and grape pips was found in jars at Mycenae. Vineyards were usually small and the property of aristocratic producers until Solon encouraged the peasantry to plant vines. This they did with such enthusiasm that for a while there was a shortage of grain in Athens. The Greek philosopher Theophrastus of Eresus (370–287 B.C.) in his *De Causis Plantarium* (*On Plant Physiology*) explained about the quality of soils and discusses the best conditions for planting, grafting techniques, and pruning methods. It was he who advised that in hot climates such as Greece the grapes should be sprinkled with soil to shelter them from the sun.

Harvesting took place in September. At first, as elsewhere, slaves treaded on the grapes in a huge vat, but in the sixth century B.C. the Greeks invented the screw and the beam presses, which allowed more efficient extraction of the juice. Wine was then transferred to jars (*pithoi*) or amphorae for transportation. The handles would be stamped with the merchant's name and perhaps names of local officials who could guarantee the quality of the wine. Beaten egg white or goat's milk was sometimes added to increase the clarity of wine, but this wine had to be thoroughly sieved before serving. The smaller the jar, the more expensive and high-quality the vintage. Pig and goat wineskins were also used. In his play *Cyclops,* the fifth-century B.C. Greek tragedian Euripides made Odysseus put wine into wineskins to ply the Cyclops, Polyphemus, and make him drunk. Polyphemus was to be despised and ridiculed because he had always drunk goat's milk.

Different areas produced a variety of wines. Some areas added seawater to the wine; some added herbs and flavorings. Theophrastus noted that the mixing of aromatic Heracala wine with the salty Erythraean wine produced a good wine. On the island of Thasos wine was mixed with honey to produce a sweet taste. This was regarded as a fine wine, as were those of Lesbos, Lemnos, and Rhodes. The cheapest wine would be akin in taste to vinegar, but this was acceptable, as was fresh grape juice. The best wines were left to mature. Odysseus's strong room contained jars of old sweet-tasting wine packed in rows along the wall. One of these wines was opened in its 11th year. The climate of Greece allowed harvests producing wine of even quality, unlike the more variable climate of northern Italy and Gaul. The Greeks added water to their wine, as did the Romans.

The Greek wine trade soon developed into a huge industry and was almost a monopoly until the second century B.C., when the Romans invaded Greece. As wine production expanded throughout the Roman Empire, prices dropped, and the wine trade became a part of the Roman economy.

THE ROMANS

The history of Rome is the process by which Rome, always conscious of its destiny, grew from being a small city on Seven Hills to ruler of a vast empire. When, as St. Luke remarked, "there went out a decree from Caesar Augustus that all the world should be taxed," (St. Luke 2:1 AV) "the world" meant the Roman world, and those within it knew of none other. Rome had achieved this position by conquering its enemies, creating friendly client kingdoms, and creating a system whereby the people of the empire—Spaniards, Gauls, Greeks, Egyptians, and many others—considered themselves fortunate to have become part of a unified Roman population. Roman citizenship was prized, and this created what the third-century A.D. Christian writer Tertullian called *Romanitas*—a Roman habit of thought and point of view. Equally prized was the *Pax Romana*—the Roman peace. Admittedly this peace was sometimes achieved by fierce warfare, but Roman citizens knew that among its benefits was a law code that applied strictly throughout the Roman world and that could adapt itself to local customs when necessary.

Roman history is usually divided into three parts: the kings, the republic, and the empire. According to tradition, Rome was founded in 753 B.C. Two legends became entwined. In the first, Aeneas led a group of refugees from Troy after the destruction of that city to settle them in Italy. They intermarried with the local population and founded the city of Lavinia. Aeneas's son, Ascanius, led a band from Lavinia to found the city of Alba Longa. The second legend became intertwined with the first, making Romulus, the grandnephew of the last Amulius, the last king of Alba Longa, the founder of the city of Rome on the Palatine Hill. Gradually six other hills were annexed and surrounded by a wall, thus creating the city named after its founder.

Archaeological evidence confirms the traditional date, showing that a few hilltop settlements were established on these hills from the end of the Bronze Age, about 1000 B.C. By 700 B.C. these settlements had expanded to take in the area that became the Forum valley. In the next century, helped by a wealthy aristocracy and a strong trading community, Rome had transformed itself into an organized city-state.

It was also situated on an important river crossing, which enabled it to attract traders and other itinerants, so that its population soon included Sabines, Latins, Etruscans, and Gauls. Literary sources based on established tradition relate that six other kings, the first three being of Latin and the last three of Etruscan origin, followed Romulus. Each king introduced his own culture to Rome, created public buildings such as temples and law courts and even an efficient sewer system, but in doing so they gave themselves more authority. The rule of the last king, Tarquinius Superbus, became so tyrannical that the citizens revolted against royal rule, deposed Tarquinius, and established a republic with Junius Brutus as its first consul. The date for this revolutionary charge was reputed to be 510 B.C.

Two praetors, later called consuls, exercised absolute power, but this power was controlled by the fact that they were elected only for one year. After their term of office ended, they retired into private life and had to account for their administration. The citizens themselves came to be divided into two groups: the patricians, who held the main offices of state, and the plebeians, who were the poorer citizens. The plebeians were made poorer by the fact that the patricians had encroached on the *ager publicus,* or the public lands, increasing their landholdings, and they suffered from devastating raids by people outside the Roman area. Debt, land hunger, and food shortages were their main problems, and to counter patrician power they set up their own assembly and elected their own officials, tribunes (*tribuni plebes*), and aediles. For the next two centuries this group sought to consolidate its power and improve the lot of its members, especially in the acquisition of land and the production of food.

But the most important group was the army, the core of which was heavy infantry. In theory the army was a citizen army, which tilled its fields until called on to defend Rome. The patricians provided the cavalry and the plebeians the infantry, which fused aristocrats and commoners into a single organization, the social foundation of the republic symbolized by the adopted motto *SPQR, Senatus Populusque Romanus* (the Senate and the people of Rome). In practice it was impossible for a farmer to leave his land for an indefinite time to become a fighting man, and the army gradually developed into a formidable professional fighting machine, which enabled the Romans to defend their city-state and extend its boundaries.

This they began to do by defeating the Latin peoples in the south in a series of bitter wars lasting until 338 B.C. To the north the Romans subdued the Etruscans in 396 B.C. and captured the important city of

Veii. By the end of the fourth century B.C., the Romans had subdued the Samnites and opened up the fertile lands of Campania, which became one of the main wine-producing areas for Rome. At the same time the Romans had had to fight successive invasions of Gauls from the north, which led to a disastrous sack of Rome in 390 B.C. The Romans were only saved because the Latins had been so weakened by the Celtic invasion that they could not shake off Roman rule.

The struggle against the Gauls and the consequent distress of many of the plebeians led to increasing agitation for them to gain more privileges and power. This finally resulted in their receiving a fairer share of conquered territory; indeed, the Pomptine lands seized from the Volscians were distributed only to the plebeians. A program of colonization and settlement began, which did much to relieve plebeian poverty and increase the fertile agricultural area. In 368 B.C. the Licinian Rogations were passed, by which the plebeians became eligible for one of the consulships. Twenty years later this was firmly in practice. No citizen was to hold more than 500 *iugera* (about 300 acres) of land, and interest paid on debts, especially that held on agricultural land, was to be deduced from the original debt.

Later Roman writers regarded this period as ideal. Seneca said wistfully that "men's bodies were still sound and strong; their food was light and unspoiled by art and luxury whereas when they began to seek dishes not for the sake of removing but of rousing an appetite and devising countless sauces to whet their gluttony, then what was nourishment to a hungry man became a burden to a full stomach."[18] Then, what before was nourishment to a hungry man became a burden to a full stomach. Frugality was promoted as a virtue, rooted in fortitude and prudence. The Roman historian Valerius Maximus commented that the greatest simplicity of the ancient Romans in eating was the clearest gauge of their good nature and self-restraint.[19] Food was basic, consisting of *puls,* far (flour made from emmer wheat), and dry legumes. Roasted grains were beaten and ground. Food was symbolic. Salt was added to flour, which could be used to make *mola salsa* sprinkled on sacrificial victims. A bride was given cakes made from far and salt.

At the beginning of the third century B.C., Rome was established as an imperial power. Its success was due to three circumstances. By founding colonies throughout Italy, it had secured strategic sites joined by a network of well-constructed roads. It had secured the cooperation of former enemies by treating them fairly and backing them with its power. Lastly, these alliances were the result of continuous wars in which the allies shared the spoils. But war was the inevitable product of an effective military machine, which had to be kept occupied. War was the raison d'être, and the Roman imperialism was the result of war.

Imperialism now spread beyond Italy. The conquest of the Hellenic south brought Rome into conflict with Carthage, another player in the fight to control the Mediterranean region. Soldiers had to become sailors because of the need to fight overseas and at sea and to bring in food supplies. The struggle against Carthage led to three Punic wars between 264 and 146 B.C., which resulted in the total defeat of Carthage. By the end of the Second Punic War in 201 B.C. Rome had gained the provinces of Sicily and Sardinia, Carthaginian possessions in Spain, and the taste for further expansion. Soon it had conquered Gallia Narbonensis (Provence) and expanded into the eastern Mediterranean. Roman troops spread across Greece, invaded the Balkans, and defeated the Macedonians. In the 140s Greece and Macedonia became Roman provinces. Carthage was finally defeated and its territory made into an African province; further annexations were made in Asia, Cilicia, and Cyrene.

This growth of empire, with greater trading opportunities leading to an importation of goods, vastly increased the wealth of the patrician class, allowing them to adopt a luxurious and sophisticated lifestyle. This was also fueled by investment in land where large landed estates were worked by war captives imported as slaves. New methods of farming also made an impact, many designed to provide absentee landlords with an income from the sale of cash crops.

But this prosperity did not trickle down to the plebeian class, who came under increasing pressure to vacate their land. Eventually, in 133 B.C., social conflict broke out when the tribune Tiberius Gracchus introduced a law to enforce the neglected limit of 500 *iugera* on holders of *ager publicus* and to redistribute the surplus lands to the plebeians. Furious opposition led to political violence and the murder of Gracchus. Ten years later his brother Gaius suffered the same fate for an attempt at even more radical reforms, including foundations of colonies to resettle the poor and the provision of state-subsidized grain for citizens of Rome. Further difficulties throughout the empire, including war in the African provinces, slave revolts in Sicily, and an invasion of Italy by the German tribes of the Cimbri and the Teutones, led to unrest between the Italian allies and political chaos in Rome.

Army reform was now essential to create a professional army serving for a set number of years and being granted land on completion of service. This was achieved in the reforms of the consul Marius, but the troops then began to identify with their generals rather than the state, and in the end they were to become the means by which military leavers gained or preserved power. In turn this would lead to civil war, and to restore order, the First Triumvirate was created between Caesar, Pompey, and Crassus. Using his command of the army, Caesar began a five-year conquest of Gaul and Illyricum, using the campaigns as propaganda value to build up his support in Rome. On the death of Crassus in 49 B.C., he crossed the Rubicon and challenged Pompey, defeating him at the battle of Pharsalus. Further campaigns in Egypt, Pontus, Africa, and Spain made him master of the Roman world, but also enabled him to bring in as many constructive reforms as possible. It was obvious that he, not the Senate, was the ruler in Rome, and an empire was established in all but name. It was this fact, together with the senators' realization of their own impotence, that led to his assassination in 44 B.C.

Power now passed to Caesar's grandnephew Octavian, but he shared this in the Second Triumvirate with Lepidus and Mark Antony. But Antony's dealings with Egypt led to his downfall, and Octavian emerged supreme. With his uncontested power, the republic ended and the empire began. Adopting the name Augustus, he created a system whereby power was concentrated into the hands of a single *princeps,* who held *potestas* based on *concensum universorum,* that is, power based on the consent of the whole population. This covered economic, political, and military power, with the emperor at the center of control but setting himself up as the patron and protector of the common people. With Augustus the system of imperial power thus theoretically encompassed republicanism, but his successors soon dropped this pretense. Power became increasingly autocratic, with the emperor often dependent on the military. It was therefore important to keep the army occupied, so until the reign of Trajan there were further conquests, Britain and Dacia being perhaps the most important.

At its greatest expansion the empire covered most of Europe, stretching from as far north as Scotland and southern Germany, across the Rhine and the Danube, westward to Spain, southward to the fringes of the Sahara Desert in North Africa, and eastward to Palestine, Syria, and Armenia. It embraced or dominated cultures, languages, and traditions, including agriculturalists and pastoralists, rich and poor. It created cities and towns out of villages and rural landscapes. If there was an overall policy, it was to bind a collection of disparate peoples into one great empire owing allegiance to Rome and aspiring to become Roman citizens, with the privileges that such a title entailed.

Roman writers explained the dominance of Rome through its military might, strong and competent administration, and the sound, moral character of its people. Rome had the right to rule other tribes and peoples. Strabo spoke of Rome's geographical position, lying between Greece and Libya. He noted, among other advantages, the length of the Italian peninsula, its climatic variation allowing the land to produce a comprehensive range of foodstuffs, providing food for men and animals.[20] There were areas where problems were encountered, such as the low level of rainfall in southern Italy and Sicily, but the diversity of products within the empire, many of which were exported to Rome, could make up for this shortfall. Pliny also extolled the physical and climatic advantage of Italy, abundant water supply, fertile soil, and rich pastures—excellent crops, wine, olive oil, wool, flax, and cloth, all exploited by the talent of the Roman people.[21]

Rome was the center, where the emperor and the administration were. Rome itself was a parasite city living off the wealth of others, but with a capacity for organization that ensured dominance of this vast empire. Italy was the only area exempt from imperial taxation and rents from public properties, until Domitian imposed property and taxation taxes in the third century A.D.

Rome governed its vast empire by centrally appointed officials, senators, and equestrians, who followed a career path that embraced military and civilian duties. Proconsuls ruled Asia and Africa. Some provinces were administered by governors, others by procurators. Civilian procurators assisted military governors by controlling taxes and custom duties. The Roman administration intended to civilize the disparate peoples in the empire, and civilization meant an urban population living in self-governing cities, which had all the amenities necessary to live a life as a citizen. In the Greek east, which had developed urban communities very early, only minor adjustments needed to be made. In the western and northern empire, cities and towns were created, and there was constant maneuvering on the part of communities to gain privileges to improve status. The main function of city administrators was to help the central government collect taxes and ensure law and order. They also had to build and maintain public buildings and aqueducts, stage festivals and games, and make certain that their citizens were fed. Most of this was done by well-to-do citizens who gave cash payments and personal services; often there was competition for public offices, as they were felt to be a mark of prestige. Only in the fourth century was there a reluctance to take on what was then considered to be an onerous burden.

Surrounding communities were expected to supply urban centers, and this might be achieved by converting a barbarian, warlike people into settled agriculturalists. This happened in Gaul and Britain, where hilltop forts were abandoned and their inhabitants resettled in lower lands. Some tribes, however, preferred to stay in their hilltop communities in an effort to follow their customary way of life. Strabo said that the Lusitanians in Spain preferred to drink beer and goat's milk, use butter, and eat acorn bread for two-thirds of the year. The Ligurians were prepared to trade flocks, hides, honey, and timber for olive oil and wine, but they did this because they were forced to rather than by choice.[22]

A well-governed urban community was a peaceful one where traders and merchants could buy and sell goods, villagers and farmers would bring produce from their smallholdings and farms to market, and householders would contribute toward taxation in Rome. Carriage of goods would be along roads laid out by military surveyors for military purposes but used by traders and travelers, who could convey goods safely to their destinations. Even so, land transport could be slow and costly, even though the Romans had developed nailed horseshoes and a horse collar. Transport by water was faster and cheaper, especially coastal trade. Sea transport depended on the seasons, but trade with the Far East developed once the Romans had mastered the vicissitudes of the trade winds. This increased the variety of spices and other foodstuffs available, thereby expanding the Roman diet.

Quite obviously, as the empire was so large, personal preference for foodstuffs and produce would depend on the area where a person lived, and even tribal origins. Soldiers and traders who had settled in one part of the empire might bring their food customs with them. An example occurred in Britain. Pottery found in forts on Hadrian's Wall is akin to that made in North Africa. Reinforcements from Britain sent to Emperor Antoninus Pius's troops in his war against Mauritania, A.D. 146–149, returned with North African soldiers and Moorish levies. These brought with them their own cooking methods, which included food cooked in dishes on portable braziers.

The main wheat of the Romans was emmer; barley was left where possible for animal food. Barley could stand winter conditions. Later emmer was supplanted by durum wheat and bread wheat, which had the advantage that these produced finer flour. Emmer grains were ground to provide meal for pottage and for *alica* (emmer groat), which was used to make a wide variety of bread and cakes. This was described by Pliny as excellent food with great nutritional value. To obtain *alica:*

> The grain is pounded in a wooden mortar to avoid the pulverisation resulting from the use of a stone mortar.... After the grain has been stripped of its coats, the bared kernel is again broken up with the same instruments. This produces three grades of *alica*—very small, seconds and very large.... The grades have not yet acquired the whiteness, which is their outstanding quality.... By a subsequent treatment—an astonishing development indeed—chalk is added which is incorporated into the grain giving colour and fineness.[23]

Alica was used to make the Punic porridge, previously mentioned. Cato used it for what may seem a very sweet cheesecake (*placenta*):

> Material: 2 pounds of wheat flour for the crust, 4 pounds of flour and two pounds of ordinary flour [*farina*] and 2 pounds of prime groats [*alica*] for the pastry layers [*tracta*]. Soak the grouts in water; when quite soft pour into a clean bowl, drain well, and knead with the hand; when thoroughly kneaded, work in the 4 pounds of flour gradually. From this dough make the pastry layers [*tracta*], and spread them out to dry. When they are dry arrange them evenly. Treat each *tracta* as follows: after kneading, brush with olive oil.... Soak 14 pounds of sheep milk cheese in water and macerate, changing the water three times. Take out a small quantity at a time; squeeze dry, put in a bowl. When you have dried out the cheese completely, knead it in a small bowl by hand to make it as smooth as possible. Then take a clean flour sifter [*cibrum farinarium*] and force the cheese through it into a bowl. Add 4 pounds of fine honey and mix well with the cheese. Spread the crust on a clean board, one foot wide, on oiled bay leaves, and form the cheesecake as follows: place a first layer of pastry [*tracta*] over the base, cover it with mixture from the bowl, add the tracta one by one, covering these with the cheese and honey until you have used up all the mixture. On the top place a single tracta, then fold over the crust. Place the cheesecake on the hot hearth in a hot crock and heap coals on top and all round the sides. See that it bakes thoroughly and slowly, uncovering it two or three times to examine it. When it is done, remove and spread with honey.[24]

Cato also made another cake, which seemingly is much lighter, called *libum,* with two pounds of soft cheese mixed with half a pound of flour and one egg, placed under leaves and baked on a warm hearth under a crock.[25]

Poorer Romans ate simple food that might take a long time to prepare. The "Moretum" described Simulus rising at cockcrow on a cold winter's morning to prepare his meal. He cleaned the quern, and then slowly turned it to mill his flour. Both hands did the work, one to feed the corn, one to rotate the upper stone. Simulus then added warm water to mix the flour to dough. He placed a piece on a part of the hearth, cleared it of ashes, put tiles over it, and covered it with ashes. While the dough was cooking, he went into the garden and picked four heads of garlic (probably much smaller than those cultivated today), parsley or wild celery, rue, and coriander. He pounded these in a mortar with water, olive oil, vinegar, salt, and hard cheese to make his *moretum*. This he would eat with his bread for his midday meal. Columella had similar recipes with additions of walnuts, pine nuts, and parched sesame seeds. The hard work necessary to produce this simple meal was a daily task.

There was obviously some variation in the quality of Roman bread. The loaves found carbonized in Pompeii were probably, when originally baked, dense in texture and dark in color. Columella said cynically, when dealing with the duties of a bailiff, that he should always eat in the presence of the slaves and eat the same bread as they do. In so doing he will make sure that the bread is carefully made.[26] Seneca, when urging a friend to try living a poor man's life for a while, said, "Let your bread be hard and dirty." He also said, "Nature does not care if the bread is of coarse variety or made from the finest wheat flour."[27] Some bread would have been excellent, being sprinkled with poppy seeds, baked with honey, or flavored with spices. Cato recommended a simple recipe for bread, using a simple method similar to that used in Greece. The crock was piled with hot ashes and the bread cooked with the dry heat:

> Wash your hands and a bowl thoroughly. Pour the meal into the bowl, add water gradually, and knead thoroughly. When it is kneaded, roll out and bake under a crock.[28]

Bread was one staple. Pulses provided another. Beans and peas were a major vegetable and a basis for pottage. Vegetables and salad produce were widely eaten. Onions and shallots were added to many dishes and bulbs that today might be considered unacceptable as a food. Gladioli, for example, were pounded or sliced, added to stews, or baked in ashes and eaten with oil and salt. Possibly this was done in times of shortage rather than as a regular occurrence.

A large variety of fruit was available. Pliny noted more than 100 new varieties of fruit trees, and Columella gave about 50. Not all these were available throughout the empire, although the Romans became adept at growing crops in a variety of regions. The exportation of the cherry tree to Britain is a case in point. Trade also helped. Evidence of trade to the farthest part of the empire came in the find of a piece of amphora from the Forest of Dean in the west of England. This had the Greek word *koyk* painted on it, indicating the contents were dates from the doum palm, a tree limited to Upper Egypt.

Meat, fish, and mainly poultry provided protein; meat might have been too expensive for some people. Game supplied food in country regions and there was no prohibition on hunting. The main condiments after salt were *liquamen* or garum, *allec,* and olive oil. These were produced in great quantities and were essential to the Romans, although not perhaps to other peoples within their empire. Their frequent use, however, both by administrators sent from Rome and the army, seems to have altered dietary habits, and these condiments seem to have gradually accepted—so much so that when the supply of *liquamen* exported to Gaul and Britain from Spain and North Africa proved inadequate during the second century A.D., local industries were established to produce this vital condiment. Olive oil had other uses than cooking, which probably accounts for its growing popularity. Gaul, Spain, and Italy were the major producers, but the eastern Mediterranean also produced olives and olive oil of fine quality. The quantity of olives carried in an amphora can be seen in the one found intact in the River Thames, which, according to the number of stones found in it, had once held 6,500 Posean olives. Sugar detected in the remains may have been a means of preservative, possibly *defrutum.*

Beer and cider were drunk in parts of the empire. Roman auxiliaries in Britain had a taste for beer. At Vindolanda in northern Britain, where Bavarian and Tungrian units were stationed, wooden tablets show that beer was part of the daily rations. On one dating to A.D. 111 the price of beer is recorded at eight *asses* a pint. A beer brewer is mentioned on one tablet, and Optatus, a *braciiarius* (maltster), is mentioned on another. Vindolanda would not have been the only fort where soldiers preferred to drink beer. The main drink of the Romans was wine, which was produced and exported wherever possible throughout the empire. Wine was also mixed with fruit juice, herbs, and spices, and new wines were softened with gypsum or lime. Wine with woodworm was recommended on medical grounds. This wine would have a bitter taste, somewhat like vermouth.

Not all the people in all parts of the empire ate and drank well. Food was more likely to be available in the towns, and as it was seasonal, more was available in summer. People living in towns also had the advantage of having "fast food" served hot in the streets, such as pottage, chickpeas, and sausages. Those persons who wished to follow a Romanized way of life, influenced by the army or civilian administrators, probably adapted their diets to those akin to the ones in Italy. The less civilized regions and those who rejected Roman influence followed their traditional ways. These might mean starvation and famine in winter or a hot, dry season. If the army as part of its food supply requisitioned crops or if there were a series of bad years climatically, this might also result in starvation conditions. Nevertheless, the expansion of the empire meant that Roman ingenuity and skills led to an increase in food supply and to some modification of original dietary identity.

The empire flourished during the first three centuries A.D. In the first century, Emperors Vespasian, Titus, Domitian, and Nerva were assiduous builders and administrators, and the fact that Nerva and his next three successors were chosen by adoption and ratified by the Senate ensured that their reigns were those of efficient administration, domestic peace, and widespread prosperity. Marcus Aurelius broke the tradition, leaving the empire to his dissolute son, Commodus. Flattered by corrupt courtiers and unpopular with civilians and military alike, his reign disintegrated. His murder in A.D. 191 led to a military crisis and the accession of a new dynasty, the Severans from the North African provinces. Despite the expansion of the tax base achieved by granting Roman citizenship to the whole empire in A.D. 212, the economic crisis and the increasing imperial despotism led to the assassination of the emperor Severus Alexander in A.D. 235, and 50 years of rebellion, disputes, and internal struggles allowed provincial uprisings and the barbarians to invade the frontier regions.

At the end of the third century Diocletian succeeded as emperor. He divided the empire into two areas, the west and the east. Systematic internal reorganization, however, led to increasingly onerous taxation, a stifling economic structure, and fragmentation in the administration of the provinces. Not everywhere suffered. Parts of the empire remained prosperous, and the empire was vast enough to switch supplies in trade if one part of the empire was in difficulties.

In the reign of Diocletian's successor, Constantine, the Christian religion was legalized by the Edict of Milan in A.D. 313, and power began to shift from the west to the east, when a new capital, Constantinople, was created on the Bosporus, where the old city of Byzantium stood. For more than a millennium, until the Turks captured the city in A.D. 1453, Constantinople prided itself on being the new Rome, and the effective capital of a once-great empire.

The former Roman Empire, however, tried to resist the repeated incursions of the barbarians. Between the end of the fourth century and the beginning of the fifth, barbarian tribes broke through the frontier regions, which had became less Roman and more cosmopolitan in their peoples. The extension of citizenship to the empire may have made all the citizens Roman in practice, but they were racially Greek, Gallic, British, Egyptian, and all other races of the far-flung empire. These peoples could either assume a strong allegiance to Rome or make common cause with the invading force. Faced with this dilemma, the empire granted military groups in frontier regions the status of *foederati,* or allies, allowing them to occupy territory and fight alongside imperial troops. It was an alliance with the Goths that forced back the Huns led by Alaric in A.D. 451, even though Rome was taken. But long before that, successive waves of barbarians had broken through the frontiers to occupy Roman territory. Rome itself was to suffer. In A.D. 410 Rome was sacked by the Visigoths, to be taken again by the Huns in A.D. 451, the Vandals in A.D. 455, and the Swabians in A.D. 472, leaving Rome devastated.

The empire, which had once ruled what was the known Roman world, was at an end. Some semblance of it lived on in Byzantium, but with a different language, religion, and tradition. In A.D. 473 the German mercenary Odoacer marched into Italy and deposed the last Roman emperor, Romulus Augustus, whose imperial name could not disguise his humiliation. On the ruins of the Roman Empire Odoacer founded a new Germanic empire based in Italy, and ruled in theory as a nominal deputy of Emperor Zeno in Constantinople. In practice he ruled openly as the first barbaric king of Italy.

THE CELTS

The Celts had no great material civilization such as the Egyptians, Greeks, and Romans. They left little in the way of permanent structures, and the remains of their goods have been found or inferred by archaeological evidence scattered over wide areas. Much of the evidence about their way of life has been deduced from grave goods, place names, and tribal names. Although nonliterate, they had an elaborate oratorical style of epic-verse speaking and singing. These included mythological legends, often with more than a grain of truth, which were written down by Irish Christian scribes. This oral tradition still survives, especially in Ireland and Wales. The Welsh *Mabinogion,* the Ulster and the Finn cycles, and the legends of folk heroes, such as Cu Chulainn, shed light on food and customs. Their archaic language still survives in the outer parts of the British Isles and in Brittany (France), and this incorporates folktales and beliefs. Celtic society also intrigued classical writers, who recorded manners, customs, and a way of life alien to them. Nevertheless, the ancient Celts were a multilayered social and economic society based on agriculture, but with production and service industries and a warrior aristocracy forming an elite at its head. Celtic society survived on the fringes of the Roman Empire, and many of its customs, social structures, and languages, as indicated, have endured to the present time, which enables conclusions to be made about its historical traditions.

The pre-Christian Celts were an innovating, iron-using people who had evolved directly from late Bronze Age societies and who were characterized by burying their dead in distinctive urns. The Celtic Iron Age society had two distinct phases, to which are given the names *Halstatt* and *La Tène*, both being derived from place names of significant find spots of Celtic material.

The Halstatt culture, dating from about 700 B.C. to 500 B.C., replaced bronze weapons and edged tools with iron ones, which gave them military and technological superiority. The site of Halstatt, near Salzburg in the Salzkammerut area of Austria, was first excavated in the 1870s. As well as a huge prehistoric cemetery of about 2,500 graves, which produced valuable evidence of aristocratic artifacts, there was also a huge salt mine in which were preserved artifacts of a more humble nature—clothing, tools, wooden platters, and food remains of barley, millet, beans, and cultivated forms of apples and cherries. The excavated salt was of great importance to the economy, being a desirable trading commodity; hence there were connections with Etruria, Greece, and Rome.

Halstatt was therefore a flourishing trading settlement with a local industry and a flourishing export trade in salt. The excavated graves revealed a tradition of people being buried in four-wheeled wagons under grave mounds with their weapons, ornaments, jewelry, and joints of meat, especially pork, which would sustain them on their journey to the otherworld and in the life they expected to live there. Similar graves have been found elsewhere, for example, in the Hochdorf region near Stuttgart in Germany and at Baden-Württemberg. A tomb at Hochdorf, dated to about A.D. 530, revealed the burial of a rich nobleman. One of the most important finds was a bronze cauldron of Greek origin. Inside was a golden drinking horn containing the remains of mead or beer, sustenance in the next world. Cauldrons for the Celts were symbolic of the social gathering, the ideal of eating together to form a social bond. Close by were several golden drinking horns. These archaeological remains confirm the descriptions in the Irish tales of Celtic feasts in which warriors drank from drinking horns while sitting around a seething cauldron. The grave also contained platters, knives, fishhooks, and butchers' tools, as well as other household goods and military equipment. Women received the same honors. At Vix in Burgundy (France), excavation of a grave dating to about A.D. 500 revealed the body of a woman, thought to be a princess or a priestess, lying on a four-wheeled cart. Among the grave goods were an Etruscan flagon, Attic cups, and a huge Greek krater weighing 280 kilograms (620 pounds) and standing 1.64 meters (5 feet 4 inches) high. This had been imported from Greece in pieces and reassembled on-site, probably by skilled workmen. Not only do these graves reveal the expectation of an afterlife, but they also show evidence of the wealth and trading connections of the Celts.[29]

Halstatt thus became the prototype for the early Celtic Iron Age period, which spread over most of Europe, from Hungary to Ireland, as far north as Denmark and southward to Spain and France. It flourished until 700 B.C., when it was overtaken by a second culture, the La Tène, which takes its name from a site on Lac du Neuchâtel in Switzerland. In 1858 the water level of the lake was reduced, revealing timber stakes and great quantities of metal and other objects probably cast into the water as an offering to some deity. Further finds followed from 1864 onward, revealing a new phase of Celtic culture. Parallels were found in the Marne region of France, Rhineland, and northern Britain. It seemed that the center of power had shifted westward and that a new dynasty had overcome the older conservative one.

The most striking difference was that a two-wheeled chariot, drawn by two horses attached to a central pole, replaced the four-wheeled wagon. This created a war chariot, enabling driver and warrior to drive swiftly into battle. Archaeological excavations confirmed the classical writers' description of British and Gallic charioteers and the existing Irish tales of the Irish heroes. The graves included andirons for roasting meat, drinking vessels, platters, and joints of pork for the journey to and continuance of life in the otherworld. The La Tène culture spread from eastern Europe into southern France and Spain. One group, the Belgae, invaded Britain before 100 B.C. and settled lowland southeast England. They introduced the deep-cut plow into Britain, created urban settlement, and dominated the old Halstatt culture.

The warlike character of the La Tène clashed with an expanding Rome. In 390 B.C. the city of Roma was attacked. In 297 B.C. the Galatae attacked Delphi, penetrated into Macedonia, and settled in the Balkans. Some Celts entered Asia Minor, creating the country of Galatia, retaining their identity into early Christian times, as St. Paul's epistle to the Galatians indicates. It was not until the Gauls were

defeated at the Battle of Telemon in 225 B.C. that the Romans began
to overcome the Celtic advance, and they swiftly began to recruit
Gallic warriors as auxiliary troops. By 192 B.C. the Romans had cre-
ated Cisalpine Gaul and started the incorporation of Gaul into the
Roman Empire, a task that was finally accomplished by Julius Caesar
in the 50s B.C. From then attention turned to bringing Britain into the
Roman Empire and the land beyond the Rhine and the Danube. The
Romans never conquered the whole of Britain, and the defeat of
Quinctilius Varus in the Teutoburg Forest in A.D. 9 meant that the
Roman advance to the north was halted. By A.D. 16 the Rhine had
become the northern frontier of the Roman Empire.

With Roman conquest came Romanization. This could be interpreted either as a drive to impose Roman ways of living on the Celtic
population or persuading people that they would be better off adopting that way of life. Romanization brought new dining habits, more
efficient agricultural practices, and better food production. Food
once obtained purely from the wild could be cultivated in gardens.
A change of lifestyle certainly happened in southern Britain in the first
century A.D., where young noblemen were urged to follow Roman
ways of living. Already, however, the Gauls in Massalia (Marseilles)
were cultivating grapes and olives to increase the wine and oil trade
to supply Roman markets.

The main drink of the Celts was beer, probably barley ale, which
was drunk in great quantities, for beer drinking is a communal activity.
Poseidonius seemed to indicate a hierarchy of drinking. In large gatherings the most important man in wealth, warlike skill, or nobility of
family sat in the center. The host sat beside him, and the others sat in
order of merit. Shieldsmen stood behind them and spearmen were in
a circle on the opposite side. Servers carried around drink in terra-
cotta or silver jars. The richer Gauls drank wine, and there were two
kinds of beer; the poorer classes drank a wheaten beer prepared with
honey, but most people drank a plain beer called *korma*. The honey
beer would be stronger and sweeter and probably more expensive.
Korma was probably barley ale, a more inferior product, although
some of the Celts added cumin to it. Pliny went further, saying that the
Gauls had many types of beer made in several ways and with various
names.[30]

Wealthy Celts developed a taste for wine before the Roman conquest of Gaul and Britain. Celtic burial tombs contained amphorae,
indicating that wine would be served in the otherworld. A Celtic
burial mound of a chieftain at Lexden, England, dating to the first

century B.C., contained 17 amphorae, some once containing wine imported from Pompeii. One amphora had a capacity of 720 liters (158 gallons).

According to tradition, the Gauls were introduced to wine about 400 B.C. Arrius of Clusium wished to avenge the seduction of his wife by Lucumo, a young prince. He therefore went to Gaul with skins of wine, olive oil, and baskets of figs, all luxurious products that the Gauls did not know. The Gauls appreciated wine much more than beer, which then seemed to them barley rotted in water. As such they were induced to cross the Alps into Italy and attack Lucumo's men. They did not stop at Clusium but went on to besiege Rome. Wine, however, was their undoing, for sated with wine, they left their camp unguarded, which enabled the Roman commander Camillus to slaughter the unsuspecting Gauls.

The Greeks, however, had introduced the southern Gauls to olive oil and wine as early as the sixth century B.C., with the trade being centered on Massalia, and finds of amphorae indicate that from at least 650 B.C. wine was being imported in Gaul. By the fifth century the Gauls were growing wines and an early wine industry was being established, which the Romans would develop so that southern Gaulish wines would be exported throughout the empire. The two major centers were Toulouse (Tolosa) and Châlon-sur-Saône (Callonum); tons of broken amphorae have been found on these sites.

Some parts of Europe, in particular northern Britain and Ireland, remained outside Roman influence and retained their old Celtic way of life. Celtic civilization was based on the tribe ruled by a chieftain. Tribes were often engaged in warfare, and the warrior class became the aristocracy. The bravest warrior received the champion's portion. Poseidonius knew of this tradition: "When the joints of meat were served up, the bravest took the thigh piece and if another man claimed it they stood up and fought in single combat to the death."[31] Bones of thigh pieces have been found in Celtic graves, indicating the honor given to a dead warrior. The Celts ate large quantities of meat. Pork was the most popular meat, but mutton, kid, and beef were also eaten. Poseidonius said that they "partake of this in a leoline fashion, raising up whole limbs in both hands and biting off the meat, while any part which is hard to tear off they cut through with a small dagger which hangs attached to their sword-sheath in its own scabbard." He added that the Gauls living beside rivers or on the Atlantic coast ate baked fish flavored with salt, vinegar, and cumin.[32]

The basic food for the Celts was simple fare. Bread was very important. Sourdough bread was made from half-baked bread soaked in water with some added fruit juice, or with a little dough kept from one batch added to the next to kept a yeast alive. Fermented wine or beer could be added to dough to produce leavened bread. Pliny commented that when the corn of Gaul or Spain was steeped to make beer, the foam that formed on the surface was the process for leavening, "in consequence of which those races have a lighter form of bread than others."[33] Carbonized remains of a flat bannock shape were found on the Iron Age site of Glastonbury in England.

Grain would be ground in the early Iron Age on a saddle quern, but by the later Iron Age the rotary quern had been introduced. Grinding grain would be a task for women or slaves, and the method produces about 80 percent stone-ground flour. This might have some grit in it, so it was sieved through wicker baskets, but the ground-down teeth noticed in some skeletal remains reveals that the method was not always successful. Even if grain was not ground, wheat sprouts can be of use. Whole-wheat grains could be soaked in water for several days and rinsed and dried at the end of each day. When kept after that in a warm place, the wheat sprouts have a liquorish taste, which would give variety to food. Irish texts, for example *Bricriu's Feast* in the Ulster cycle, mention wheaten loaves baked in honey, which might be considered to be loaves baked with honey or wheaten honey loaves. Experiments, however, of balls of dough cooked in bowls of honey showed that the dough soaked up the honey, making something akin to a rum baba without the alcoholic content. Honey formed an important part of the diet, and bees were kept in wicker or pottery hives to ensure a plentiful supply.

Grain was also used to produce pottage. Lindow Man, so called because the body was found in a peat bog at Lindow Common in England, had eaten a pottage of wheat, rye, oats, and barley, which also contained wheat seeds. Pottage can also be made from beans or fat hen, the latter plant being rich in iron and albumen and probably serving as the main green vegetable. Seeds of fat hen were collected for future use, and it was found in the stomach of the bog burial Tollund Man (Denmark), indicating its value as a food. Charlock, a member of the cabbage family, is palatable when young. Black bindweed seeds, similar in appearance to buckwheat, were ground into flour to make acceptable bread. Silverweed could be boiled, roasted, or ground up to produce meal. Other vegetables gathered from the wild included nettles, wild celery, chickweed, and burdock. Even young beech and hawthorn leaves could be eaten in the spring. Pollen grains and carbonized seeds indicate the vegetables and fruits that were eaten. Peas and beans have been found on Iron Age sites. The beans are a small variety that appear to have been cultivated, while the peas seem to be a variety gathered from the wild. Peas, beans, and lentils could be baked into cakes and fritters. They could be stored for the winter and were useful for thickening stews. Fruits gathered from the wild included blackberries, strawberries, and crab apples. Nuts included hazelnuts and walnuts. Food would be given flavor by the addition of wild chervil, chives, mint, myrtle, and tansy. Oil from seeds, in particular gold of pleasure, was useful for cooking and lighting.

Dairy products were essential. Milk from cows, goats, and sheep was drunk or used to make butter or cheese. Strabo commented that the Belgae had large quantities of food including milk. Milk would be available all year round, but it was richer and sweeter in the spring. Columella said that for nomadic tribes that have no corn, sheep provide their diet; hence the Gaetae (or Getae, a tribe living north of the lower course of the Danube) are called "milk drinkers."[34] In this he was doing the Celts an injustice, as they did grow corn, but classical writers believed that the drinking of milk and eating of butter were the marks of barbarian tribes. Pliny commented that the barbarians considered butter their choicest food, the differing quantities of which distinguished the wealthy from the lower orders. Cow's milk was commonly used, but sheep's milk gave the richer butter. Strabo said that the Celtiberians in Spain ate butter instead of olive oil with their bread, even though they had access to olive oil. Wooden casks containing a fatty substance given the name "bog butter," some containing as much as 18.2 kilograms (40 pounds), have been found in Irish and Scottish peat bogs. Although this is suggested to be adipocere, a waxy material formed from animal fat, some is conceivably butter, pale yellow in color and having a grainy consistency, put into a bog to preserve during summer months and removed when required in autumn or winter.

Pliny stated that the barbarians had lived on milk for centuries but that they did not know the blessings of cheese. He was wrong, as cheese was made in great quantities. An Irish poem written in the twelfth century A.D. but believed to be part of an earlier tradition described a fort in culinary terms as being surrounded by a sea of new milk, and having thick breastworks of custard, fresh butter for a drawbridge, walls of curd cheese, and pillars of ripe cheese.

The Celts, therefore, had a rich diet, especially where diary produce was concerned. Those Celts conquered by the Romans or who developed trading relations with them could improve their diet with new products. The Romans introduced many new vegetables and fruits or improved the quality of those originally gathered from the wild. Farming methods also improved existing stock. New cookery methods were introduced. The Romans had a distinct dietary identity, and this they brought to other lands. In turn, the polyglot nature of the empire meant that their diet was also altered. It continued to alter throughout the time of the empire. Yet the Irish poem cited above shows that some parts of the Celtic world still retained their own dietary habit.

NOTES

1. Tacitus, *Agricola* 21; Tacitus, *On Britain and Germany,* translated by H. Mattingly (West Drayton, England: Penguin Books, 1948).

2. Diodorus Siculus, 1.34.2–5.

3. Diodorus Siculus, 1.34.10.

4. Nicholas Reeves, *The Complete Tutankhamun* (London: Thames and Hudson, 1990), 202–203.

5. Athenaeus, *D* 33d.

6. Athenaeus, *D* 8c–9b.

7. Athenaeus, *D* 268b.

8. Horace, *Epistles,* translated by H. R. Fairclough (Cambridge, Mass.: Loeb Classical Library, 1929), 2.1.156.

9. Athenaeus, *D* 402c.

10. Athenaeus, *D* 402a.

11. Hippocrates, *Regimen* 9, *Epidemics* 7.62; Galen, *AF* 6.664.

12. Varro, *Saturae Menippeae (Menippean Satires),* 4 vols., W. A. Krenkel (St. Katharinen, Germany: Scripta Mercaturae Verlag), 403; Galen, *AF* 6.664; Apuleius, *Metamorphoses* 7.22.

13. Galen, *AF* 6.664.

14. Athenaeus, *D* 399d.

15. Homer, *Odyssey* 7.112–121.

16. Xenophon, *Anabasis* 2.3.15.

17. Athenaeus, *D* 371b.

18. Seneca, *Ad Lucilium Epistulae Morales,* 3 vols., translated by R. M. Gummere (1917–1925), 95.15.

19. Valerius Maximus, *Facta et Dictu Memorabilia,* 2 vols., translated and edited by D. R. Shackleton-Bailey (Cambridge, Mass.: Loeb Classical Library, 2000), 2.5.5.

20. Strabo, 6.4.1.

21. Pliny, *NH* 37.201–202.

22. Strabo, 3.3.7, 4.6.1.

23. Pliny, *NH* 18.87–96, 112. Chalk was added to flour in England in the nineteenth century in an adulteration of flour to bulk it out, but during the Second World War in 1941, the British government decreed that calcium carbonate, readily obtained from refining ordinary chalk, was to be added to flour to provide extra calcium. This was added in the proportion of three ounces to each sack (280 pounds) of white flour.

24. Cato, *DA* 76. An easier version is to be found in Andrew Dalby and Sally Grainger, *The Classical Cookbook* (London: British Museum Press, 1996), 95–96.

25. See also Dalby and Grainger, *The Classical Cookbook*, 93–94.

26. Columella, *RR* 1.8.12.

27. Seneca, *Epistulae Morales* 18.7, 119.3.

28. Cato, *DA* 74. The author has seen a similar method in modern Ireland, where dough, put into a clay pot, was piled around with hot ashes, which allowed the sourdough bread to cook slowly until perfectly baked.

29. Jorg Biel, *Der Keltenfürst von Hochdorf* (Stuttgart, Germany: Konrad Theiss, 1985); R. Jeffroy, *La Trésor de Vix (Cote D'Or)* (Paris: Presses Universitaires, 1954).

30. Pliny, *NH* 22.164.

31. Athenaeus, *D* 154c.

32. Poseidonius, quoted in Athenaeus, 152a–b.

33. Pliny, *NH* 14.149.

34. Columella, *RR* 7.2.1.

CHAPTER 5
EATING HABITS

MEALS

The sun and the hours of daylight conditioned the working day in the ancient world. In the Mediterranean regions, people rose early to get as much work as possible done before the sun became too hot, then rested, returning to work hard before darkness fell. In the northern areas as much work as possible had to be done during daylight hours. The poor in society might not have been able to afford much artificial light in the evening, although time would be made for a more relaxing meal than any eaten during the day. People cannot indulge if they need to keep their wits about them for hard or official work. In a hot climate, a smaller meal during the day is advantageous to the digestion; it also takes less time away from work. Mealtimes also depended on areas. In the town a longer time might be available for a midday meal than in the country. A wider variety of food, especially fast food, was available in towns. Men could stop in taverns to get a snack; in the country agricultural laborers or slaves wished to use the hours of daylight as much as possible. The landowner would have more time for a leisurely meal midday, but the general impression remains that it was the evening meal that was most appreciated. For the wealthy the evening would be the time for feasting and banquets.

In Egypt banquets started in the early or middle afternoon, but few details are available about the eating of ordinary meals. The basic Egyptian meal was beer, bread, and onions, which the peasants ate daily, probably as a morning meal before they left to work in the fields or on works commanded by the pharaohs. Another simple meal would be eaten in the cool of the evening, probably boiled vegetables, bread, and beer; possibly wild fowl, obtained by hunting, would be added. The wealthy would expect to eat two or even three meals a day comprising vegetables, wild fowl, fish, eggs, and beef. Butter, milk, and cheese were also easily obtainable. Dessert would consist of fruit—grapes, figs, dates, and watermelons. In a Saqqara tomb of the Second Dynasty, a full meal was found that had been laid out for an unnamed noble. It included pottery and alabaster dishes containing a porridge of ground barley, a spit-roasted quail, two cooked lamb's kidneys, pigeon casserole, stewed fish, barbecued beef ribs, triangular loaves of bread made from ground emmer, small round cakes, a dish of stewed figs, a plate of sidder berries, and cheese, all accompanied by jars that had once contained wine and beer.

In the Old Kingdom, the Egyptians ate around a small table a few inches high, using their fingers to eat. Normally dishes were placed in the center of the table, and each person sitting around it dipped bread or a spoon into it. The lower classes continued this form of eating in the New Kingdom, but the upper classes then preferred to sit on tall cushioned chairs. Servants brought around water in small bowls so that guests could wash their hands before and during the meal.

More evidence is available for meals eaten in the classical world. Bread and pulses formed the chief ingredients. Homer indicated that humans were bread eaters, and bread formed a major part of the Greek diet. Meat was a rarity, usually only obtainable in abundance on feast days. Most of the Greeks ate two meals during the day. For the lower classes they were both probably frugal and monotonous. The first meal (*ariston*) might be a breakfast or a light snack postponed until noon. In the *Odyssey*, Homer describes Telemachus arranging breakfast for his father, the returned Odysseus, at dawn in a swineherd's hut. The swineherd sets before father and son a platter of roast meat saved from the night before, served with a basket of bread, and with honey sweet wine to drink.[1] This could have been *akratísma*, which was a little wine with some food taken early in the day.

The evening meal (*deipnon*) could be followed by the symposium. Both were social occasions, a time for relaxation after a hard day's work. There might be a first course of appetizers (*paropsides*), but the Greeks usually went immediately to a main course (*sitos*) containing a cereal such as bread, usually made from barley, served with a relish (*opson*), a thick soup or a pottage, or a baked cereal such as a form of polenta. Meat was cut into slivers or gnawed from the bone. Fish and softer foods would be eaten by tearing off pieces by hand. These were usually eaten without a drink. Wine came with the last course, the *tragemata,* which meant chewy foods such as nuts, sesame seeds, chickpeas, dried fruits (especially dates), beans, cheese with a little honey, and cakes. Chestnuts, eaten boiled or roasted, were particularly appreciated. As the only implements were knives and spoons, most of the food was eaten in the form of stews or porridge. As napkins were not available, fingers were cleaned with pieces of bread, which were then thrown to the dogs.

Details of Roman meals are more easily obtainable, and the Romans ate more food and more frequently than the Greeks. In theory, and probably in practice, most Romans ate three meals a day. During the day, food prepared the body for hard work by satisfying hunger and providing energy; in the evening food had a social and relaxing purpose. This was a time for leisure and relaxation. Breakfast (*ientaculum*), the breaking of the nightly fast, was little more than cheese or fruit and a piece of bread washed down with water or wine. In the poem the "Moretum," Simulus, a poor peasant, wakes at cockcrow. He does not bother with breakfast, but prepares a meal to take with him to the field by grinding corn, making dough, baking bread, and pounding herbs, salt, cheese, and nuts into a kind of pesto.

Lunch (*prandium*) could be taken at any time between 10 A.M. and 2 P.M., according to when breakfast had been taken. It was not necessarily the time that mattered as the importance of what was eaten and the keeping to a strict regime. Lunch was usually a snack meal eaten quickly—bread, cheese, meat, vegetables, and a drink. Fast foods, such as sausages or chickpea soup, bought from street sellers or eaten in bars were cheap and nourishing; lukewarm chickpea soup was cheap at a cost of one *as.* People working in the fields or shepherds took their food with them. Some physicians stressed that some people found it better to eat once a day; others should have a meal at noon or in the evening. People must follow their usual custom. If lunch was always taken, then it should not be omitted. If they ate lunch when they were not used to it, they became bloated, drowsy, and mentally dull. If they ate a large lunch and then had dinner, they could suffer from flatulence and indigestion. Whatever was eaten had to be digested by dinnertime, and if people were going to exercise in the afternoon, they must either not eat lunch or restrain their appetites; otherwise they would have severe problems.

The evening meal (*cena*) was the principal social meal, a time for relaxation after a hard day's work, eaten any time after 4 P.M. The eighth or ninth hour was common, eating at about 5 p.m. Small private dinners were taken with the family and perhaps a few guests or clients. Clients would accept with alacrity, as such a dinner might be a means of social advancement or the granting of a request. Even so, they might dine on poorer food than the host or the important guests. Sometimes recreation was taken before the meal; a visit to the baths would be deemed appropriate. An unexpected invitation to dine could be issued at the baths. Petronius's *Satyricon* began with such invitations.

Dinner comprised three courses. The first (*gustatio*), consisting of vegetables, shellfish, and eggs, was a taster or appetizer course. The main course (*primae mensae*) included roasted or boiled meats, poultry, sausages, and vegetables, probably sharply flavored with herbs and *liquamen*. The last course (*secundae mensae*) usually comprised sweet dishes—small cakes sweetened with honey, fruits, egg custards, or puddings made with pulses. It could include savories—shellfish, oysters, and snails. Soft dishes or those that would not keep a long time were regarded with special favor. Drinks could be taken with any course, but the more abstemious preferred not to drink until the second course. Wine was mixed with water, for only barbarians drank undiluted wine. The meal might be followed by modest entertainment, possibly reciters of poems, dancers, or musicians.

Martial offered six guests a first course of mallow leaves (good for the digestion), lettuce, chopped leeks, mint (to help with belching), rocket leaves, mackerel garnished with rue, sliced eggs, and sow's udder marinated in tuna brine. The main course was tender cuts of kid with beans and early greens, a chicken, and ham left over from three previous dinners. The dessert was fresh fruits and vintage wine from Nonentan, which had no dregs. This was to be followed by a merry entertainment, free of malice, with no unpleasant talk and nothing said that the next morning his guests might regret.[2] On another occasion he invited Toranius to share an appetizer of cheap Cappadocian lettuces, strong-smelling leeks, chopped tuna, and sliced eggs. This would be followed by green broccoli, fresh from the garden, served on a black plate, together with sausage on snow-white pottage and beans with rare bacon. The dessert was to be grapes "past their prime," Syrian pears, and Neapolitan roasted chestnuts. Wine followed to rouse the appetite for choice olives from Picenum, hot chickpeas, and warm lupines. Martial ended by calling this a modest little meal, which would not have courtesans but merely a flute player.[3] Allowing for the sarcastic note, it provides an insight into the meals given to guests during the early years of the empire.

Apuleius described a luxurious dinner given by a lady who was the leading light of the city, where the tables were draped in cloths sparkling with gold. The guests drank from glass, crystal, amber, and gold goblets. Even more splendid were the cups made from hollowed-out semiprecious stones, which were filled with vintage wine by boys whose hair had been specially curled.[4]

Pliny the Younger reproached Septicius Clarus for not coming to dine. He could have given himself and his guest a lettuce, two eggs, three snails, a barley cake, olives, beetroots, gherkins, and onions, together with similar delicacies. A comic play, a reader, or a singer (or all three, if he felt generous) would follow the meal. Instead Septicius went where he could have oysters, sow's udders, sea urchins, and Spanish dancing girls. Pliny indignantly said that Septicius might have richer food elsewhere, but nowhere would he find such free and easy enjoyment as with Pliny.[5] The inference is that a meal is not enjoyable without additional entertainment.

These meals could be served in dining rooms in town houses and country villas. They had a different arrangement than the Greeks in their dining habits. The triclinia usually held three couches fitted together around one table. Outdoor or garden triclinia, which were a common feature at Pompeii, had stone couches, which could be covered with cushions. These might be surrounded by fountains, or even a jet of water springing out of the middle of a table. Indoor areas had wooden couches with bronze fittings, usually having a foot or headrest. In the first century B.C. and the first century A.D., the normal arrangement was for three guests to be seated on each couch. The traditional place of honor was on the left-hand side of the middle couch, where the guest could easily receive messages or transact business without disturbing the company. The host sat on the left-hand couch at the end so that he could easily direct proceedings. The aim of these meals was not necessarily companionship and good fellowship, but deference, patronage, and political networking. This arrangement was the ideal form of dining, but more guests might be accommodated. Some triclinia had U-shaped couches, a style that became popular in the fourth and fifth centuries A.D., probably because it allowed a larger space for the entertainment. In country areas the couches might face onto a courtyard or an atrium or overlook a magnificent marble floor like the one in the Lullingstone (Kent) villa in England. Larger rooms might lack intimacy, but they allowed for greater displays of wealth and more accommodations for guests.

Mosaics from the first century onward often have panels showing food products. These include live animals, birds trussed up for cooking, seafood (live or in baskets), vegetables, fruits, and baskets of snails. A large one from a villa at Thysdrus (North Africa) is divided into 24 panels, each showing live birds or animals and food products, together with one showing gamblers sitting around a table. Another at Antioch includes several dishes set out with food. One small corner has a carefully arranged tray on which are placed two eggs in egg cups and the spoons with which they are going to be eaten, two artichokes, and two pig's trotters; in the center is a small bowl containing a sauce. Next to it is a plate on which rests a fish, a roast fowl, a ham, and some kind of cake. Rolls of bread, garlands, and cups of wine are scattered between other plates.

The mosaic may represent the order in which dishes were to be eaten. As well as knowing the etiquette for reclining, guests had to be careful in what order they ate their food. Their uncertainty might be compared with guests today mastering which cutlery to use at a grand dinner. The second-century A.D. traveler and lecturer Lucian of Samosata mentioned how embarrassed he was at not knowing in what order to eat dishes at a dinner that he attended and, like a modern counterpart, he stealthily watched his fellow diners to see what he should do. This, he thought, was essential if he was not to be mocked.[6]

Walls could be decorated with banqueting scenes but, as in Pompeii, most participants are depicted as drinking. Food does appear, but seemingly no elaborate meals. Mosaic floors are more revealing. It was usual to throw debris on to the floor, which slaves had to clear up later. Mosaics began to depict *asartos oikos* (the unswept room), which became a talking point for guests. Pliny said that the Hellenistic mosaicist Sosos at Pergamum in the second century B.C. was the first to create a floor representing the debris from a dinner table.[7] A copy of this in the Vatican Museo Gregoriano Profano shows debris of food on a white ground. Bones of fish, chicken, shells, and fruits are depicted, as well as a mouse gnawing a nut. It depicts a floor difficult to clean and therefore fixes a banquet in a moment of time.

This view of the debris on the floor introduces a note of caution into descriptions of the behavior of diners and the conduct of eating. Food was eaten at a table with one's fingers. Bread was dipped into sloppy stews, and spoons used to sup broth or pick out chunks of meat. Any drops would soon make a table messy. The food might have been well cooked, but it could have been overspiced and served in a sloppy and careless manner. Slaves who were not particularly careful in their habits could have cooked it in a smoky, untidy kitchen, under the eyes of a cook who shouted and bullied them. The pots might not have been washed carefully. There was rarely a supply of running water; buckets of water had to be fetched from a fountain in the street. Martial mentioned a guest asking for warm water, but cold water had not yet been fetched to the house.[8] Kitchens excavated in Pompeii and Herculaneum were small, mean places with little or no ventilation. Guests may have felt somewhat queasy after a meal, not because they had eaten too much but because of food poisoning.

The term *cena* was applied to meals associated with ritual ceremonies, such as a boy coming of age, a marriage ceremony (*cena nuptialis*), or a death (*cena novendialis*). A *cena recta* was a formal dinner given by the emperor or a wealthy private citizen and provided anything, as the saying went, from eggs to apples (*ab ovo usque mala*). A *cena publica* was given by a prominent citizen to mark a special occasion, such as a *cena adventicia* to announce arrival in a town. A *cena aditialis* was a meal offered by a newly elected priest or a magistrate on assuming office. Varro said that Quintus Hortensius, to mark his augurship, gave such a dinner, serving peacocks for the first time.[9] Someone paying for a gladiatorial show might give a free dinner (*cena libera*) to the public on the night before. These meals, however, grew in importance, so that they became more like feasts than private dinners.

FOOD FOR SPECIAL OCCASIONS

Ceremonial eating and drinking is an indication of a civilized society. The host's main aim is to give pleasure to guests, who could be familiars, clients, patrons, and social equals. It can be a private or public event, but there are often hidden agendas. Eating in groups implies the understanding of a code. Even the act of giving pleasure to people implies that the giver expects something. This might be gratitude or social acceptance as an equal. Peer-group dinners sound out social relationships and political alliances. Client-patron dinners are fraught with tension. Patrons demand loyalty from clients; clients become obsequious to patrons. Each group must know their place. Protégé dinners test potential recruits aspiring to a higher social grade. Banquets give opportunity for displays of conspicuous consumption and wealth on a grand scale, as well as being a means of gaining favor or buying loyalty. These may also allow the host to display contempt for social inferiors. Only, perhaps, in Celtic society did the sheer enjoyment of eating and drinking for its own sake with no inhibitions become commonplace, but even here these events seem to be confined to the warrior class.

The Egyptian Banquet

For Egyptian peasants there were some feast days, as at the New Year and after harvest and local religious festivals, but the peasants preferred to be offered sports and pastimes rather than elaborate dining. Meat was probably given to them after religious sacrifices. Dinner parties or banquets appear to have been one of the favorite entertainments for the middle and upper classes of the Egyptians, but literary evidence is scarce. There is no word for banquet in Egyptian; the nearest is one meaning "to make a festival" or "make a holiday." The information for feasts or banquets comes almost entirely from scenes found in tombs. In the Old Kingdom they seemed to be mainly family gatherings, when presumably banquets were held to celebrate or commemorate family occasions, birth, marriages, and deaths. Banquets in the New Kingdom were more elaborate, with family and guests enjoying the meal. Pharaohs gave official banquets; Horemheb, the last pharaoh of the Eighteenth Dynasty, gave his officials a banquet every month.

Banquets usually began in midafternoon at a time when the blue lotus flower opened to its fullest extent. Theban tombs show this flower placed on people and wine jars as if there were some significance attached to it. The flower closes at sunset, which may have indicated the end of the banquet. It may be significant that when the biblical Joseph, who by then was "governor over all the land," asked his brothers to dine with him, he invited them for noon (Gen. 43:16 AV).

The tomb scenes show the guests being greeted by their hosts and servants coming forward to offer garlands of flowers. Next basins of water are offered for the guests to wash their hands. The guests are ornately dressed in robes, jewels, and wigs. The Egyptians wore wigs or hairpieces woven from natural hair, and those worn for the feasts were most elaborate. On top of the wig was placed a perfumed cosmetic cone, made by steeping flowers in layers of fat. The cones were usually depicted as white with streaks of orange-brown, probably representing the perfume, running down from the top. During the banquet the heat of the wig and that of the room caused the cone to melt, so that the wax ran down. The result would be a sweet, cloying (if not overpowering) scent and a very sticky mess. When the cone had melted, the servants, who also wore similar cones, replaced them. The smell of the cones might have had the additional purpose of repelling insects, but could also be a sign of resurrection.

Tomb scenes show men and women on alternate panels as if they ate in separate groups or in separate rooms. A painted scene from the tomb of Nebamun at Dra Abul Naga, Thebes, who was an official during the Eighteenth Dynasty reign of Amunhotep III, shows the more honored women guests seated on chairs being waited on by servants. Guests could also be seated on stools or cushions. They ate from small tables, but side tables were seemingly loaded with food in almost buffet style, although servants would bring the food to the guests and offer them napkins to wipe their mouths. Jugs and basins were placed on stands nearby, ready for washing of hands and feet. Herodotus mentioned a golden foot basin that was used by King Amasis when guests were eating at his table.[10] After eating, guests washed their mouths out with water containing natron as a disinfectant and to clear the breath. The main food would be bread, fruits, pulses, and vegetables. Fruits would include dates, figs, melons, and possibly fruits imported from other countries. Meat could be in abundance at banquets. Whole oxen were roasted; ducks, chickens, geese, and pigeons were served. Fish seems to have been less popular, although fish were shown in paintings in the tomb of Horemheb. Cakes would be sweetened with honey and dates. Honey was a precious food, mainly the preserve of the wealthy, and therefore expected at feasts.

Jars underneath the table held beer, wine, and fermented fruit drinks that were poured into pottery, alabaster, or silver cups. One beer, called *zythos,* was reputed to be as good as wine. The main drink, however, was probably wine served undiluted, as this was a prestigious drink. Alcohol content varied from vintage to vintage, but usually the alcoholic content was low. Osiris is mentioned as the "lord of wine," probably in connection with the renewal of the vine after the annual flood, as ancient authors noted that the Nile seemed to be red during the annual inundation (from the iron-rich alluvium washed into the Nile from the Atbara branch), and one legend was that the Nile turned into wine. Servants poured wine from small jugs into shallow goblets. In a painting in the New Kingdom tomb of Nebamun, he; his wife, Ipuky; and his daughter are offered wine in a shallow vessel with a pronounced foot. Queen Nefertiti pours wine through a strainer for her husband, Akhenaton. In some tombs, drinking sets of bronze jugs, goblets, and strainers have been found. Toasts were drunk to the goddess Hathor, who was associated with music and alcohol, because she had been tricked into becoming drunk with beer dyed red to look like blood to stop her from destroying humanity.

Even though the alcoholic content of both beer and wine was low, so much was drunk that intoxication was inevitable, but this did not mean that it was regarded with disapproval. As long as people did not lose control it was tolerated, if not encouraged, as intoxication was believed to be a means of communication with the dead. Many of the gods were associated with drunkenness. In the tomb of Paheri at el-Qab, a lady is depicted saying to her servant, "Bring me eighteen cups of wine. I love to drink to get drunk; my inside is as dry as straw." The servant approves: "Drink. Do not refuse. I am not going to desert you. Drink, do not spoil the entertainment; and let the cups come to me." There were some warnings against it: "Drink not to excess. The words come out of thy mouth thy cannot recall. Thou dost fall and break thy limbs and no one reaches out a hand to thee. Thy drinking comrades say, 'Away with this fellow who is drunk.'" A schoolboy is told ca. 1400 B.C.: "Thou art like a broken steering oar in a ship that is obedient to neither side. Thou are like a temple without a god, and like a house without bread. Know thou that wine is an abomination."[11] Intoxication enhanced the pleasure of the banquet and allowed people to communicate more easily with their neighbors. Some banquets might have been devoted more to alcohol than food. Two festivals at Thebes were called the Festival of Intoxication and the Offering of the Festival of Intoxication.

Although drunkenness was regarded more with amusement than contempt, excessive drinking might result in loss of self-control. A tomb at Beni Hassan has a painting of guests carried out of a banquet on the shoulders of servants, obviously incapable of going home on their own. A painting from an Eighteenth Dynasty tomb shows a man looking over his right shoulder to vomit. That both sexes did this without any inhibition is revealed by a painting in a Nineteenth Dynasty Theban tomb where a woman sits on the ground, her head turned over her shoulder as she vomits profusely. A servant rushes to catch her spume, but too late.

The meal would be accompanied by music. Reliefs from tombs in the Old Kingdom show groups of two musicians, usually a harpist, a flutist, and one or two singers. In the New Kingdom reliefs, the number in the groups increase to include men or women playing a lute, a tambourine or a drum, clappers, and a double oboe. One from a tomb at Thebes shows a double oboe and three women clapping, probably in rhythm to accompany the dances. After the meal there might be storytelling or

Scene from a wall painting in a tomb at Thebes. A woman wearing a perfume cone on her head is depicted vomiting during a banquet. Her slave has not managed to catch her spew. Redrawn from Sir John Gardner Wilkinson, *The Manners and Customs of the Ancient Egyptians*, 1837.

acrobats. Professional dancers performed energetically, often scantily clad. An inscription in one tomb read, "Be merry all through your life and do no more work than is necessary."[12]

There might be a sober ending to the meal. According to Herodotus, a model coffin was carried around containing a wooden effigy of a corpse. This was shown to each guest in turn with the sobering words uttered "Gaze here and drink and be merry; for thou shalt look like this when thou art dead."[13]

The Greek Symposium

The Greek symposium was an all-male aristocratic social drinking party. There are some vase paintings of women enjoying a symposium, but these are probably indications of male fantasies. The normal symposium was usually held after an evening meal with a carefully chosen guest list. This was not always possible. A guest might ask to bring a friend or even turn up with one, and there were always gate-crashers seeking a free drinking session. Women were expressly forbidden to attend, although courtesans could be brought in toward the end of the evening as part of the entertainment. The aim of these gatherings was to release tension, forget the cares of the outside world, and promote good fellowship among the guests. There were also betrothal symposia, usually held in the spring, at which eligible bachelors discussed girls who might be their brides with fathers or brothers. The girls were not present, but had been considered beforehand. On the island of Delos, this became an important festival, where games and sacrifices were followed by symposia at which suitors were chosen and girls betrothed. Alexander the Great took with him a large tent that could hold more than a hundred couches, which he used for lavish symposia and other entertainments, including the one when he forced his troops to marry Persian women.

The formalities of the evening symposium were strictly observed. These usually took place in a square or oblong private dining room (*andron*), which opened directly onto the street or a courtyard and provided an intimate drinking place. A small raised platform ran around the walls, and this seemed to have supported one side of the couches, usually 7, 9, or 11, which lined the walls. Guests sat on these, one or two to a couch, and in front of each couch was a table. Shoes were removed and feet washed before the room was entered. Guests might be crowned with garlands of flowers or have them hung around their necks. The first couch to the right of the entrance was the place for the chief guest, who was seated besides the host. Reclining on couches was a custom that seemingly had been adopted in Greece as early as the seventh century B.C. from the Near East, where it had been a royal prerogative. There was an art in reclining. In Aristophanes' play *The Wasps*, a sophisticated young man, Bdelykleon, exasperatedly instructs his father, Philokleon, in the method of reclining and rearrangement of the legs. Reclining at meals set elite society apart from the lower classes and slaves. In Macedonia no man was allowed to recline until he had captured or killed a boar without the aid of nets.

A *symphosiarchas,* or organizer of the symposium, kept a strict watch on the proceedings, controlling the pace of drinking and the entertainment. According to Plutarch, the same spirit was required in marshalling a line of battle as in presiding at a symposium.[14] The organizer might even expel a guest who became objectionable. The host sprinkled wine on the floor and the guests commended themselves to each other in a fixed order. Refreshments and drinking vessels were placed on low tables, and at the beginning three toasts were made. The first could be to the Olympian gods, the second to the heroes, and the third to Zeus Soter. The *symphosiarchas* decreed the ratio of wine to water and the speed of drinking.

Wine and water were mixed in a ratio of 1:3, 1:5, or 2:5—that meant large quantities could be drunk. To drink wine undiluted was the action of a barbarian. Athenaeus said that King Cleomenis of Sparta, urged on by Scythian envoys, drank wine undiluted and as a result had a fit of madness, slashing himself to death with a knife.[15] In Sparta wine from the first pressing was given to the Helots so that they would reel through the streets vomiting and making obscene gestures. This would be a warning to Spartan youth as to what could happen to them if they drank unmixed wine. Plato thought that no one under the age of 18 should drink, as it might inflame his high spirits. From 18 to 40, wine should be drunk in moderation. After 40, a man could drink as much as he liked to revive his youthful spirit and forget every-day worries.[16]

Decorated amphorae carried the wine from storage to the symposium, and the wine could be chilled in a *pskter,* a vessel with a rounded body, short neck, and high foot that could be placed in a large krater filled with cold water. The water was brought in a bronze or pottery two-handled *hydria.* The mixing was done in a large krater, which was placed in the center of the room. This was usually an elaborately

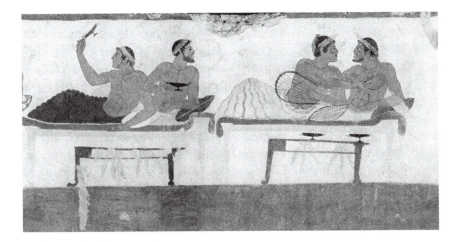

Two revelers at a Greek symposium displayed on a wall painting at Paestum, Italy. Courtesy of the author.

decorated piece, for it was the focal point and symbol of the symposium. The liquid was drawn from the krater by a ladle (*kyathos*) and
placed in a shallow two-handled pottery drinking bowl (*kylix*) or a
two-handled cup (*skyphos*) of gold or silver. Usually the revelers drank
three kraters full each evening.

The aim, however, was not drinking per se but to promote discussion. Plato's symposium was asked to define the meaning of love.
Athenaeus said that Homer's account of the symposium of Menelaus
has young men "proposing questions to each other as though they
were in the company of learned men; they held civilised conversations.
They cut a roasted chine of ox and talked quietly to each other about
Menalaus' rich possessions."[17] Plutarch in his *Banquet of the Sages*
made Thales say, "We do not attend a symposium like vases to be filled
but to speak seriously and to jest, to hear and deliver speeches that
occasion requires of the participants if they are to take pleasure in
conversing amongst themselves."[18] Not everyone enjoyed symposia.
Pericles consistently declined invitations; he made one exception, for
celebrating the wedding feast of his cousin.

Toward the end of the evening things became less decorous, when
entertainment took place. Courtesans, who had been well trained for
their roles, played instruments, danced, or otherwise entertained the
guests. Youths also took part, and these could be from distinguished
families. Euripides had done this in his youth. Xenophon recorded
that once two dancers acted a love scene between Ariadne and Dionysus
so realistically that the embarrassment caused made this symposium
end very quickly.[19] Hippocleides caused great offense by standing on
his head on the table and beating time with his legs. An alternative
entertainment was playing games. A myrtle wreath was passed from
one man to another until the host decreed a stop. The last man had to
recite or sing. *Kottabos* entailed hitting a target with drops of wine. The
target was usually a metal disc placed on top of a column. Below was
a larger disc. A guest hooked a *kylix* around the index finger of his right
hand and spun it around in the air. Drops of wine would be flung out
with the aim of knocking the disc off the column to hit the larger disc
and make a great noise. The elegance with which a cup was handled
was taken into consideration. The prizes offered were simple—eggs,
fruit, sweets, a pair of sandals, a cup, and cake.

Sometimes the evening ended raucously. Guests were reported to
have vomited and danced drunkenly through the streets and to have
gate-crashed other symposia, resulting in fights. At Agrigentum in
Sicily, a party of young men grew so wild when overindulged with

liquor that they imagined they were sailing in a trireme in a bad storm, tossing all the furniture and bedding out of the house to lighten the presumed ship. A crowd gathered outside and began to run off with this supposed jetsam. Even then the revelers did not stop, but poured out of the house into the street. Next day, when still only half sober, they were questioned by the magistrates and explained that they had only been trying to save themselves and the ship. Possibly remembering bouts of drinking when they had been young men, the magistrates pardoned the revelers, but said they must never drink so much again, and this was promised. From then on, however, the house where the festivities had occurred was known as the Trireme.

An even greater disaster occurred when Alexander, inflamed at a symposium by a passionate speech of the *hataera*, Thais, led his companions on a drunken revel and set fire to Persepolis. In Plato's *Protagoras,* Socrates deplored this kind of behavior, saying that where the drinkers are worthy and cultured men, there will be no dancing or music or even dancing girls.[20] These men would enjoy their own company without any frivolity, using the occasion to speak and listen in turn to each other. Yet in Xenophon's version of a symposium, Socrates loved watching the dancing girls and even tried to copy their movements.

Symposia also might have been places for plotting, for men were off their guard. Plutarch said that when Pelopidas and his companions wished to get rid of the tyrants at Thebes, they proposed to do this at a symposium.[21] They wore women's clothing over their armor and garlands of pine and fir to hide their faces. The Romans also adopted the custom of the symposium, and Livy recounted that when L. Quinctius Flaminius was campaigning in Gaul he entertained a Boian chieftain who had come seeking Roman protection. But during the meal, when all were relaxed, he accused him of treason and engineered his execution. For this and for abusing the rights of hospitality, Flaminius was expelled from the Senate.[22]

Not all the Greeks held symposia. The Spartans ate in dining groups or messes (*syssitia*) of 15 once a day, which were compulsory for all males, who sat divided by age and social status. Where the women ate is not clear. Admission to the mess was by lot. When a candidate was proposed, each Spartan grasped a piece of bread and put it into a bowl. If he had screwed up the bread, this meant he disapproved of the candidate, who would be rejected and excluded from the messes. The meals were intended to promote equality, and the men did not recline but were seated on hard wooden benches. *Syssitia* were designed by the state to promote the Spartan ideology and male bonding among equals.

The main food consisted of barley bread, cheese, wine, figs, and the infamous black broth, a basic pork stew consisting of pork, pig's blood, and vinegar. According to Plutarch, "a certain king of Pontus hired a Laconian cook so that he could serve black broth. When the king tasted it, he spat it out whereupon the cook said, 'King, this soup should only be taken after a dip in the Eurotas,'" a remark that seemingly indicates that the Spartans were in the habit of taking a bath before a meal.[23] Athenaeus said that a Sybarite, after dining in a Spartan mess, remarked that it was reasonable for the Spartans to be the bravest of men, because any sensible man would choose to die 10,000 deaths rather than have to eat such a wretched diet again.[24]

The food was not provided entirely by the state. Each man had to bring to the mess each month a bushel of barley, eight gallons of wine, five pounds of cheese, and two and half pounds of figs together with *opsonion*, that is, relishes that could be meat, fish, and vegetables. When any person made a sacrifice to the gods, it was expected that he would send a portion to his mess. No olive oil was included in these rations, but it must have been contributed by the state, as the Spartans ate barley cake soaked in olive oil. The mess would include boys taken from their mothers at the age of seven. Each Spartan warrior also had a helot who served him. Calculations of the food provided assume that there was a large surplus, especially of wine. Some food was given to the boys; other may have been passed to the women. Food and drink were also passed to the helots, who were encouraged to drink as much as possible, so that their drunken behavior would be a warning to Spartan warriors.

Cretan men also sat to eat and ate their meals in common. The younger men served the older ones. Sons sitting at the feet of their fathers' chairs were served half the food of the father. All the food was served plain, without any sauces. A separate table was allotted to strangers and foreigners. Plato admired this type of meal as being ideal for a state, but also praised the symposia for encouraging free discussion among equals. The symposium, however, never lived up to Plato's ideals. Once Greek freedom had collapsed under the Macedonian conquest in the fourth century B.C., the symposium became, if it had not been before, little more than a talking shop and a vacuous drinking session.

The Roman *Epulum* and the *Convivium*

In the early days of the republic the Romans prided themselves on self-reliance and frugality. Eating and drinking on a large scale later became part of the Roman way of life. The change probably came after the conquest of Sicily in 241 B.C., when the Romans could indulge in the more exotic tastes of the Near Eastern regions. The term *epulum* was the name given to a Roman feast and was first a meal associated with some religious function, such as the Ludi Romani, which included a feast in honor of Jupiter. In time its religious connotation diminished, and the term was associated with an opulent meal provided by a man, and occasionally by a women, from the emperor down to a wealthy citizen for friends or for the public. The *convivium* in its simplest form differed from the symposium of the Greeks, although this dining custom too was adopted. It was a meal for friends and was intended both to express a relationship between equals as well as to be an opportunity for patrons to entertain clients and probably show off their wealth. Freedmen and slaves could eat together, solidarity could be expressed in guild (*collegium*) dinners, and funerary meals could be held for the dead.

Cicero says that Cato the Elder praised the early Romans for choosing the term *convivium* (*con-vivere*) to describe the relaxing and reclining of friends at feasts, as it implied "a communion of life which is a better designation than that of the Greeks who call it sometimes a drinking together [symposium] or an eating together [*syndeipon*]." Cicero said that he enjoyed even an afternoon banquet, that is, one that began early and cut short business days, possibly the modern equivalent of the long lunch.[25] In time *epulum* and *convivium* both came to mean large public feasts in a variety of contexts, for feeding and entertaining many more people than simply friends of the host.

The Greeks separated their main meal (*deipnon*) from the symposium. The Romans did not, although there might have been a drinking party after a meal in private houses, and some Romans were said to follow this custom. The dictator Sulla followed a dinner with a drinking party, where dancers and musicians entertained. Drinking was part of the Roman meal, and as much attention was paid to this as to the food and the talking. Wines from different regions might have been served with different courses.

Women sometimes participated in the *convivium* and could recline together, although the practice varied. In 7 B.C. Livia, the wife of Augustus, entertained the wives of senators while her son Tiberius entertained the senators at a dinner. She had wanted to entertain both together, but Tiberius insisted on the separation of the sexes.

The Romans adopted the custom of reclining from the Greeks, possibly from the third century B.C., when they came into contact with the Greeks of southern Italy, although the Etruscans had also adopted the custom. Livy indicated that a number of foreign customs flowed in from Asia Minor, and that the triumph of Cn. Manlius Vulso in 187 B.C. intensified this when he brought with him couches, precious hangings, furniture, gold and silver vessels, and even specialized cooks. These seem to have been the first triclinia couches to be seen in Rome. The art of fine dining increased, characterized by this show of wealth. Boys might recline when they assumed the *toga virilis,* but this also implied that they had to restrain their teenage passions and submit to guidance in the rules of dining. Plutarch attempted to answer a question about the possible squashing together of diners on couches. He suggested that diners first lie flat on their stomachs to allow the right hand to reach for the food. When they had taken the food, they lie on their sides to give their neighbors more room.[26] Probably people were so used to this way of dining that they thought nothing to it. If there were any discomfort, it would be worth it for a good meal.

Slaves might recline during the festival of Saturnalia, when roles were reversed and slaves were masters for that festival. Columella advised that a bailiff should encourage farm workers to take meals with him in his house, but he should not recline except on feast days.[27] Martial despised Maximus Syriscus not only for dissipating his fortune of 10 million sesterces but also for sitting on tavern stools and not reclining while he talked.[28] Not all Romans agreed with the custom. Cato the Younger, on hearing of the defeat at Pharsalus, as a sign of his Stoic displeasure, refused to recline in the future except when sleeping. From then on he always sat upright at meals.

Private banquets became notorious for their ostentation. In the first century B.C., Lucullus's extravagance became notorious. Once, when Caesar and Pompey met him in the forum, Lucullus invited them to make a petition. They said they would dine with him that day, but they would not allow him to give notice to his servants, hoping that he would be forced to give them a simple meal. Lucullus outwitted them, for he merely told his servants he would dine with them "in Apollo." Each of his dining rooms had fixed allowances for dinners, and Apollo served the most costly. All was therefore ready when the two guests came to dine. Such extravagance was satirized by Petronius in his description of Trimalchio's banquet in the *Satyricon,* with its seven courses of 62 items, some served with Falernian wine said to be a hundred years old. Some banquets were a trial to guests. Seneca knew a freedman, Calvisius Sabinus, who paid his slaves to memorize the works of Hesiod and Homer, but he bored the guests by repeating half-forgotten lines learned from the slaves.[29]

Public banquets, often on a lavish scale, were held by magistrates before elections and by family members to commiserate on deaths or celebrate birthdays. Generals feasted their troops after battles, senators fed their clients, and decurions and aediles entertained fellow citizens or their peers. Distinguished citizens provided these for the populace. Such feasts may be regarded as indicating both the realities and the emphasis of the social order. To take part was to acknowledge, whether consciously or not, the superior power of the provider as well as the achieving of a collective identity. The three-day festival of the Arvel Brethren, a high-status brotherhood in Rome, made sacrificial offerings to the Dea Diva. After a libation had been made to the deity, the president ate, followed by other members in order of status. On the third day slaves and freedmen were allowed to eat, but they were provided with good white bread instead of meat.

In Rome it was expected that generals and senators would provide feasts. To celebrate his triumph over Mithradates and Tigranes in 62 B.C., Lucullus is said to have given a banquet for the Senate and provided sacrificial feasts for the people, which included a million jars of Greek wine, probably equivalent to four million liters. Crassus in 70 B.C. feasted 10,000 tables of people after a sacrifice to Hercules and gave each person an additional allowance of grain for three months. In 45 B.C. Julius Caesar gave a feast with 22,000 dining couches. Allowing three people to a couch this would mean 66,000 people were feasted. Such generosity was not confined to the elite. An inscription at Ostia records that P. Lucilius Gamala gave a feast on 217 dining couches, and on two occasions provided a lunch (*prandium*) for the *coloni*. C. Iunius Priscus at Arles gave two days of shows and a wild beast hunt for the citizens, a feast for the decurions on 13 triclinia, and another on 34 biclinia for the advocates and other officials.

It is not surprising that feasting was linked to fierce competition for both public and private support and that emperors sought to gain favor by providing public banquets in addition to private dinners. Claudius entertained hundreds of guests and even went so far as to pass an edict allowing flatulence at banquets after he learned that one of his guests was acutely uncomfortable through modesty. One of the most memorable was that given in the Coliseum by Domitian in A.D. 84 on the Kalends of December. Slaves handed out white napkins to the crowd. Fruits included luxurious ones from the east—plums from Damascus, dates from Pontus and Palestine, figs from Asia Minor, and apples and pears from Amorica. Pastries distributed included some in the shape of human figures. Flamingos, pheasants, and guinea fowl were tossed into the crowd for people to take home. Wine flowed freely, and the crowd was entertained by troops of dancing Lydian ladies, troops of Syrians, and gladiatorial fights, including several by pygmies. Caligula's banquets were welcomed for their opulence but feared for what could happen. The senators might be stripped of their togas and dressed as slaves, then made to wait at tables. On one occasion in A.D. 40, Caligula suddenly burst out laughing. The two consuls present nervously asked the reason for his mirth. Caligula replied that this was because he had just thought that he could have had their throats slit before they had finished the meal. Nero's excesses were notorious. His banquets included those getting rid of rivals and enemies with tricks and dramas played on senators. Banquets were no longer means of discussing political and other matters.

Nero also preferred handing out other gifts. Suetonius recorded the emperor's decree that every day his officials should hand out 1,000 birds of every kind, food parcels, tokens for corn, clothing, gold, silver, farm beasts, wild animals, and even agricultural lands.[30] Seemingly it was potluck what was received. Wealthy patrons, giving distributions of bread and wine and pastries and sweet wine to the populace to celebrate their election to office or when a building was dedicated, emulated these gifts in a less extravagant way.

Collegia held feasts partly for solidarity and partly because some collegia were composed of slaves or freedmen who had no family ties. Varro complained that "such dinners are now so countless that they make the price of provisions go soaring."[31] Collegia buildings have been identified at Pompeii and Ostia. One building at Ostia founded in the reign of Hadrian seems to have been the collegia of the carpenters (fabri tignuarii). A central court, surrounded by rooms, is extended by a wing containing four triclinia with masonry couches, indicating that dining activities were one of the main functions of the collegium. Livy said that when in 312 B.C. the censors forbid the guild of flute players from holding these regular feasts, they promptly went on strike and decamped to Tibur. The Romans tried to entice them back, to no avail. So the Tiburtines plied the players with drink until they were intoxicated and fell asleep, packed them into carts, and sent them back to Rome. They congregated in the Forum, but their appalling hangovers soon sobered them.[32]

Inscriptions on reliefs bear out the munificence of the feasts provided. In Gabii decurions and members of the priestly college of the

Severi Augustales were to banquet in public on their separate triclinia. Individuals also left money for feasts. M. Cacius Cerna, who lived at Sinuessa in the Campania after a distinguished political and military career, founded a feast for the people of his locality to be held each year on his birthday. He gave explicit instructions that the feast was to be held in public. Cocceia Vera from Cura allocated money for a feast to be held in public on her birthday, with the guests arranged strictly in order of status. Decurions should be placed on 10 triclinia, *seviri* being seated on 2 or more, and so on, thus reflecting the social spectrum. In Corfinium, a donor left a legacy to set up a fund for both the city council and the populace, with the interest to provide a feast to remember him on the anniversary of his birthday. But the fund was carefully delineated. The decurions and their children got 30 sesterces each for a feast where they reclined. The Severi Augustales got 20 sesterces each, and the plebeians 8 sesterces each for a dinner. The different choice of words indicates the different ranks of society. Only the decurions are reclining; the rest are sitting. This indicates the privileged setting and the reinforcement of a social hierarchy.

The evidence is clear that the plebeians loved being feasted and always appreciated this. Valerius Maximus said that "for a while the people approved of private frugality, publicly they set more store by an handsome show."[33] Seneca qualified this, implying that the Roman people loathed luxury but loved public splendor: "They do not like extravagant banquets but much less do they like shabbiness or meanness."[34] Cicero said that Cato the Elder disapproved of feasts, indicating that it was wrong to promote goodwill by providing food. He added that some feasts went terribly wrong. Quintus Aelius Tubero was asked by his cousin Quintus Fabius Maximus to organize a funerary banquet for the people of Rome on the death of his uncle, Scipio Aemilius. Tubero, however, was a Stoic, and therefore covered the couches with shabby goatskins and provided poor Samian ware, which was declared by the people to be more appropriate for the death of Diogenes the Cynic than to honor the death of the mighty Scipio Aemilius (also known as Scipio Africanus). In consequence, the people voted against Tubero when he stood for praetor in the next election.[35]

Others incidents at feasts might be used as a warning or as propaganda. Mark Antony once had the heads of defeated enemies brought before him at the end of a banquet, but in doing so was accused of following foreign habits. After the Roman defeat at Carrhae in 53 B.C., the head of Crassus was brought before the Parthian king Orodes when he was feasting.

Feasts also had to be provided for unexpected guests. In 45 B.C. Cicero wrote to Atticus that Julius Caesar had stopped overnight at Philippus's "place" on his route from Pozzuoli. He then moved on to Cicero's. Unfortunately, this included all his retinue, who had to be entertained in three dining rooms, and 2,000 soldiers, although Cicero probably did not have to feed the soldiers. Caesar had a bath, oiled his body, and came into dinner. As he was "following a course of emetics," he was able to partake of "a fine well appointed meal," and he indicated that he had dined well. Cicero provided his guests with all they had wanted and boasted that "I showed that I knew how to live." He added wryly "that they were not the kind of person to whom one says, 'Do come again when you are next in the neighbourhood.' Once is enough. It was a visit or should I call it a billeting, which was troublesome to me but not disagreeable."[36] Caesar, however, was reported to be indifferent to food. At one dinner party, where the host used rancid oil by mistake, Caesar poured it on lavishly to show that he did not consider his host a boor.

Any feast had to be serviced by large numbers of servants or slaves. They approached guests with bowls of water and napkins, so that guests could wash their hands. Trimalchio's slaves kept pressing the guests to food and drink, anointed their feet, spread coverlets, and in an extravagant gesture, offered the guests wine in which to wash their hands, but they served their master warily, as they did not know what might happen to them By the late empire handsome youths with long flowing hair were preferred, especially to pour out wine, and these "luckless boys," as Seneca said, had to "suffer shameful treatment" after a banquet was over.[37] He also mentioned slaves standing silently while their masters dined: "When we recline at a banquet, one slave mops up the disgorged food, another crouches beneath the table and gathers the leftovers of the drunken guests. Another carves priceless game birds, and this is his only job."[38]

At the end of the meal slaves had the right to consume leftover food and drink, if they still had the stomach for this. Trimalchio's slaves were allowed to crowd onto the couches and displace the guests. But slaves might suffer minor punishments for dropping a cup or spilling food, or more brutal punishments, such as that given to a slave at one of Caligula's feasts who stole a silver plate. He had his hands cut off and was forced to parade among the guests with a placard around his neck proclaiming his offense. Guests were also humiliated, but in more subtle ways. T. Vinius stole a golden cup at a banquet given by the emperor Claudius. The emperor noticed the theft, invited him back, and ordered the servants to serve Vinius alone with earthenware pottery.

A server dressed in woman's clothes had his beard plucked out by the roots. One slave, a *vocatur,* had to watch the guests for their behavior to see who might be invited again; another surveyed what they were eating to note what food might be served next time. A *vocatur* issued invitations and allocated place sittings. He could be bribed, and a wealthy provincial secured an invitation to one of Caligula's *convivia* by paying a *vocatur* 2,000 gold pieces.

Such moneys made certain slaves very wealthy, and slaves might progress in their careers. Most were men, although women servants or slaves wearing long dresses appear on banqueting scenes on sarcophagi. A tombstone of M. Ulpius Phaedimus, who died in Rome at age 28 and was a freedman of Trajan, recorded his career. He began as a server of drinks and moved on to become a *tricliniarch,* an organizer of feasts, before being chosen to carve roasts and fowls for state banquets.

Celtic Feasting

The Celts loved feasting. The Celtic year in Ireland was divided by four great festivals, and it is probable that similar feast days were held in other parts of the Celtic world. Imbolc (February 1) was dedicated to the god Brigit, later Christianized as St. Bridget. This marked the renewal of spring and the coming of the first ewe's milk. Hence it was a festival dedicated to fertility. Beltain (May 1), linked to the Celtic god Belenos, was a cleansing festival when fires were lit or renewed in houses. Fires were also lighted in the fields so that cattle could walk through them and be cleansed. All grass and rush bedding was burned, so that household tasks started afresh. This, although possibly the Celts did not realize it, was the best way to stop infection, as pests were burned with the straw. Lughnasa (August 1), lasting for almost 40 days, was the greatest festival, when food and drink flowed in abundance. It was concerned with the harvesting of the crops and was dedicated to the god Lugh (Ireland) or Lugnos (Gaul). The last festival of the year, although it was the first in the Celtic calendar, was Samain (November 1), which was more a sober and dangerous time. It marked the end of the old year and invoked the dead, who could become visible to the human world; hence the Christian church transmuted it to All Souls' Day (November 2), when it was propitious to remember deceased relatives and friends.

Feasting was a time to exhibit the prowess of Celtic heroes. Diodorus Siculus said that the Celts cut off the heads of their enemies slain in battle and fastened them to their horses.[39] The heads of their most distinguished enemies they kept in chests and showed to strangers. These might be the ones that Strabo said were embalmed in cedar oil and exhibited to guests at feasts.[40] These customs, and that of human sacrifice, was one reason why the Romans proscribed human sacrifice when they overcame a Celtic region and put down the Druidic priest-hood, which had encouraged it.

Poseidonius commented that the Celts sat on straw and ate from low tables, although Diodorus says they sat on wolf skins, forming a circle with the bravest warriors sitting in the middle, making sure that those warriors had the best cuts of boiled or roasted meat.[41] The youngest children served the warriors. The Celts were hospitable, inviting strangers to their feasts and waiting until after the meal to ask them who they were and what they wanted.

The Irish tales are the best evidence available for descriptions of Celtic feasting. The amount of food gathered for a feast could be prodigious. In an Irish tale of the Ulster cycle, *Bricriu's Feast*, Bricriu made a feast for the men of Ulster and their chieftain, Conchobar mac Nessa. For this he gathered food for a year and built a house at Dun Rudraige from which to serve it. But Bricriu's aim was to show he could set the men of Ulster at odds, which was done by his prepa-ration of the contest for the champion's portion, the hindquarters or thigh of a pig, which was given to the bravest warrior. Bricriu knew that the Ulstermen would fight for this, and incited the heroes of Ulster to challenge one another. The fight and difficulties connected with the contest extended beyond Bricriu's house, until eventually the sovereignty of the heroes of Erin was given to Cu Chulainn. Although Conchobar knew what Bricriu intended, the Ulstermen had to accept the invitation to his hospitality or run the risk of being thought cowards.

Nothing was lacking, so that during the evening, the heroes got drunken and merry. The food eaten in the first course was unspecified. It was the second course that was the most important. The food included a cauldron filled with wine, and a seven-year-old boar that had eaten only fresh milk and fine meal in springtime, curds and sweet milk in summer, the kernels of nuts and wheat in autumn, and beef and broth in winter. To this meat were added five score cakes of wheat cooked in honey. The story of Lludd and Llefelys in the Welsh *Mabinogion* mentions a year's provision of food and drink for a feast, but this was taken by a supernatural being who packed it into a huge basket to carry it away.

Chieftains were expected to entertain their followers at great feasts. Poseidonius commented on the feasting habits of the Avernian leader Lovernius, father of Bituis, who was dethroned by the Romans. He was said to have driven a chariot over the countryside distributing gold and silver, causing thousands of Celts to follow him. He held a great feast lasting many days for his followers set in a large square enclosure, one and a half miles each way. Within this "he filled vats with expensive liquor and prepared so great a quantity of food that for many days all who wished could enter and enjoy the feast prepared, being served without a break by attendants."[42] This was both an indication of power and an example of conspicuous consumption on the grandest scale. In Galicia, which was also settled by the Celts, Ariamnes gave a feast that was said to have lasted a year, held in temporary halls throughout the country, to which even travelers were invited. An important person at the feast was the satirist, who was allowed great license, being able to insult or make fun of the warriors' foibles.

Drink played a large part in the feasting. The Irish tale *The Intoxication of the Ulstermen* describes how, on the feast of Samain, the tribal king Conchobar gave a feast at the stronghold of Emain Macha. This included a hundred casks of every kind of ale, which led to the indulgers leading a furious ride through Ireland, leveling every hill, clearing every forest, and drying up every river. There are few wilder descriptions in literature than the one of this drunken ride, but allowing for the hyperbole, both this and the preceding tales indicate that if food and drink were available, the Celts indulged themselves to excess.

Diodorus Siculus said more credibly that the Gauls, who were normally deprived of wine and oil, became addicted to wine when it was imported into the country, drinking it unmixed, and "since they partake of this drink without moderation by reason of their craving, when they are drunken they fall into a stupor or a state of madness. Consequently, many of the Italian traders, induced by the love of money which characterizes them, believe that the love of wine of these Gauls is their own salvation.... they receive in return for one jar of wine a slave, a servant in exchange for a drink."[43] He added that the fulsome Celtic mustaches were so long that they acted as a kind of strainer. Diodorus's disapproval of this drinking habit is revealed by his comment that the wine was drunk unmixed. Poseidonius also said that the wine was unadulterated, although sometimes a little water could be added. In fairness, Ammianus Marcellinus, a fourth-century A.D.

historian, reported that Cicero said in an aside, when defending Fonteius in 121 B.C., that the Gauls did mix wine with water, which they had once thought was poison. He added that the Gauls were "a race fond of wine, and disposed to numerous drinks resembling wine." Some, when drunk, rushed around in "aimless revels."[44]

Evidence has to be sought in archaeological remains. Beer drinking was a social activity, and so it was drunk in great quantities. The Hochdorf burial reveals that Celtic aristocracy had suitable equipment to indulge in feasting on a grand scale. The cauldron could contain up to 500 liters (110 gallons) of honey beer or mead. The site revealed two U-shaped trenches containing a large amount of pure hulled barley, which was probably deliberately germinated as if there were a brewing establishment there. A tomb at Apremont in France also contained a huge cauldron together with drinking cups. Finds at sites in central and southern Gaul, such as Corent and Mont, indicate that consumption of beer or wine was on a heroic scale. The site of Beuvray has produced vast quantities of amphorae, most imported from Italy, which indicates the prodigious amount of wine consumed by the Celts. Archaeological discoveries are supplemented by literary evidence. Poseidonius noted that the Celts drank from a common cup, drinking a little at a time but rather frequently. The Celts drank a wheaten beer mixed with honey, which was probably mead, although Diodorus commented that they drank water with which they had cleansed honeycombs.

FOOD FOR SPECIAL GROUPS

Warriors and the Military and Athletes

The aristocracy and the elite ate more and better food than the poorer classes. The Celtic warrior class took the best portions of meat, especially the thighs of pork—the champion's portion. The Egyptians did not have a standing professional army; pharaohs drew on local aristocracy and officials to provide an officer class, and troops were recruited on temporary conscription at a local level. They therefore fought after the harvesting time and might return to their land in time for planting crops. Some landless men were not released and could serve in the army for a number of years. There was no commissariat, and the army requisitioned food and fodder from their allies or by force. This could be done because Egyptian campaigns lasted only a short time.

Wheat, barley, and other supplies were carried on the backs of donkeys on campaign. The baggage train also included sheep and goats to provide meat for the officers. The pharaohs often supplied food. The pharaoh Seti I (B.C. 1318–1304) ordered his regimental commanders to provide daily supplies, including fish and wine, to 1,000 men. The campaign of Tuthmosis III in the Eighteenth Dynasty against the Prince of Qadesh in 1458 B.C. relied on an army of 100,000 men that would require at least 20 tons of grain and 95,000 liters (20,900 gallons) of water a day. The organization and logistics for this were the duty of scribes who fulfilled the role of quartermasters and recruiters.

The Spartan army survived on basic rations. When the Spartans invaded an area they took what they needed in terms of supplies, laid the rest to waste, and then went home. Spartan wars were always as short as the Spartans could manage. They were taken by surprise at least once. When they were facing the Argive army at Sepeia near Tiryns, they decided to break for a midday meal. While they were eating, the Argives attacked. Many Spartans were killed, and the rest only escaped by taking refuge in a nearby woods.

The fifth-century B.C. Greek historian Thucydides in his account of the Spartan attack on Pylos in 425 B.C. wrote that the hoplites (the standard heavy Greek infantry) on Sphakteria were allowed during a truce just under two Attic *choinikrs* (two kilograms, or 4.4 pounds) of ready kneaded barley, moistened and eaten without baking, and two *kotylai* (half a liter) of wine, which would have been mixed with water, together with some meat, for each hoplite, and half that amount for each Helot. Presumably the quantities refer to each day. Later some Spartans were trapped on the island, so provisions were smuggled to them. These included flour, cheese, wine, and "other food; while swimmers brought skins containing poppy seed mixed with honey and pounded linseed." When, however, the Athenians occupied the island after the Spartan withdrawal, they found a large quantity of food. Either the Spartan commander had curtailed the rations in accordance with Spartan tradition, or he had kept back half the rations to eke out in case the siege should be prolonged. One of the surprises was that the supplies included wheat flour, which was not part of the Spartan diet.[45]

The Greeks seem to have had no regular arrangements for feeding the army. As early as the Trojan War, plundering was deemed acceptable for the provisions of Greek troops. Each soldier was expected to provide his own rations for three days on the march, although sometimes these rations were provided at public expense. There were no large supply trains, as was made for the troops at Plataea in 479 B.C., and arrangements could be made for traders to obtain supplies. Later soldiers might be given an allowance to exchange for food. That mainly covered basics, such as barley bread, but without reliance on adequate rations there might be problems with discipline. On the march soldiers were allowed to forage or plunder. When the Ten Thousand were returning to Greece in 401 B.C., it was not part of the duty of their leaders to provide for the army. Every man in the army therefore provided food for himself by foraging and buying from traders.

Along the route, traders quickly seized their opportunity. It would have been foolhardy to allow the soldiers into the towns, so markets were quickly organized outside the walls and boundaries of towns, to enable soldiers to buy provisions. Those who could not afford to buy food had to rely on fellow soldiers. Soldiers who had the foresight to have fuel for a campfire would not allow others to come near unless they paid for this privilege in food. On other campaigns, markets were allowed to be set up in or around the walls of the camp with the agreement of the leader. If stalls were set up in the camp, it would serve the dual purpose of giving employment to traders and encouraging them not to leave the camp.

The Greeks encouraged athletes to have special diets of simple foods. At first these were light meals—grain, soft cheese, and fruits, especially figs. About 500 B.C., the diets became heavier, with meat being included. The change is ascribed to Pythagoras, but he was better known as encouraging a vegetarian diet. Some athletes were said to have had a very heavy diet. The wrestler Milon was said to have consumed huge quantities of meat, including a whole bull in a single day. Heavy athletes were praised, and Philostratus, a Greek from Lemnos who wrote on athletic training in the third century A.D., made fun of physicians and trainers who gave men specially prepared food—bread sprinkled with poppy seeds and pork from pigs fed only on acorns.[46] Plato prescribed a regime for warrior athletes, which included plenty of fish and roast meat.[47] An athlete who had won honors for his city was often allowed to have free meals when he retired.

In the Roman Empire, one of the best-fed groups was the gladiators, who were also encouraged to eat heartily. Their everyday food consisted of barley gruel with beans, which gave them the nickname of *hordearii*, or barley-porridge eaters. The Roman poet Propertius referred to them eating *sagina* or a "foul mash."[48] This was supposed to build up their strength and keep them in the best possible fighting condition. Regular meals also ensured that they were free from variations in food supply and the food shortages that affected the Roman Empire. Galen, who was appointed physician to the gladiators in Pergamum in A.D. 157, advised them on their diet as well as treating their wounds. Although he thought that the diet made them fat and flabby, he had to admit that it gave them one advantage. The fatty layer afforded some protection against minor wounds.

The Roman army had the best commissariat and arrangements for feeding in the ancient world. It was an important agent in transmitting the Roman way of life to the provinces, and in doing so it revolutionized the economy and provided new foods. Its demands caused native populations to increase food production from subsistence farming to an agriculture that produced surpluses. On the march, it was supplied with rations of wheat and other foods, and when established in the forts it could expect regular supplies. The army created a network of contacts and an efficient transport system and it constructed roads, which allowed goods to be moved quickly throughout the empire as well as locally from fort to fort and country to town.

Standard food would consist of bread, bacon, cheese, vegetables, and the lowest quality of wine. For these commodities, a fixed amount was deducted from a soldier's pay. Emperor Hadrian followed the example of his troops and in camp ate the basic food of bacon, cheese, and sour wine. A soldier could supplement these rations by buying supplies elsewhere, but the army also supplied extra food, including *liquamen,* salt, and olive oil. The last was more than a food, for it could be used to oil joints on armor, as a lubricant for the body, and for lighting. Special rations would be issued at festivals and other occasions. Nevertheless, a camp commandant had to make sure that sufficient supplies for fuel and food must be provided at all times, and the fourth-century A.D. military writer Vegetius, whose manual on the organization of the Roman legions is invaluable, devoted a whole chapter to the commandant's duties in this area. Excavations of camp hospitals in Rhineland have produced evidence of fruit and vegetables, part of invalids' diet. Vegetius's manual also indicated that a diet of eggs, meat, and oysters was the best diet for sick troops.

Bread was a basic commodity, fresh loaves being provided daily in camps or forts. Unlike Greek soldiers, the Romans did not eat barley bread. To eat this was regarded as a disgrace. The Emperor Augustus punished soldiers who broke ranks by executing every 10th man and making the rest eat barley. Meat—beef, pork, goat, and mutton—was provided by the commissariat or by hunting wild boar, deer, hare, and fowl. Writing tablets discovered at the fort of Vindolanda in Britain show that chickens were ordered in large quantities for the officers, either for eating or for religious sacrifices.

Soldiers encamped near the seacoast included fish in their diet, but fish bones found on inland sites indicate that transportation of this food was probably relatively easy. Care had to be taken with seafood. Terentius, a legionary stationed in the early second century A.D. at Alexandria, wrote to his father apologizing for not meeting him, as he and other soldiers had suffered a violent attack of fish poisoning. Oysters and other shellfish were popular. At the legionary fort at Caerleon in Wales there seems to have been a snack bar in the baths serving lamb and muttonchops, chicken, pork ribs and trotters, and oysters.

Food could be supplemented in other ways. It might be bought from passing traders or from a shop in a *vici* that had been established around the camps. Letters written on *ostraca* found at Wâdi Fawâkhir in Egypt thank relatives for gifts—bread, vegetables, corn, and fish. Others from Mons Claudianus in Egypt refer to buying food. Clemens wrote to Antoninus the centurion that he had bought three suckling pigs for him. Soldiers might take individual cooking preferences with them from province to province. On the Antonine Wall in Scotland, pottery has been discovered akin to that in North Africa. It has been suggested that reinforcements from Britain sent to Emperor Antoninus Pius in his war in Mauritania, A.D. 146–149, returned with additional North African soldiers and Moorish levies. These brought with them their own cooking methods.

The variety of army diet is revealed by the Vindolanda writing tablets. A list covering the payments and supplies over a period of eight days in June sometime between A.D. 92 and 105 includes fish sauce, pork fat, roe deer, piglets' trotters, ham, venison, olive oil, plums, eggs, semolina, honey, twisted loaves, beans, lentils, salt, and spices, including garlic paste. Drinks include sour and good wines and a native beer. A fragmentary papyrus from Egypt dating to A.D. 199 seems to have been part of a survey given as payment in kind to support the army in Egypt. The foods include wheat, lentils, cattle, calves, goats, pigs, hams, wine, and radish oil. This oil was a staple cooking oil in Egypt, and the soldiers must have adapted to its use. Hay and other fodder crops were also supplied for the animals.

Regular meals were important. Vegetius said that regular and adequate meals for soldiers were important so that they would not be weak from hunger.[49] Livy recorded that the consul Aemilius, before engaging in battle with the Etruscan army in 311 B.C., insisted that his troops were fed, a tactic that succeeded, as the Romans won against superior numbers.[50]

Archaeological evidence from military sites along the Rhine indicates the consumption of a variety of grains, pulses, vegetables, nuts, and fruit. The fort at Neuss, dated to the first century A.D., has revealed evidence of wheat, barley, wild oats (probably used as fodder), eggs, meat, oyster, broad beans, lentils, garlic, grapes, elderberries, and hazelnuts. In addition, there are four foods that must have been introduced to the area by the army—rice, chickpeas, olives, and figs. Barrels, which had contained imported wine, were found. At Dura-Europos, on the Euphrates, papyrus records show solders engaged in tasks of collecting, purchasing, and escorting supplies of corn, food barley, and special supplies for banqueting. Analysis of food remains at other sites and the evidence in literature show that the food provided was adequate in quantity and quality, and it is certain that soldiers never went hungry.

Food in Religious Practices

Food had a part to play in religious belief and practices. Apart from food presented to the dead for their use and placed within the tomb, this included food consumed by religious groups or eaten during the course of a ceremony, the result possibly of tradition or an imposition by a ruling or priestly caste. Religion in Egypt was interwoven into daily life. The pharaohs constructed and maintained temples, sometimes to the detriment of the rest of their polity. The great temples and the building of the pyramids consumed an enormous amount of administrative time and money. Ramses III's funerary temple at Medinet Habu had a calendar giving the number of bread loaves, cakes, and quantities of beer and meat that should be presented at various times. There was also a garden containing olive trees, date palms, and argun palms. Dates and date palms, which were sacred to Ra, the god of the sun, and symbolized life after death and resurrection, were planted in the forecourt of temples. Doum palms, sacred to Thoth, the moon goddess, were also planted, for these were regarded as a source of water provided for the deceased. The sycamore fig, sacred to Nut, the sky goddess, was planted to take care of the deceased. Inscriptions record this: "I am Nut. I have come to thee bringing gifts. I allow thee to imbibe of my milk and to live and have nourishment of my two breasts; joy and health are there. I present to you my bread, my beer, my milk, my figs."[51] Some illustrations show Nut giving out bread and other foods.

Many tombs have vine leaves painted as if growing across ceilings; the grapes were symbols of rebirth. Some have inscriptions: "May you pluck papyrus plants, rushes, lotuses and lots buds, There shall come waterfowl in thousands, lying in your path; you cast your throwing stick at them."[52] Papyrus was important. At the New Year festival celebrating the beginning of the agricultural year, papyrus was offered to the gods for the produce of the marshes—birds, fish, and vegetables. In addition, corn mummies or ritual figures stuffed with a mixture of earth, sand, and barley represented the annual cycle of birth and renewal. Old figures were destroyed each year and new ones made to ensure a good crop in the new harvest.

Offerings were made in temples, and the walls were inscribed with lists of these. One list at the great temple of Medinet Habu, instituted by Ramses III, indicates the vast amounts given. These included, every day of the year, 3,229 loaves of bread, 24 cakes, 144 jugs of beer, 32 geese, and many jars of wine. On festal days still more was delivered. For example, over 11 days in the month of Choiakh, dedicated to the Memphis god Ptah-Sokaris-Osiris, the temple received 60 jars of wine, 242 geese, 10 oxen, 1,357 jugs of beer, 1,972 cakes, and a large number of loaves. This was more than the priests could eat. Some of it could be stored, but most probably fed the crowds who took part in the festival.

Fishing scenes are common in tombs. The tomb owner is often represented as spearing a fish and presenting it to guests, just as fish were presented to priests at the temples. On the tomb of Horemheb, a painting depicts a ship with dried mullet hanging from the rigging. This was a desirable and expensive fish. It was exported to Syria and traded for cedar. Ramses II is said to have donated some 474,660 fish in honor of the god Amun at Thebes. Fish found in the kitchens of the priests at Karnak suggest that the priests' servants ate fish, although the priests were forbidden to eat it.

In the calendar of lucky and unlucky days, however, it was forbidden to eat fish on holidays and certain other days, such as the 22nd day of the first month of the season of inundation. This seems to be connected with the god Ra. He ate other gods, but when they upset his stomach, he spat out their bodies in the form of fish and their spirits in the form of birds. Fish burials are common. At Gurob a whole cemetery was given to fish, mostly Nile perch. They were placed in pits packed in a fine ash, which may have acted as a preservative. The mouth and the openings behind the gills were also packed with ash.

Some of the paintings in the temples were of gardens. A garden might be shown as three rows of rectangular plots with raised borders. Waterfowl and fish splashed in water. Outside the temple tomb of Queen Hatshepsut, four raised oblong tanks were offering tanks for milk. Priests plunged burning torches into these tanks to extinguish them, and libations of milk were offered for purification. Elongated lettuces are painted on the walls. Lettuces were important because they were sacred to Amun-Min, as its milky sap represented the semen of the fertility god. They were thus regarded as an aphrodisiac. Lettuces were often left to grow to a huge size, sometimes to the height of a meter.

Gardens at temples had the practical purpose of growing plants as offerings for deities and food and drink for priests, who also acted as agents of the gods in passing on food and drink to the deity. Olives provided oil to light their lamps. Vines produced grapes that were pressed to provide wine for libations. The temple of Tuthmosis III at Karnak had a symbolic indoor garden with a T-shaped offering center. The walls were decorated with plants, animals, and birds. The garden also symbolized a place of rebirth. A pharaoh was reborn after death. He had passed through the rooms of the pyramid representing death and had been rejuvenated in a new life.

The priests who served the temples might be full-time or part-time. Rituals were performed, often several times a day, before a cult statue. The statue was washed, anointed with perfumes, dressed with clothes, and decorated with jewelry. Food and drink were presented to it, and the common populace provided this on a daily basis. The god took spiritual nourishment; physical nourishment was available to those who served the god. These included the major and minor priests, the servants, and funerary workers and might include those who hung around temples seeking temporary employment or merely scrounging for food. Priesthoods were often sold or inherited, and one of the great attractions was the edible gifts supplied by worshippers.

All religions had a number of festivals at which food and drink were provided for certain groups. The Egyptians believed that the gods joined the worshippers at the great festivals. The calendar of Efu said that the gods, together with their followers, sat down and celebrated before the venerable god Efu. All drank, anointed themselves, and praised the god loudly. Special personnel were employed to butcher cattle, which were being killed for sacrifice. The cattle had their throats cut; the heads were cut off, and they were bled and skinned. The meat was jointed and select pieces were presented as offerings. Some meat was given to the poorer classes, a rare treat for them.

Greek public dining was linked to religious ceremonies and the veneration of a deity. The Theseia, celebrated in honor of Theseus, included sacrifices and a huge banquet paid for by the wealthy of Athens. To participate was to belong to the community. Once Greece had been overcome by Rome, these occasions increased. Epaminodas revived the festival of the Ptoia in Boeotia, instituting an annual dinner for magistrates and councillors. Every fourth year food and drink were given to all the citizens and resident foreigners. Between the 20th and 30th of each month, Epaminodas's wife provided lunches for citizens' wives, female children, and even female slaves. The food was carefully chosen to relate to the status of the participants. Cleanax of Cyme gave wedding feast banquets to all free men, feasts in honor of the dead, and feasts in honor of Dionysus for citizens and visitors, with the food carefully delineated to each social group.

The Romans organized festivals to a number of gods as part of the Roman calendar. On two of these, the Saturnalia and the Compitalia, the feasting was open to the public; hence Domitian's great feast at the Saturnalia. Usually the Saturnalia began with a sacrifice in the Temple of Saturn and was followed by a banquet (*convivium publicum*) open to all Roman citizens. This had been established in 217 B.C. The Compitalia had begun when farmers offered sacrifices at the end of the agricultural year to the Lares Compitales, the protector of crossroads. By the mid-60s B.C. a Collegia Compitalicia was responsible for organizing these festivals. They were banned in the late republic but were revived by Augustus, who linked them to the Genius Augusti to enhance his own image. The festival linked sacrifices, processions, and theatrical displays with a sacrifice of a bull and a pig. At other festivals, food was used to emphasize distinctions among citizens. The Ludi Romani (September 4–19) and the Ludi Plebei (November 4–17), for example, included processions, games, and sacrifices, followed by banquets, which were open only to senators. Augustus allowed even senators expelled from the Senate for any reason to come to dine. Originally the food had been eaten on wooden tables and from earthenware dishes, but, in the time of the empire, far more luxurious tableware was provided.

Other festivals were simpler. In Rome the Penates looked after the larder, its contents, and its replenishments. Statuettes of the gods, kept in the larder or in a *lararium*, were put on the table at meal times. Vesta was the Roman goddess of the hearth where food was prepared. During a meal a portion of food was thrown into the fire as an offering. The state festival of Vesta was in June. On June 9 the mill donkeys were hung with garlands of violets, decorated with loaves, and given a day free from toil. On June 15 married women came barefoot with offerings of food to her shrine.

A popular ceremony begun about 399 B.C. was the *lectisternium,* where images of gods were placed on couches as if participating at a banquet. Another festival was that of Anna Perenna on March 15, when the plebeians celebrated by singing, dancing, and drinking in a grove near the Tiber on the Flaminium Way. Each person was reputed to have to drink as many cups of wine as the number of years they wished to live. The Vinalia Priora on April 23 was linked to the offering of new wine to Jupiter and was celebrated when new wine was brought to market.

At most of the religious festivals where a large number of animals were sacrificed, the meat must have been distributed among the poor. For those Egyptians, Greeks, and Romans to whom meat was a rarity, these festivals were always welcome. The ritual slaughter of large numbers of animals—bulls, cows, sheep, goats, and oxen—meant that some meat was given to the gods, the priests got the choicest pieces, and the rest was divided among the worshippers. At the Greek festivals dedicated to Dionysus, a huge number of bulls was killed; in 333 B.C. this was reputed to be 240. Before the sacrifices, copious amounts of wine were drunk with dedications to the god of wine. Sometimes fish were sacrificed. Meat was either given directly to worshippers or, as in Greece, roasted or boiled before distribution. Sometimes it was used to provide a communal banquet. In Boeotia huge eels from Lake Copais were decorated with garlands and scattered with barley seeds before being sacrificed. The meat from animals sacrificed to gods of the underworld had to be burned or eaten before nightfall by the worshippers. If this was not done, then generous portions of meat were handed out to the general public.

Food in Funerary Practice

The Egyptians believed that the soul of a person had three aspects. One was the *ka,* which represented the life energy of the person and was essentially his double. As such, the *ka* had the same needs as the person and so had to have food and drink. A common funerary inscription decreed that the *ka* should have a "thousand of bread, a thousand of beer, oxen and fowl."[53] The second aspect was the *ba,* represented as a bird with a human head. The *ba* stayed with the dead person in the tomb during the night, but during the day went out into the sunshine, thus ensuring contact with the living. When it returned each night it had to know its own body and home; hence the mummification of bodies and a tomb provided with contents that had formed part of a person's life. The third aspect, the *akh*, was the actual spirit of the person that survived death. It was a luminous element, and in this aspect it mingled with the gods.

In the First and Second Dynasties the simple stone or mud mastabas provided the resting place of the dead. Food and drink had to be left here, as the relatives of the dead were expected to make provision for the continued well-being of the *ka* of the dead person. As the meal was never consumed, it was presumed to be available for all time. At first real food and drink were provided, thus provisioning a house of eternity. This provisioning affected the evolution of the tomb, because the resting place of the dead was linked with a mortuary chapel in which priests officiated. There were offerings niches, which were gradually extended deeper and deeper into the superstructure until they became internal chambers forming part of the chapel and filled with food, drink, and other possessions. Later these more simple tombs surrounded the grandiose pyramids of the dead pharaohs, where food and drink offerings were on a lavish scale. These offerings included large amounts of wine. At Abydos (ca. 3150 B.C.) one tomb contained 360 jars, which had probably contained good-quality wine. Some offerings appear to be of a ritual nature. The shaft entrance to Khufu's pyramid contained two wine jars, the horned skull of an ox, and three leg bones wrapped in reed matting.

Later, as provisions became a burden on the living, tomb paintings served the same purpose as the actual objects. First came a painting of the deceased sitting at a table on which food and drink were placed. This was then elaborated into showing the production, gathering, and hunting of food as well as the provisions with which the deceased was nominally supplied either for the journey to the afterlife or within the tomb. Even entertainment was provided, with paintings of musicians playing instruments before the dead. An inscription on a stela at Abydos emphasized the good fortune of the person: "How well established are you in your place of eternity, in your everlasting tomb. It is filled with offerings of food. It encloses every good thing."[54]

In the Egyptian *Book of the Dead,* the deceased upper-class Egyptian who had never toiled in the fields faced questions when he came before Osiris and his assessors. He had to give negative answers and admit ignorance. "Nor have I desolated ploughed fields, nor have I made inroads into the fields of other peoples, not have I driven away the cattle, which were upon their pastures, nor have I turned back water at season, nor have I cut a cutting in water running."[55] If he were judged to have passed this test, he had to spend time in the Field of the Reeds, the landlike delta where the deceased plowed, sowed, and harvested. This was not considered a punishment but the ideal state for them, for it was considered eternal prosperity. In the time of the Middle Kingdom a figure, the *shawabti*, was placed in tombs. This was a small statuette showing the deceased as a wrapped mummy. This, together with agricultural tools placed in the tomb, were intended to do the work in the afterlife in place of the deceased.

In the Greek world it was accepted that the living would maintain a close relationship with the dead, since their acceptance into the afterlife might be dependent on the attention they received in their former life. On funerary monuments, a man would be shown reclining, attended by women, for he was regarded as the host at his own funerary feast. Food and drink were necessary for the welfare of the dead, so provision was made to provide food for them on the journey to the afterlife and their eternal stay in that place. Herbs such as marjoram were scattered on the bier to ward off evil spirits, and the body was laid on vine leaves, myrtles, and laurel leaves. The scent of these would have helped to combat the smell of the corpse but would also have indicated that the body was to be returned to the ground. Libations had to be poured when leaving the house and at the tomb, usually about three *congii* of wine and one of oil (about 18 pints of wine). The offerings also included milk, honey, water, oil, and *pelanos* (a mixture of meal, honey, and oil).

Animals could also be sacrificed by the grave. A bull would be exceptional; normally poultry, sheep, and kid would be sacrificed. These had to be killed over a ditch so that the blood would run into the earth, thus emphasizing the dead person's contact with the dead. This was part of a feast offered to the dead, but the sacrificial meat was burned by the grave. Festivals were arranged on the 3rd, 9th, and 30th days and then on the anniversary of death, with visits being maintained at intervals throughout the year, especially on certain festivals when the emphasis was on propitiating the spirits of the dead. Gifts were deposited in their tombs. These included wine, olives, olive oil, milk, honey, *pelanos*, *kollyba* (first dried fruits of crops), cheese, bread, and cakes.

Funerary feasts by the tomb or the family memorial (Greek bodies were usually cremated) included these foods as well as small honey cakes and wine, often mixed with bitter herbs. The pots and cups used could be smashed after the meal, possibly to indicate to the dead that the food and drink had been made for their benefit. In addition, wreaths and branches of myrtle were common. As the Greeks were more reserved in their attitude to death, there were neither the same outpourings of grief nor the continuity of funerary feast rituals, which were common elsewhere in the Roman world.

Roman funerary customs were more elaborate. The funeral meal was an essential part of the funerary process, taking two forms—the funerary meal during or after the burial ceremony and the period of mourning, and the meal provided to sustain the dead in the tomb and on their journey to the afterlife. The latter was important because it was believed that the dead continued to reside within the tomb. Even when people were cremated, their spirit still resided within or close by the burial place, so that the dead retained all the needs, desires, and feelings that they had had in life. The funerary cult was based as much on fear as on piety, for the dead were prone to resentment, even vengeance, if they felt they were neglected. To forestall this, the correct rites had to be carried out. In these rites food played an important part.

Once the deceased had been cremated or placed in the tomb, a libation of wine to the Manes (spirits of the dead) was poured out. Offerings of food were placed at the tomb to be eaten in a funerary meal (*silicernium*) by members of the family. Sometimes the hungry poor waited close to the tombs to partake of the feast after the mourners had departed, even though this was considered sacrilege. Slaves, freedmen, and soldiers who had no family usually belonged to a burial club (*collegia funeraticia*) whose members met once a month to pay contributions toward their funerals. They would dine together for convivial friendship, to have a commemorative meal for their deceased colleagues. The college could purchase communal columbaria for the ashes, where meals were held on specific anniversaries.

The period of mourning included purification ceremonies and meals eaten by the grave nine days after the funeral and then on personal anniversaries, such as birthdays, and annual festivals when the dead were commemorated. These had a dual purpose, ensuring that memories of the dead survived in the minds of friends and relations, and reassuring the dead that they were not forgotten by inclusion in the refreshment provided. Often money would be left in a will for the necessary food and drink—bread, cakes, meat, fruit, and wine.

The Parentalia, held February 13 to 21, was the feast of parents and kinsfolk, when the dead were appeased by food offerings, including a family meal eaten at the grave. The Parentalia ended in the public festival of the Feralia, when the Manes were honored. The Lemuria, held on May 9, 11, and 13, was when hungry ghosts (the *lemures* and the more dangerous *larvae*) gathered around the house. Meals were prepared for them. At midnight, the head of the family washed his hands in clean water and threw away black beans, while keeping his face averted, saying nine times, "These I cast, with these I redeem me and mine."[56] As he made his way out of the house, touching water on his route, the ghosts were believed to pick up and eat the beans.

On anniversaries, relations and friends ate commemorative meals at the tomb, with a share provided for the dead person. The fact that it was not eaten did not mean that the dead spirit was not partaking of its share; it would be nourished either within its bones or its ashes. To prepare such meals, kitchens were sometimes provided at mausoleums, so that the food might be as elaborate as when eaten by the deceased when alive. The dead might be jealous if they thought they were now held in less regard. Kitchens can be seen attached to certain tombs at Isola Sacra, the cemetery attached to Ostia, the port of Rome. These tombs present the appearance of the dwellings of well-to-do bourgeoisie.

Meals could be eaten in the funerary gardens, which were sometimes created around a tomb. In the *Satyricon,* Trimalchio, when giving directions for his future tomb, says that he would like to have an orchard with "various kinds of fruit growing round my ashes and plenty of vines."[57] The Romans had a passion for gardens, which the dead in the tomb were assumed to retain. The Elysium Fields were regarded as an idyllic landscape with abundant flowers and heavenly banquets.

Inscriptions on tombstones mention walled gardens with refreshing water, vines, fruit trees, and flowers. There are references to *cenacula* (dining rooms), *tabernae* (taverns), *triclae* (summerhouses), *horrea* (store houses), and even *stabula* and *meritoria* (brothels and rooms to let). An inscription at Langres directs that the *pomaria* (orchards) should be tended by three gardeners and their apprentices. At Nimes, one man made his mausoleum fruitful with vines, trees, and roses. Marcus Rufius Catullus, *curator nautarum Rhodianeorum,* who died at Géligneur, had made for himself, his son, and his daughter a tomb with a vineyard and enclosure walls. Publicius Calistus from Die left precise details. His tomb was to have a "vineyard two-thirds of a half an acre in area from whose yield I wish libations of no less than fifteen pints of wine to be poured for me each year."[58] Presumably they should be poured into the tomb or onto the ground, so as to sustain him in the afterlife.

The tomb of the baker Marceius Vergilius Eurysaces, *pistor et redemptor* (baker and contractor), and his wife, Atistia, which still stands outside the Porta Maggiore in Rome, has a burial chamber in the upper part of a trapezoidal tomb. At the top is a frieze displaying the process of baking, from the sifting and grinding of the corn to the weighing of the finished loaves. The series of vertical cylinders may represent corn measures and the horizontal ones ovens. That the tomb was meant to represent the bakery is shown by a nearby inscription mentioning the tomb as a *panarium,* a breadbasket or a bakery. Two figures, carved in relief, found close by represent Eurysaces and Atistia.

Tomb of the baker M. Vergilius Eurysaces, and his wife, Antistia, outside the Porta Maggiore, Rome. A relief showing the stages of baking encircles the top. The holes represent the ovens. Courtesy of the author.

Some tombstones show the *totenmahl,* or funerary banquet. The deceased lies on a couch, holding out a cup as if to toast the living. A small, three-legged table is in front, on which rests food. Such tombstones were popular in Rhineland and eastern Gaul. One of the finest tombstones is at Cologne: Gaius Julius Maternus, a veteran of Legion I Minervia, reclines on a high-backed couch, raising his cup in his right hand and holding a serviette in his left. His dog is at his feet. A three-legged table covered with a fringed cloth is placed in front of him, on which is set a meal of fruit and bread. Servants stand to the left and right to wait on him. His wife, Maria Marcellina, seated in her basket chair, holds a bowl with more fruit. The dead were expected to be nourished by these meals. Even so, none could escape the implacable reality that the pleasures of eating and drinking were ephemeral. Titus Flaminius, a soldier of Legion XIV Gemina, on his tombstone in Britain at Wroxeter (Shropshire) was uncompromising: "I did my service and now I am here. Read this and be either more or less fortunate in your lifetime. The gods prohibit you from the wine-grape and water when you enter Tartarus."[59]

The Romans believed in a life beyond the tomb, but also held the view that meals shared at the tomb with the dead might not be enough to satisfy them. Food had to be placed within the tomb at the moment of interment or on the funeral pyre. There were two premises. The first was that the tomb was the home for the dead, where they would expect all that they had had in life; the second was that food replenished their energies.

The premise of the tomb as an eternal home was constant in the Roman world. Trimalchio was going to decorate his tomb carefully: "It is wrong to look after the house in which you live and to neglect the house in which you will stay much longer."[60] Containers for ashes were placed in urns shaped as houses. The elaborate tombs at Ostia and those south of Rome, along the Via Latina near its convergence with the Via Appia Nuova, are large square buildings, which take the form of rectangular houses, some having an underground burial chamber surmounted by a two-story building.

In the catacombs of Kom el-Shuqqafa at Alexandria, Egypt, dating from the second century A.D., the dead were interred in a vast necropolis, reached by a spiral staircase, descending to a depth of 35 meters. A triclinium with three stone benches was provided, where meals could be eaten before the dead persons underwent the ritual of evisceration and mummification, graphically represented on the wall of the principal tomb. Anubis, the Egyptian god of the dead, but here dressed as a

Roman legionary with a serpent's tail, representative of a Greek divinity, Agathodaemon; and Sobek, the crocodile god, also depicted in Roman military dress, guarded the embalmed body before it was incarcerated within one of the many niches carved out of the rock. When the catacombs were first excavated, wine amphorae and tableware were found on a central wooden table in the triclinium.

An elaborately carved sarcophagus found at Simpelveldt, Holland, emphasizes the belief of the tomb as home. Around the interior walls are carved all the accompaniments that the deceased lady required in the next world. She herself lies on a couch. By her side is her basket chair, shelves displaying glass or metal vessels, cupboards, cabinets and chests, and a three-legged dining table. Even her bathhouse is placed there, so that she should feel at home in her tomb, and food and drink were probably placed there.

The second premise was that the dead are hungry and thirsty and must be nourished by offerings either burned on the funeral pyre or placed in the grave. It was believed that the dead depend for their nourishment on the libations that are poured in our world and the burned offerings at the tombs; accordingly, a shade who has no surviving friends or relations on earth goes about in the otherworld as an unfed corpse. This nourishment could be delivered through pipes. For poorer people this meant the mouth of a flagon protruding above the ground serving both as a grave marker and an entrance for liquid nourishment. These can still be seen in situ at the Isola Sacra cemetery.

It was not only wine that nourished the dead. The Celts placed joints of meat in the grave to sustain warriors on the way to their Celtic Valhalla, as revealed by burials at Snailwell, Cambridgeshire, and Danes Graves, North Yorkshire. The pig was particularly important in Celtic mythology. Pork was characteristic of the feast served to dead warriors. A man carrying a pig on his back often represented the Lord of the Feast. Pigs were also sacrificed to Ceres, goddess of corn and germination.

Roman cemeteries have revealed food offerings and eating equipment. Food found in tombs in France includes the remains of dates, pears, plums, cherries, figs, apples, apricots, nuts, cereals, beans, peas, and cabbages. French archaeologists consider that the food selected may have been symbolic. Vegetables, especially beans, symbolized the world of the dead. Beans and lentils had a nutritional value to sustain the dead for their journey, but they were also a mark of regeneration, for within them is the embryo giving promise of new life. Fruits represent the principle of immortality. Nuts, such as almonds, symbolize the buried sense of wisdom. Cereals were sacred to Ceres-Demeter, goddess of corn and germination. Apples are symbolic of femininity. Dates, figs, and pine nuts, on the other hand, are potent masculine symbols, relating to Attys, consort of Cybele. These products ensure immortality. Attys transformed himself into a pine tree, a god dying each winter and renewing himself.

It was equally valid to burn food on the cremation pyre or even at the side of the tomb, for burning released the life spirit of the object. Lucian in his essay "Charon" depicts Charon asking Hermes, the messenger who led the dead to the underworld, why corpses are placed in receptacles called tombs: "Look, there is a splendid banquet laid out and they are burning it all; and pouring wine and mead, I suppose, into ditches? What does it mean?" Hermes answers that "the souls arise from below and get their dinner as best they may, by flitting about in the savory steam and smoke and drink the wine in the trenches." Charon replies, "Eat and drink when their skulls are dried bone? What folly, the idiots! They little know what an impassable frontier divides the world of the dead from the world of the living."[61]

NOTES

1. Homer, *Odyssey* 16.2–56.
2. Martial, *Epigrams* 10.48.
3. Martial, *Epigrams* 5.78.
4. Apuleius, *Metamorphoses* 2.19.
5. Pliny the Younger, *Letters* 1.15.
6. Lucian, "On Salaried Posts in Great Houses," in *Lucian*, vol. 2., translated by B. O. Foster, F. Gardner, E. T. Sage, and A. C. Schlesinger (14 vols.) (London: Loeb Classical Library), 15.
7. Pliny, *NH* 36.184.
8. Martial, *Epigrams* 8.67.
9. Varro, *RR* 3.6.6.
10. Herodotus, 2.172.
11. Leonard H. Lesko, *King Tut's Wine Cellar* (Berkeley, Calif.: B.C. Scribe Publications, 1977), 229.
12. See article on Banquets in *The Oxford Encyclopedia of Ancient Egypt*, Donald B. Redford, editor in chief (Oxford: Oxford University Press, 2001).
13. Herodotus 2.78.
14. Plutarch, "Aemilius Paulus," in *Parallel Lives*, vol. 6, 28.9.
15. Athenaeus, *D* 436e–f.

16. Plato, *The Laws,* 2 vols., translated by R. E. Bury (Cambridge, Mass.: Loeb Classical Library, 1926), 2.666a–e.

17. Athenaeus, *D* 188e–f.

18. Plutarch, "Dinner of the Seven Sages," in *Moralia,* vol. 2, 2.147e.

19. Xenophon, *Symposium,* translation and commentary by A. J. Bowen (Warminster, England: Aris and Phillips, 1998), 9.7.

20. Plato, *Protagoras,* translated by W.R.M. Lamb (Cambridge, Mass.: Loeb Classical Library, 1924), 347c.

21. Plutarch, "Pelopidas," in *Parallel Lives,* vol. 5, 9.4–11.

22. Livy, 39.42.5.

23. Plutarch, "Lycurgus," in *Parallel Lives,* vol. 1, 9.8.

24. Athenaeus, *D* 138d.

25. Cicero, *De Senectute,* translated by W. A. Falconer (London: Loeb Classical Library, 1923), 13.45.

26. Plutarch, *Moralia* 679e–680b.

27. Columella, *RR* 11.1.19.

28. Martial, *Epigrams* 5.70.

29. Seneca, *Epistulae Morales* 27.5.

30. Suetonius, *Nero* 11.

31. Varro, *RR* 3.2.16.

32. Livy, 9.30.5–10.

33. Valerius Maximus, 7.5.

34. Seneca, *Epistulae Morales* 95.72–73.

35. Cicero, *Pro Murena,* translated by L. L. Lord (London: Loeb Classical Library, 1946), 74.

36. Cicero, *Letters to Atticus,* 4 vols., translated and edited by D. R. Shackleton-Bailey (London: Loeb Classical Library, 1999), 13.52 (353).

37. Seneca, *Epistulae Morales* 95.24.

38. Seneca, *Epistulae Morales* 47.5–8.

39. Diodorus Siculus, 5.29.

40. Strabo, 4.4.5.

41. Poseidonius, quoted in Athenaeus, *D* 151e; Diodorus Siculus, 5.28.4–5.

42. Poseidonius, quoted in Athenaeus, *D* 152d.

43. Diodorus Siculus, 5.26.2–3.

44. Ammianus Marcellinus, 3 vols., rev. ed., translated and edited by J. B. Rolfe (London: Loeb Classical Library, 1950), 15.12.4.

45. Thucydides, *History of the Peloponnesian War,* translated with an introduction by Rex Warner. Notes by M. I. Finley (Harmondsworth, England: Penguin Press, 1990), 4.16.1, 4.26.8; J. F. Lazenby suggests that the wine would have had water added to it. See Lazenby, *The Spartan Army* (Warminster, England: Aris and Phillips), 118.

46. Quoted in M. Golden, *Sport in the Ancient World from A–Z* (London: Routledge, 2004), 52; Philostratus, *On Athletic Exercises* 43–44.

47. Plato, *Republic,* 2 vols., translated by P. Shorley (London: Loeb Classical Library, 1930, 1935), 410b.

48. Propertius, *Elegies,* translated by G. P. Goold (Cambridge, Mass.: Loeb Classical Library, 1990), 4.8.25.

49. Vegetius, *Epitoma De Rei Militaris (Epitome of Military Science),* translated with notes by N. P. Miller (Liverpool: Liverpool University Press, 1993), 3.11.

50. Livy, 9.32.

51. Quoted in N. de G. Davies and H. R. Hopgood, *The Tomb of Ken-Amun at Thebes* (New York: Publication of the Metropolitan Museum of Art Egyptian Expedition, Volume 5, 1930), 53.

52. Quoted in Alix Wilkinson, *The Garden in Ancient Egypt* (London: The Rubicon Press, 1998), 78.

53. A. I. Spencer, *Death in Ancient Egypt* (Harmondsworth, England: Penguin Press, 1982), 58.

54. Quoted in Spencer, 73.

55. Quoted in Spencer, 146.

56. J.M.C. Toynbee, *Death and Burial in the Roman World* (London: Thames and Hudson, 1971), 64.

57. Petronius, *Satyricon* 71.

58. *CIL* 12.1657.

59. R. G. Collingwood and R. R. P. Wright (eds.), *The Roman Inscriptions of Britain* (Oxford: Clarendon Press, 1965), no. 292.

60. Petronius, *Satyricon* 71.

61. Lucian, "Charon," in *Lucian,* vol. 2, 22.

CHAPTER 6

CONCEPTS OF DIET AND NUTRITION

THEORY OF EATING

Why did people in the ancient world eat what they ate? This was obviously to keep fit and well, but also, more so than in present-day Western society, to keep alive. To avoid starvation people even ate grass or twigs. Crises of food shortage and hunger dominated an insecure life, so that a search for food or its production was the immediate priority. Primitive people in prehistoric societies avoided eating poisonous plants or other noxious substances. Slow poisons, such as food cooked in lead pans, however, could cause death without a person realizing the cause.

A second reason for eating certain foods was that people ate according to a belief or to follow a prescriptive regime. A belief in the humoral theory dictated some people's choice of food and when they ate it. Religious belief and celebration in festivities played a large part in what was consumed. This could be linked to supply. Poor people in Greece and Egypt ate most of their meat from sacrificial animals. Culture and tradition can determine what food should and could be eaten. Preference could be influenced by what one had as a child or the culture of the family or tribe. The Celts had a tradition based on butter, milk, and cheese. The Greeks and Romans preferred to use olive oil; in Egypt oil was obtained from seeds. People were influenced by or obeyed taboos, sometimes from choice or tradition, sometimes, as in the case of priests, because it was a condition of their profession. The Stoics practiced asceticism. The followers of Pythagoras, who believed that the souls of humans transferred after death to either humans or animals, practiced vegetarianism.

A third reason centered on taste and preference. Taste is determined in childhood, when children build up a visual prototype of favored foods. They will reject foods that do not match the prototype, probably because of an ancient survival mechanism that sets the pattern for future eating preferences. Thus foods that are harmful, such as poisonous toadstools, would be avoided. Some foods appealed more than others. Sweet tastes dominated, linked to ripe fruits and breast milk; a dislike of bitter tastes was linked to alkaloid toxins in plants. Scarcity would extend the range of foods that people were forced to eat. But when food was available in larger quantities or when people had the means to procure a greater variety of food, then choice would dominate. People might have preferred savory or sweet foods, meat, or vegetables, but choice was probably confined to the wealthy. Poorer people had little or no choice and ate what was available within their area. Conspicuous consumption of food was a sign of power and privilege. The rich could indulge themselves by tasting exotic foods unavailable to the poorer classes.

Taste is linked to a fourth reason: availability. Making food available was often a political necessity. The Egyptians stored corn in granaries so that it would be available in times of famine. The Roman emperors provided the citizens of Rome with a constant food supply to avoid unrest. Availability and the extension of choice of food often was subject to the weather. When St. Paul was being brought to Rome on a corn ship from Alexandria (Acts 27 AV), the ship was wrecked in a tempest and the wheat cast out to try to lighten it. The Alexandrian corn fleet usually traveled in convoy, so if there were delays, the corn supply in Rome was often running dangerously low. Emperor Tiberius expressed forcibly Rome's dependence of food supply on the hazards of the weather.

Availability also depended on extending the distance from which food could be brought. Imports into a country and the introduction of new plants to supplement those gathered from the wild provided wider choice. The growth of long-distance trade was the area in which the Romans excelled. The expansion of the empire increased the availability and choice of food. Traders, under the protection and with the encouragement of an authoritative regime, were able to transport their goods along well-made roads to towns and cities where market halls and retail outlets were supplying agents for the buying public. In addition, soldiers stationed throughout the empire had to have supplies of food and money sent to them. This might mean the introduction of new foods such as *liquamen,* wine, or olive oil, but, more importantly, the system put ready cash into the local economy, which could encourage trade not linked to a barter system.

HUMORAL THEORY

Health in the ancient classical world, as described in the writings of Hippocrates and Galen, was linked to the harmony of four bodily fluids, or humors. These were blood (hot and dry), phlegm (cold and moist), yellow bile or choler (hot and dry), and black bile or melancholy (cold and dry). In turn these were linked to the four elements of earth, fire, water, and air, analyzed in terms of cold, hot, wet, and dry, and from there transposed to the seasons.

These explained disease and human behavior in terms of interactions and the relative proportions of these fluids. The food and drink that a person consumed and therefore his or her diet could influence the humors and health. If blood was in the ascendant, then the person was sanguine; if phlegm dominated, the person would be melancholic. The humors determined what should be in a person's diet, what illness or disease he or she could catch, and what might be his or her personality. The theory even applied to plants and animals, so that matching the right type of food to the person was essential. Hot and moist people had to eat similar foods except when they were unbalanced, in which case they had to eat cold and dry foods to correct the balance, and the reverse therefore followed. There was therefore a constant battle to achieve the correct diet.

A physician could control the humors by prescribing a regime of certain foods and drink or giving medicines counter to the type of humor. Bitter almonds and garlic neutralized phlegm, cabbage counteracted black bile, and honey and sweet liquids were the remedy for yellow bile. Hippocrates in his *Regimen in Health,* as well as discussing cooking methods, exercises, and bathing, prescribed a seasonal regime. In winter a person should eat a great deal but drink little. If he has wine, it should be diluted. Bread, meat, and fish, cooked dry, and a few vegetables would keep the body dry and hot. In spring liquid could be increased and bread and cereals reduced, and meat and fish should have more liquid in them. When summer comes, drinking liquids should be increased, foods made more watery, and vegetables eaten raw. In autumn the eating of cereals should be gradually increased, meat and fish should be cooked drier, and drinking should be more sparing. Even when traveling, a regime should be followed, and here the advice seems to be sensible. The Greek physician Diocles of Carystus in the fourth century B.C. advised that if undertaking a long journey in summer, there should be a pause for lunch and a rest after this. If this is impossible, only a little food and drink should be taken, and the food should include some salt. In winter he advised that there should be no break, and, rather curiously, indicated that no food and drink should be taken. He might have intended that it would be as well for a person to ignore breaks and refreshment to reach the destination quickly before night set in and the cold weather increased.

There were some sensible theories dictating a regime. Some foods were prescribed to strengthen a stomach and stop it rumbling. These included quinces, olives in brine, raisins, and mustard. To prevent flatulence, chickpeas, beans, barley cake, lupines, fresh dates, figs, and beer should be avoided. Simple meals should consist of bread, cheese, and fruit. Attendance at a banquet or a rich meal was allowable, providing this was not done too regularly.

How many people followed these theories is problematic. Most poor people would have been more concerned about getting anything to eat than regulating a diet, but wealthy people who were under the control of a physician might have subjected themselves to a prescribed regime. Women, for example, were believed to have a cold and wet constitution. This could be corrected by prescribing hot and dry foods, which are those that had little liquid and were not saturated with spices. Women should avoid fish, fat, and anything from a new-born animal. They were not to drink a great deal of wine, although a little could be allowed. They were often denied meat, as this would raise the quality of heat and thus their sexual allure.

Physicians, however, had realized correctly that women require less food than men. Modern nutritionists have decreed that women need 2,000 calories per day while men require 2,500–4,000, depending on the degree of work they undertake. The ancient world, however, was a patriarchal society, and so it was inevitable that women, of whatever class, always got less food than men, unless they were in the more wealthy ranks of society.

FOOD SUPPLY

Two groups of people in the ancient world might eat better-quality meals with improved provision of food. The first was the army. Even in Egypt, where there was no organized commissariat, commanders made sure that the men were fed before campaigns. The Spartans ensured that their men relied on as little food as was required but enough to keep them fit. The Greeks did allow foraging, but it was the Roman army that had an excellent commissariat to supply food. The second group were the people who lived in towns, who ate well except in times of famine. Towns developed thriving and lively daily markets supplied by traders and people bringing in food from the country, who were only too eager to sell a cash crop. Some parts of Italy followed a nine-day cycle for their markets; other parts of the empire followed similar patterns. There were also occasional markets held as part of fairs and festivals. The Greek agoras and Roman forums were built specifically to be lively centers for buying and selling of all kinds of goods and food. Some markets specialized in fish or meat. The Forum Boarium and the Forum Holitorium in Rome were the centers of a meat trade. The Greeks had markets on the quayside, so that when a ship came in fresh fish were for sale. Urban dwellers could obtain food easily and had the advantage of fresh fast food, bread, cooked meats, and sauces. They could eat reasonably well, with an increased variety of diet, or even more elaborate dishes if they had the advantage of hiring one of the cooks who waited in the marketplace to seek employment. They might even have a cook who knew some of the sophisticated recipes gathered in Apicius's book.

Food was a priority. If supplies were scarce, people would eat whatever they could; quantity, not quality, was the criterion. When food became more plentiful, consumer choice and discrimination were possible. In the towns and at culling and harvest time in the countryside, the problem might not be lack of food but a surplus. The gorging of food and indulgence in wine could result in liver complaints, heart attacks, and obesity. A rich diet, especially if laced with *liquamen,* caused bad breath. Worse could occur. Juvenal told the story of one woman who, arriving late for a dinner party in Rome, slakes her thirst with "a couple of pints before dinner to create a raging appetite; then she brings it all up again and souses the floor with the washings of her insides."[1]

Self-indulgence and gluttony were both attributed to the Romans, not least because of Seneca's contemptuous and rather unfair comment that "from every quarter the Romans gather together every known and unknown thing to tickle a fastidious palate; the food which their stomachs by weakened indulgence can scarcely retain is fetched from the farthest oceans. They vomit that they might eat;

they eat that they may vomit. They do not deign even to digest the feasts for which they ransack the whole earth."[2] The Greeks also warned against shameless consumption of food, although it might be difficult to distinguish between gluttonous consumption of food and drink and gastronomic extravagance. Moralizing against both came from critics such as Seneca and Cicero. A warning against gluttony came from the Roman poet Persius, where a patient ignored the advice of his doctor: "Bloated with food and queasy of stomach he goes to bathe with sulphurous belching issuing from his throat. But as he drinks his wine a shivering fit comes over him and knocks the hot glass from his hands; his bared teeth chatter, the savoury morsels drop from his slack lips. Then follow the trumpet and the candles and last the dear deceased, laid out on a high bier, and smeared with greasy unguents, sticks out his stiff heels towards the door."[3]

Examples of obesity occur in Egyptian mummies, probably a consequence of eating too much fat, honey, and sweet cakes and excessive drinking. Mummies of Pharaohs Amenhotep III and Ramses III have large folds of skin on them, indicating that they were very fat. This may have been due as much to inflammation of the gallbladder as to overeating. Queen Hatshepsut is depicted on the wall of her temple at Deir el-Bahari as being grossly overweight. That obesity was not confined to the wealthy is shown by a wall relief of the Middle Kingdom where a grossly overweight harpist strains to reach the strings of the harp as he plays before Prince Aki.

People also become accustomed to types of food. Galen describes traveling near Pergamum when he was a young man. One day he came across some peasants who had already eaten their supper. Now the women were going to make bread. One woman put some wheat and water in a pot to boil, and then added some salt. Some of the mixture was scooped out and given to Galen and his companions to eat. This they felt they had to do partly out of courtesy for this hospitality and because they were hungry. When they had eaten they felt "it was as heavy as mud in their stomachs," and the whole of the next day they had very bad indigestion, no appetite, and were full of wind. "We also had blackouts before our eyes as nothing of what we had eaten could be evacuated," and this, he added, "is the only way by which indigestion can be relieved." The effect on Galen's stomach would be equivalent to eating newly baked bread, which, washed down with water, tends to swell. The peasants were more used to eating this simple fare than people who ate a greater variety of food.[4]

DIET

The Mediterranean diet has been assumed to be a healthy diet, comprising mainly pulses, cereals, vegetables, fruits, olive oil, cheese, fish, and only a little meat. To reduce this even further, cereals, vines, and olives are considered to be the essential parts of a dietary regime. But the benefit of this diet depends upon its availability. Food may not be equally gained or shared. Vines and olives may not be grown everywhere with equal success. Some products may be left out or substituted. In Egypt, sesame oil was used instead of olive oil. Even in Greece and Italy, wine and olive oil might not be readily available, although they could be provided by the wealthy as charity and at feasts given on festive occasions. People living near the seacoast or along the banks of a river would eat more fish, a good protein source and high in lysine, a vital amino acid. Those people living farther inland could have a supply of salted fish, but would be more dependent on land animals for their protein or, like the poor, eat more bread and pulses, which often led to indigestion and flatulence, an antisocial effect. Cereals and pulses were dominant foods, for there was no rival staple in the ancient world. Grain provided the bulk of food for the poor, rations for the soldiers, and supplies for urban residents. The superiority of the wealthy over their inferiors lay in their ability to obtain and consume other food than cereals and pulses.

The Celts living in the northern Europe could have a high-protein diet based on animal products. Meat is also rich in the B vitamins, especially B_{12}, which combats anemia and tiredness. This diet would be adequate in good summers, less so in the winter. Lack of fodder entailed killing of cattle, ensuring a feast of meat in the autumn while the culling was taking place, but little thereafter. Presumably every part of the animals would be used. Offal, although lower in energy value because of its lower fat content, has a protein content of high biological value and a high content of nicotinic acid, folic acid, and vitamin D.

Such a diet would be richer in fat and protein in summer than in winter. The fat content of the meat would be lower, because free-ranging animals have five times less fat than domesticated breeds. The carbohydrate content of the subsistence diet could be high in winter if its basis was the thick pottage. Pieces of meat and fish added to it would provide protein; so would the eggs of chickens and those collected from wild birds. This type of diet, although rich in fiber, could lack certain vitamins and minerals, and as the science of nutrition was not known, supplementary foods would not be eaten, thus making the diet somewhat debilitating.

Though berried fruits, and dog rose hips in particular, can be used to make healthy syrups, rich in vitamin C, there would certainly be a lack of that vitamin in winter in northern Europe, so that scurvy would be a constant threat. Both Hippocrates and Pliny knew of this disease from their description of gum ulceration. Iron deficiency, which causes hemoglobin levels to fall, resulting in anemia, would probably be avoided if iron cooking pots and cauldrons were used and a diet eaten containing pulses and wheat-germ cereals. A diet containing a large amount of indoles present in the cabbage family, dried beans, and lentils inhibits the formation of tumors. If lentils were part of a diet, then these would provide an excellent source of vitamins A, B, C, and D together with iron, phosphate, and potassium. Fat hen is particularly nutritious, providing iron, calcium, and vitamin B_1. Walnuts, hazelnuts, and other nuts can provide a valuable source of vitamin A.

One problem with a mainly cereal diet and especially the eating of bread made with a high fiber content is that as well as fiber it contains phytate; the consumption of this component interferes with the absorption of calcium and vital minerals such as iron, thus predisposing individuals to rickets and osteomalacia. Although rickets was not mentioned as a disease or as a specific ailment in parts of the ancient world, except as a deficiency in children, both it and osteomalacia have been found in bodies in Roman cemeteries, indicating a lack of vitamin D. No case of rickets was found in skeletal remains in Egypt. Children of the upper classes in Greece and Rome were swaddled and kept indoors rather than allowed to run free, which would have created a propensity toward rickets. Children of the poorer classes would have had more freedom but were probably more subject to an early life of hard labor helping their parents, and this could have caused other problems. Rickets, however, arises out of dietary deficiencies, along with other disorders, including anemia and dwarfism, and these are more likely to occur in people who eat a largely cereal diet.

Vitamin D is essential for the uptake and utilization of calcium in the skeletal structure and for the absorption of calcium from the gut. Egg yolks, liver, and fish oils can provide this, but the best source is the action of sun on steroids in the skin. Lack of sun in winter could be a problem in the northern European regions. On the other hand, the inhabitants would spend more time outdoors, and thus skin would be more exposed than is the case today. In Mediterranean lands exposure to sun might cause other problems; in Egyptian texts there is mention of skin being like the hide of a crocodile.

Calcium intake would be higher in summer than in winter because of the availability of green leafy vegetables and more fresh milk and cheese. Milk has a high calcium content essential for strengthening bones, small amounts of phosphorous and potassium, and a significant amount of protein. Retinol, or vitamin A, essential to repair surface body tissue, is more present in summer milk than winter milk, and this is when milk production would be more prolific. The Celts, as a milk-drinking and butter-eating people, would benefit from this. The Greeks and Romans, who disliked milk and butter and regarded them as food for barbarians, would lack this benefit.

This, together with a lack of liver, kidneys, and fish oils, could result in eye diseases such as night blindness and keratomalacia, a softened, perforated cornea. Roman oculist stamps with their carved retrograde inscriptions are testimony to the numerous cakes of eye salve into which they were pressed and that were given to recipients hoping to use them for a cure. A good cure for eye problems was eating liver, which was prescribed regularly by classical writers, although it took some courage to eat goat's liver on an empty stomach, as prescribed by Herophilus, a physician of Alexandria in the third century B.C.[5] As he also recommends an ointment of crocodile feces, vitriolic copper, and hyena bile mixed with honey, it was perhaps no wonder that his suggestion of goat's liver was equally regarded as questionable.

The Greek and Roman dislike or possible problem with milk might indicate a degree of lactose intolerance. The problem with unpasteur-ized milk is that it can carry disease-causing organisms, especially tuberculosis and brucellosis. Several examples of tuberculosis of the bone have been found in skeletons excavated from Roman sites; three were noted at the Roman town of Poundbury (England), which could have been caused by infected milk. In Egypt, bovine tuberculosis was rife from Neolithic times and was probably caused by close contact with livestock.

Fish provide an excellent source of protein, as it is rich in lysine, a vital amino acid lacking in a high-cereal diet; traces of vitamins C and D; and iodine. Calcium can be gained from eating the bones, and fluorine helps to prevent tooth decay. Fish need, however, to be transported, sold, and consumed rapidly. Growth of bacteria means that it deterio-rates, becoming both smelly and dangerous to health. Fastidious eaters would avoid it, and even those who were short of food would be wary of its nausea-producing effects. Pliny and Columella warned against eating fish that is anything less than fresh. In the second century A.D. Terentianus, a soldier stationed at Alexandria, wrote to his father, apologizing for not meeting him. He, with almost all the garrison, was unable to leave the camp for several days because of "so violent and dreadful an attack of fish poisoning."[6] Fish preserved in brine, however, kept for about a year and could be consumed during late winter and early spring, when food was scarce, or as a short-term response to famine. Iron is found in mollusks, so the huge consumption of oysters would be beneficial.

Roman adult taste tended toward the spicy and the robust. The Romans disliked bland tastes and added contrived sour, spicy, and bitter tastes by the use of herbs and spices. They countered those flavors by adding *liquamen* or olive oil. The oil blunted the bitter phytonutrients and, unknown to the Romans, had the added advantage of containing vitamin E. Care had to be taken, as oil could deteriorate, producing a rancid taste. Elaborate cuisine required that food should be civilized, or that wild food, as in the case of game and certain fruits, should be made more civilized. The trick of doing this was to bring them into the civilized area without overcooking; hence the use of condiments and sauces. Expert cooks made natural products unrecognizable, either in the specific dish or by misleading the diner. Hence vegetables were made into star and fish shapes. Roman cooks disguised meat as fish, indicating their patrons' preference for eating one product masquerading as another. One Apician entrée was shaped like a fish and made to taste like a fish, but was in reality well-salted liver; another—pounded cumin, pepper, and *liquamen* with ground walnuts poured into brine—resembled a dish of salt fish.

Plants and vegetables, if used quickly, would provide much-needed nutrients especially vitamins A and K, found in leafy greens. Slow transportation results in overripe vegetables, so the quicker the transfer of food from garden to table or from supplier to consumer, the better. Salmonella and listeria can occur through eating tainted food, and fertilization with sewage can lead to *E. coli* infection. Apicius gives advice on preserving food and preventing it from going bad. The problem often lies with food storage, especially with fish sauces. Food poisoning need not result in death, providing that immunity has been built up. It is with people who are unused to bad food that problems occur. That people survived infestation has been revealed by the analysis of fecal remains from a cesspit at Carlisle and sewers at York (England). Whipworms and roundworms, both of which live in the intestines, were present in huge numbers. Heavy infestation of these can cause dysentery.

In Egypt, as elsewhere, many plants had medicinal as well as nutritional uses. The sycamore fig aided stomach and intestinal disorders. Its crushed leaves were used as a laxative and to cure hippopotamus bites. The sap was placed on scars to darken them. Leeks also darkened scars and relieved bites. Watermelon had a purgative effect. Garlic, cooked with honey and vinegar, was used to expel tapeworm and parasites. Roasted in oil, garlic could be used to treat bruises. Garlic and goose grease were used as an eye drop, although the efficacy of this treatment may be doubted. Onions boiled in water were used as antibiotics, diuretics and expectorants, and even as vaginal douches. Even more problematic was a paste of peas, acacia leaves, honey, and moringa oil, which was used to stop bleeding from the womb. Eating peas was believed to combat heart trouble. Lupine beans were used for mouth rinses and dressings and as a paste used for softening stiff limbs. Bean-meal paste mixed with honey was used for a prolapsed rectum. Lettuce-seed oil was used to mix ointments, which would soften limbs, and when applied to the head would cure headaches. Celery was given to retain urine, which was puzzling as celery juice was also given as a diuretic. Mixed with sweet beer it was said to relieve toothache, while mixed with oil and sweet wine it could be used as a contraceptive.

In order to keep well, people would rely on plant and folk remedies, which would provide additional nutrients to the diet, as in the case of fat hen. Coughs and colds were relieved by the traditional method of milk and honey. A more efficacious remedy was mixing horehound with wine. An amphora that had contained this mixture was found in the Roman fort of Carpow in Scotland, presumably having been issued to the troops to combat coughs in the cold climate.[7] Fats with a high caloric value obtained from seeds were part of the Egyptian diet. The Greeks and Romans preferred olive oil, which was one of the main fats that helps to make a cereal diet palatable. A diet high in olive oil helps prevent coronary heart disease as well as mitigating the effects of arthritis, but probably few people lived long enough or lived such a sedentary life for heart disease to become a chronic health factor.

SCARCITY, FAMINE, AND MALNUTRITION

Food would be scarcer in winter. Meat and soft cheese might be in short supply, but grain would be available. The Egyptians and the Romans provided huge granaries for storage of grain. The Celts stored their grain in pits, lined with clay and covered with wooden or clay covers. Experimental archaeology has proved that when the pit is opened during the winter months to remove some grain, it is fresh and suitable to be ground into flour. Barley and spelt, roasted, pounded, and cooked with water in a cauldron, would make a thick pottage. Salting, drying, smoking, and steeping in brine would preserve some foods, but survival would depend on the weather; a harsh winter meant hunger. Galen mentioned that famine was more prevalent in rural areas than in the towns where people collected and stored food. Country people took a great deal of their produce to the towns to sell as cash crops and often finished their supplies before the end of winter; therefore they "had to fall back on unhealthy foods during the spring." These might even be "twigs and shoots of trees and bushes; and bulbs and roots of indigestible plants; they filled themselves with wild herbs and even fresh grass."[8]

This would not necessarily be true of all areas and all conditions. Possibly Galen was discussing severe crisis conditions in winter. His comment on grass might mean that country people were also eating edible weeds, which could have provided some nourishment. If Galen were being told these facts rather than witnessing conditions for himself, there might have been an element of political cunning in such descriptions. The peasantry, particularly in the Roman Empire, was heavily taxed. By exaggerating their misery they might avoid having their crops taken as part of the amount they were taxed.

Yet the large gulf between rich and poor in the ancient world was obvious. The diet of the poor was frugal, with a basic repetition built around staples of cereals, legumes, and occasional meat. Wealthy people in Egypt had a varied diet of fish, fowl, ox meat, fruit, vegetables, milk, beer, and wine. Poorer people survived on bread, onions, radishes, some vegetables, and beer, although they could obtain fish and wild fowl from the Nile regions. In Athens humble fare could consist of pottage, pressed olive skins, and sprats. Salt fish was considered food only for the lower classes. Food for poorer people usually consumed the best part of an income, the whole of the crops grown on a plot of land, or time given to preparing a meal. The Latin poem of the "Moretum," probably written to present an account of the heroic poor, nevertheless indicates the effort needed to get a simple meal. The Greek poet Hesiod's poem *Works and Days* dealt with friendly advice for the workingman, but underlying this theme was the hard life of a countryman and his vulnerability to hunger and shortage. Country people would rely on wild crops. Athenaeus has a telling story of the hardship faced in Greece by a poor family: "My husband is a pauper and I am an old woman with a daughter and a son, this boy and this nice girl, five in all. If three of us get a meal, the others must share only a small barley cake. We wail miserably when we have nothing and our faces grow pale with lack of food. The elements and the sum of a livelihood are these: a bean, a lupine, herbs, a turnip, pulses, vetch, cicada, chickpea, wild pea, beech nuts, an iris bulb, a wild pear and that god-given inheritance of our country, darling of my heart, a dried fig."[9]

She might have added that the poor relied heavily on food gathered from the wild or scraps left over from feasts given by the wealthy. They also suffered not only because of the difficulties in getting the product, but also in storing it and being able to cook it. Cooking implements and tableware needed storage places. Larger homes had cupboards where eating vessels could be placed. These were lacking in poorer homes, where reliance might be on one unhygienic pot.

Famines did occur in all areas of the ancient world. This could be the result of disease, warfare, climatic conditions, neglect of agriculture, or breakdown of food supplies. Virgil in the first book of his poem *Georgics* mentions the problems that farmers could face. These included delay in the arrival of rain or too heavy a downpour and diseases such as mildew or rust. Production of food crops in one area did not mean that the surplus was sent to relieve famine in another. Poor transport, bad roads, and climatic variation might result in famine; lack of political will meant that little was done to combat starvation conditions. War and sieges could also produce famine conditions. The destruction of crops was an offensive tactic in warfare. The main crops that suffered were vines and fruit trees, as they could be hacked down, and grain crops just before the time of harvest. Troops could reap these for their own supplies, as Caesar did in Gaul. Armies practiced a scorched-earth policy against enemies, commandeering all supplies and driving away cattle, leaving farmers without this year's harvest and next year's seed crop. Food prices in besieged cities and other places affected by famine would be subject to enormous increase. The poor would suffer the most, having to curtail their meager rations even more. Humans would consume edible weeds intended for cattle, thus depriving cattle of fodder. In Greece some states helped others by sending supplies of wheat, and the network of roads created by the Romans throughout their empire allowed supplies to be moved more easily. The poor might rely on their patrons for help, but many would starve or suffer malnutrition.

The early Egyptians suffered from a large number of famines, many being the result of too-great inundations of the Nile or its insufficiency. Peasants had to abandon their fields or neglect the irrigation dykes when called up for war. A seven-year famine, the result of the failure of the Nile to flood, in the reign of the Third Dynasty pharaoh Djoser about 2700 B.C., is recorded on a granite stone on the island of Sehel: "Children wept. Grown-ups swayed. As to the old their heart was sad, their kneels buckled, they sat on the ground, their arms swinging."[10] Bad harvests in 1116 B.C. led to peasants eating boiled papyrus leaves to avoid starvation and workmen at Deir el-Medina going on strike because their food wages were not paid. At the end of the Sixth Dynasty, about 2200 B.C., the system failed when large floods coincided with an adverse climate. The result was starvation on a large scale. In A.D. 99 the opposite happened. The Nile flood was only a small one, and therefore food was scarce. Emperor Trajan ordered ships coming from Egypt laden with grain for Rome to return so that the Egyptians could have basic food.

To try to combat years of shortages, the pharaohs built huge grain storehouses to conserve supplies ready for emergences. Other measures were taken. Amenimhet, the nomarch of the Oryx nome in the Twelfth Dynasty reign of Sesostris I (ca. 1971–1927 B.C.), had inscribed on the walls of his tomb, "When the great hunger appeared I then cultivated all the fields of the Oryx name as far as the southern and northern boundaries, giving life to the inhabitants and providing food. No man went hungry in it. I gave to the widow as equally to her who had a husband and made no distinction between the great and the small in all I gave. The came great inundations, bringers of crops and of all things, but I did not exact the years of land tax."[11]

Where there was grain there were fungal diseases, especially rust, and these could attack grain at any time. References in the Bible show that people in the Near East were aware of them. Rust was the result of too much moisture in a warm climate. Roman writers knew of it, and the Romans devised the festival of Robigalia, offering prayers and sacrifices to Robigus, the protecting god of farmers, and the Cerealia, for Ceres, the grain goddess.

Malnutrition is a deficiency disease, the result of the lack of availability of food and specific nutrients, especially nourishing foods and vitamins. It was a condition rather than an event, thus being constant even when there was no famine, especially among the lower classes and during the winter months. Studies of skeletal and teeth evidence of both adults and children have proved this. Radiological studies of the long bones of Egyptian mummies often reveal transverse calcified zones, known as Harris's lines, which are indicative of arrested growth, suggesting malnutrition or periods of vitamin deficiency. Children are especially prone to malnutrition, which could cause stunting, and this applied to both the wealthy and the poorer classes. Child-rearing practices undermined health, not that their parents realized this. The Roman upper classes regularly gave their babies into the care of a wet nurse, who might not have as rich breast milk as the mother, and were weaned very early, often onto unsuitable foods. Soranus, a Greek physician who practiced in Rome in the second century A.D., recommended they be weaned onto cereals, crumbs softened with milk or sweet wine or a soup made from spelt, and an egg.[12] Galen rather vaguely preferred "first bread, then vegetables, meat and other things grinding them before putting them into the babies mouths."[13] Both therefore recommended a cereal diet that would be low in nutrients. Boiled honey was recommended rather than milk. The babies were also swaddled, which denied them exercise and sunlight. The poorer classes probably weaned their children early so that the mother could get back to work. In either case, resistance to disease would not strengthened. Problems would occur if feeding vessels were not cleaned properly, leading to gastroenteritis or death.

Another problem caused by early weaning is bladder-stone, which can be a result of substituting poor milk and infected water for breast milk. Classical writers realized there was a problem. Pliny said it was "the most painful of all afflictions," but his remedies did not encourage confidence. Mouse droppings rubbed on the stomach was one.[14]

In times of hunger, people cannot be fussy, and it is as well to remember that the tastes of people in the ancient world might vary considerably from those in Europe and North Africa today. Food that was half rotten or "high" would be eaten as part of a normal diet. Many foods that tasted bitter, acrid, or astringent would be eaten because they provided nourishment or were what are known a "belly fillers." Recent work at the University of Washington Nutritional Sciences Program in Seattle, Washington, has determined that many people today do not like vegetables, and the feeling is mutual. Plants protect themselves against being eaten by producing bitter-tasting phytochemicals that are often toxic. Children almost always dislike bitter flavors, even if they develop more sophisticated tastes later. The prejudice against bitter flavors may protect people from poisoning themselves, but when food is scarce or when they are hungry, they may need to distinguish the toxic from those they merely dislike.

Not everyone suffered from malnutrition. Inhabitants of country regions would be aware of the abundance of plants, roots, and other crops, which would be useful. In the Roman period new varieties of crops were introduced to different parts of the empire, and some crops would be crossbred with these to give a better crop. Better breeding of sheep and cattle ensured finer animals. People might know nothing of nutrition, but of necessity they knew what they liked, what plants made them feel well, and which they thought were harmful to them. There would be a wide variety of taste tolerance, of necessity far more than there is today. People would produce their own palatable diet of foods associated with texture, smell, color, and taste—savory, sweet, and neutral. This food choice would, in general, give them a reasonable balance of protein, vitamins, minerals, and calories, which would suffice, providing that food was available. It was famine conditions that inevitably led to crises in diet and to poor nutrition.

TABOOS

The Romans seem to have been uninhibited in their eating habits, apart from not eating cats, dogs, or horses, although horses could be eaten in cases of extreme provocation. Galen said that some people of necessity ate the flesh of young asses, that snakes were eaten in Egypt, and, with some exaggeration, that the Greeks ate tortoises every day.[15] Both tortoises and turtles could be a food source, but not a popular one. Some parts of these reptiles were used in medicine. Galen, for example, made use of turtle blood and turtle bile.[16] Caesar commented that the Celts did not eat hare, geese, or chicken, but reared them for amusement and pleasure.[17] The remains of gnawed bones of these creatures on habitation sites prove that this taboo was ignored. The followers of Pythagoras and Empedocles in the late sixth and early fifth century B.C. would not eat animal flesh. They believed in the immortality of the soul and its reincarnation into another body. This could be either human or animal, and, if the latter, killing would be murder and eating could be cannibalism. Empedocles went even further and envisaged reincarnation into plant life. Porphyry of Tyre in the third century B.C. made a case for vegetarianism but was not concerned with the doctrine of reincarnation. He was more concerned with not eating animals because they have a soul. He regarded eating meat as not helping either the body or the soul, as it intensified human passions.

Pythagoras issued a specific taboo on eating beans. If a bean was split and exposed to the sun, it could smell of human semen. Pliny was also wary about eating beans because they could contain the souls of the dead. This would explain the use of beans in Roman rituals associated with the dead and their subsequent commemorating feasts. Herodotus claimed that the Egyptians did not eat beans, but beans have been found in Egyptian tombs, and although not as popular as other pulses, the broad bean was cultivated from the time of the Old Kingdom.

Herodotus was also responsible for present day Egyptologists believing for a long time that pork was taboo for the Egyptians. He said that any Egyptian who accidentally touched a pig would have to purify himself in the Nile. Egyptian priests were certainly forbidden to eat pork, which might have been self-denying ordinance rather than a taboo. Pigs were associated with the forces of darkness, especially as the god Seth, the enemy of Osiris, transformed himself into a black boar in his conflict with the sky god, Horus. Pigs were, however, kept on farms in the New Kingdom, and these are illustrated on tomb paintings. Although pork is not mentioned among offerings for the tomb dead, the pharaohs gave offerings of pigs to temples. Excavations of the workers' village at Tell el-Amarna have revealed a large pig farm and a considerable number of pig bones scored with knives. Possibly this meant that pork was eaten by the less wealthy as a cheap, low-status food. Pig bones, similarly scored, have also been found in excavations of other villages in Egypt. The distaste for pork may have been more to do with the unclean habits of pigs that wallowed in dirt and smelled or with the diseases that resulted from eating pork. Pork can transmit parasitic worms to human intestines, which cause trichinosis, resulting in pain, sweating, insomnia, and even death. Pork also spoiled more quickly than other meat and was probably taboo only to certain groups or, more understandably, at certain times of the year.

Egyptian priests considered it a religious duty to avoid salt, so they refused to eat food cooked with it. Plutarch made the sensible suggestion that they did this because eating salt sharpened the appetite and made them more inclined to eating and drinking.[18] Sea salt was taboo to most of the population, as it was associated with the kingdom of Seth. Salt was brought from the Siwa oasis and elsewhere for the general population. Priests were reputed to avoid eating beans, onions, and garlic. Paintings in tombs show priests receiving offerings of these, but they may have passed them on as gifts to worshippers. They did eat very well of other foods. Herodotus said that "they have no expense and trouble in everyday life. The grain is ground for them and they enjoy a plentiful food supply of beef and goose; they also have proper wine."[19] Wine was offered to Egyptian deities, but occasionally, as in the temple at Heliopolis, wine was strictly forbidden even in libations, and the priests were forbidden to drink it. Plutarch said that in other places the priests poured it on the altars of the gods, "in imitation of the blood of those enemies who had formerly fought against them. Sometimes the wine was merely sprinkled on the ground."[20]

If Herodotus is correct, priests abstained from eating fish, and for some people eating some kinds of fish was also taboo: "Therefore on the ninth day of the first month when all the rest of the Egyptians are obliged by their religion to eat a fried fish before the doors of their houses, they [the priests] only burn them not tasting them at all."[21] This taboo was because of damage that fish had done to the god Osiris. Osiris had been attacked by his brother Seth, who cut up the body and scattered the pieces. All were recovered by Isis, Osiris's wife, except for the phallus, which had been eaten by three fish, the lepidotus (the carplike barbus), the phargus (probably a catfish), and the oxyrhynchus (a common fish with an elongated snout). Isis created a replacement for the phallus and impregnated herself, producing Horus, who avenged Osiris, who became ruler of the underworld. In some parts of Egypt, priests trampled on and mangled fish as part of festival ritual.

At Esna, perch were not eaten. Thousands of mummified perch were found in tombs there. Sometimes the catch was dedicated to the spirit of the deceased and presented as a gift to the marsh goddesses Sekhet and Hathor. Animals were sacrificed to the gods. These included goats, poultry, and fish. The animals had their feet tied, were put on the ground, and then had their throats cut. The shoulders, thighs, ribs, rump, heart, and kidneys were put on the altar. The head was taken to market, sold to strangers, or given the poor. The altar offerings were burned at first. Later only certain portions were burned. The remainder was given to the priests or sometimes to those who had presented the sacrifice.

Roman priests also had food taboos. These included raw flesh and beans. Priests of Jupiter were forbidden to eat bread fermented with yeast. Sometimes they avoided wine because of drunkenness and or its association with Bacchic revels. Plutarch asked why priests did not touch flour or yeast. The answer was because they were incomplete foods.[22] Flour and yeast had not yet become bread or attained the usefulness of food. Yeast was itself the product of corruption and produced corruption in the dough with which it was mixed, for the dough becomes flabby and inert. The priests also avoided raw meat because it was not a living creature and had not been cooked. It was repulsive, like a flesh wound.

TEETH: DIET AND HYGIENE

Dental care was always a problem in the ancient world. That there was a fear of toothache and loss of teeth is indicated by the Egyptians believing that dental caries could be attributed to a worm: "After Anu made the heavens, the heavens made the earth, the earth made the rivers, the rivers made the canals, the canals made the marsh, the marsh made the Worm. The Worm came weeping unto Samas, came unto Ea, her tears flowing. 'What wilt thou give me for my food, what wilt thou give me to destroy?' 'I will give thee dried figs and apricots.' 'What are those dried figs and apricots to me? Set me amid the teeth and let me dwell in the gums, that I may destroy the blood of the teeth and of the gums chew the marrow. So shall I hold the latch of the door.'"[23] This lament for the state of the teeth is from early dynastic Egypt, where extreme tooth wear resulted in pulp exposure and abscess formation, and this is confirmed by the bad state of a woman's teeth whose repast was provided in her tomb at Saqqara. She had lost all her teeth on one side of her mouth.

A high-fiber diet protects the teeth because it is more abrasive and scours the teeth more than does a highly refined diet. The drawback was that if flour was not sieved well, the grit remained in the baked loaf. In the "Moretum," after Simulus had milled his grain, he sieved the flour carefully. The refuse stayed in the sieve while the pure flour was sieved out, cleansed of impurities. Lucretius, the first-century B.C. Roman poet and philosopher, stated that the teeth have a share in the sensations of the body, as is shown by toothaches and twinges from cold water and biting on a sharp stone in a piece of bread. Seneca noted that "a benefit rudely given by a hardheaded man was like a loaf of gritty bread, which a starving man needs must accept but which is bitter to eat."[24] Horace, on his journey to Brindisium, mentioned stopping at a place to buy water and fine bread because "later in Canosium [modern Canosa] the bread is gritty and the water poor."[25]

Grit in bread was a factor in grinding down the teeth, as was evident in skulls found in Egyptian tombs. Some skulls had their teeth so ground down that it was suggested that sand was deliberately added to grain as a cutting agent to speed up the process of grinding flour. Microscopic grains of sand also came from using saddle querns. Querns imported into Roman Britain from the Eifel district of Germany were notorious for producing a huge amount of grit. The grinding surfaces on some teeth found in skulls in Roman cemeteries as at Cirencester (England) were almost completely worn down; at Trentholme Drive and Chigwell (England), many skulls had teeth that showed evidence of abscesses in the alveolar bone. These would be painful and make chewing difficult. Examination of the teeth of many adults found in 1980 in the boat shelters at Herculaneum in which they had taken refuge showed enamel hypoplasia (stress marks), which indicates the consequences of arrested growth due to poor nutrition. At Poundbury (Dorset, England) the teeth of many young people unearthed displayed hypoplasia (growth deficiency).

Early loss of teeth would have an important effect on diet. This would be exacerbated by having no false teeth to replace the lost or damaged teeth. Juvenal presented a pathetic picture of an old man who prayed to the god Jupiter for a long life. His prayers were answered, but he soon found that old men have "voices as shaky as their limbs, with the smooth head and the runny nose of babyhood; their voices tremble as much as their limbs and they mumble their bread with toothless gums."[26] They were a burden to their wives, their children, and themselves.

Oral hygiene was a problem. Pliny had advised that teeth could be cleaned with a toothpick and a mixture of ground-up oyster shells and charcoal. As this was unpleasant, it was mixed with honey, which would undo any of the good work. In Egypt, periodontal disease was prevalent, leading to loss of teeth and subsequent problems with chewing. Attrition of teeth leads to the dental pulp being exposed, which in turn leads to abscesses. Many Egyptian skulls have jawbones with small holes drilled in them. This may have been to drain the pus or the result of the pus dissolving the bone. Either way, the abscesses would have caused great pain and made the breath smell. Similar evidence of abscesses in the alveolar bone has been found in Roman skulls in Europe. A remedy in an Egyptian papyrus advised a mixture of cumin, frankincense, and carob-pod pulp to relieve toothache. A mixture of frankincense, myrrh, cinnamon, and other fragrant spices and plants boiled with honey and shaped into a sweet was used to combat bad breath.

Not everyone in the ancient world lost his or her teeth. Sometimes people kept them into middle age or even until they died. Teeth in skulls in Roman cemeteries at Chichester, Cirencester, York, and Ilchester (England) indicate a lack of dental caries. This may have been due to a lack of sweet foods and a complete absence of sugar, but these areas also have a high natural fluoride content in the water, and absorption of fluoride would be a factor.

CEMETERY AND TOMB EVIDENCE

Skeletal evidence can show a connection between diet and disease. At Cirencester (England), out of 362 Romano-British skeletons examined in 1969–1976, 80 percent revealed evidence of osteoarthritis, a similar number to those who had suffered from this disease in the Trentholme Drive cemetery at York.[27] This is a "wear and tear" disease, often the result of a lack of calcium in youth. It can cause immense pain and eventually disability. Those who had it could be a burden on the community. Pliny the Younger mentioned that Domitius Tullus was crippled and deformed in every limb, so that he could not turn in bed without assistance and had to have his teeth cleaned for him.

Some skeletons in Romano-British cemeteries and at Herculaneum have a high bone-lead content. This could have been caused in a soft-water area by the drinking water running in lead pipes, but many skeletons reflected a lifetime accumulation. Some children had died of lead poisoning; the unborn may have absorbed it through their mothers' milk. Those persons surviving into middle age had ingested it from food cooked or resting in lead pans or through fruit juices and wine prepared in lead or pewter vessels. The acidity of the fruit caused traces of lead to dissolve. Fruit juices could be added to wine so that the amount of lead intensified in the solution. Persons suffering from lead poisoning develop a metallic taste in the mouth and experience lack of appetite; lead ingestion results in digestive trouble and diarrhea. To counter lack of appetite, victims eat more highly spiced and seasoned food, which Roman cookery provides. Inhumations in Selinunte in Sicily show that adults and children have furrows in the eye sockets, indicating a lack of iron, possibly due to food shortages. Some of the skeletons at Herculaneum had high zinc readings, which can be interpreted as resulting from a high consumption of crustaceans, oysters, dry fruit, and legumes. This diet, which lacks meat protein, can also be responsible for cases of anemia.

Skeletons found in a Roman cemetery at Dorchester (Dorset, England) have recently been examined to determine the protein composition of bone material. The carbon and nitrogen ratios in bone can be measured to give average protein intake and the proportion of shellfish, vegetable, and meat protein consumed by a person over the last 10 years of life. Two periods were studied. In the first century A.D., when Roman influence was just beginning to be felt among the Celtic population, people were buried in simple graves with few grave goods. The carbon-isotopes ratio in their bones revealed that they had eaten average amounts of animal and plant protein. They were still eating food that could be hunted and herded or grown and gathered easily.

By the fourth century those buried in the cemetery had lived in the prosperous Roman town of Durnovaria. Some people were being buried in stone coffins with more personal possessions, and those of the higher social strata had stone tombs. This wealthier part of the community apparently ate very well and much better than those buried in wooden coffins. Shellfish had been eaten frequently and the diet was high in meat. The carbon ratio of two people was, however, so high that it might imply they were recent immigrants or administrators from Rome or southern Gaul, the warmer Mediterranean regions, where carbon is absorbed at a higher rate.

Lack of good hygienic habits, especially with regard to foodstuffs, can lead to problems ranging from mild discomfort to chronic sickness. Good hygiene always matters where food is concerned, but this was impossible in most parts of the ancient world. Oribasius, quoting Diocles, recommended cleaning whatever was uncooked, stripping off everything that was of no use, and "removing anything which was troublesome about them." Food should be boiled, soaked, and washed several times if it had an impurity. How far these recommendations could be adhered to was an individual matter.[28] Even allowing for tolerance for poor or bad food, there would be cases of food poisoning and dysentery, causing weakness or death.

Infestation sometimes caused death as well as debilitation. A woman in the Orton Longueville cemetery (Cambridgeshire, England) died from drinking impure water. A calcified hydatid cyst the size of a chicken's egg, caused by swallowing the larvae stage of a tapeworm, had found its way into the thoracic cavity. The bursting of the abscess in the lung or the plural cavity probably caused death. In Egypt a similar cyst was found in the lung of a female mummy, seemingly named Asru, which may not have killed her but would have caused a chronic cough.

The Egyptian mummy of a male weaver called Nakht from the Twentieth Dynasty, who died before he was 18, showed he had chronic liver cirrhosis and a ruptured spleen. He had been infested by the parasite *Trichinella spiralis,* a result of eating poorly cooked pork. Lack of accurate medical records can only give rise to speculation regarding the fate of the population in the ancient world. It is impossible, for example, to say how many women died in childbirth of hemorrhage, puerperal fever, or lack of nourishment after giving birth. The number of infants buried with mothers in Roman cemeteries suggests that risks of childbirth were great; descriptions of birth from Egyptian papyri suggest the same.

The large number of leg ulcers affecting the fibulas and tibias of skeletons in Romano-British cemeteries can indicate a lack of vitamin C, probably arising because the inhabitants lacked fresh fruit and vegetables or because of climatic conditions or deterioration in living standards. In the Chigwell (England) cemetery, out of 36 burials, there were 11 cases of hypoplastic development of the tooth enamel, showing lack of growth due to disease or malnutrition. Four cases of cribra orbitalia and four cases of porosity of the cranium indicated diet-deficiency anemia.

At times resistance was weakened by causes other than lack of good nutrition. Plagues struck Egypt several times, killing many of the population. A particularly vicious one swept the Nile valley in 1500 B.C. Classical literature tells of plague sweeping through Athens in 430 B.C. while Spartan armies besieged the city, and in the Roman Empire in the fourth and fifth centuries. About A.D. 443 there is mention of a *pestilentia quae fere in toto orde diffusa est* (a plague which spread through the whole society), and the British cleric and historian Gildas in the sixth century also recorded a *pestifera lues* (disastrous plague).[29] The black rat (*Rattus rattus*), whose fleas carried the bubonic-plague bacillus, was known to have existed in the ancient world, but plague also manifested itself in the form of infectious viral hemorrhagic fever. Pestilence, no matter in what form, would have had a debilitating effect on the population. Malaria and tuberculosis were common. Survivors, weakened by disease and perhaps infested by parasites, would find it difficult to regain their strength and therefore would succumb through weakness or a secondary ailment. Famine would exacerbate the condition. Toward the end of the fourth century A.D. and into the fifth, when disease seems to have begun to be commonplace, no amount of good food could provide immunity from endemic diseases.

Evidence from skeletons in Roman Britain shows the extent to which undernourishment and a life of unremitting hard labor took its toll. This is seen in skeletal evidence for the heights and life expectancy of men and women. The average height for men was 1.69 meters (5 feet 7 inches) and for women 1.63 meters (5 feet 4 inches), but many men were about 1.5 meters (4 feet 1 inch) and women below that height. The low stature is confirmed by skeletal evidence from Herculaneum, where the average height for men was 1.68 meters (5 feet 6 inches) and for women 1.5 meters (4 feet 1 inch). At Pompeii it was 1.67 meters (5 feet 5 inches) for men and 1.5 meters (5 feet 1 inch) for women. The same seems to have been the case in the classical period in Athens.

Evidence from Greece and the Roman Empire seems to indicate that few people achieved a ripe old age. Life expectancy in Greece about 400 B.C., seems to have been about 30 years. In Rome, where overcrowding was rife, life expectancy was even lower—about 25 years. The skeletal evidence for death in Roman Britain reveals that middle age could be considered old age and that few people reached beyond the age of 55. Out of 21 adults in the Chigwell cemetery, the average age of death was 35 for males and 28 for females. Few in Cirencester had lived beyond the age of 50. At Ilchester (Somerset), out of 49 adults, the oldest male was 45 and the oldest female 50. The average age of death at the Lankhills cemetery, Winchester (Hampshire), was low; only 52 out of 284 adults seem to have survived beyond the age of 36. The average age of death of persons in the Dorchester (Oxfordshire) cemetery was 33. At one Chichester cemetery, the adult males had all died in their mid-30s. Added to this, there was a very high rate of infant mortality, caused by poor hygiene and lack of adequate medical help.

In Egypt, the average life expectancy was even lower, averaging between 22 and 27 years of age. Excavations of shelf tombs at the cemetery of the Late Period (747–332 B.C.) to the Ptolemaic period in the mastaba of Ptahshepses at Abusir found that the average age of death was 19.5 years for women and 21.5 for men.[30] Investigation of mummies revealed that a few had reached the age of 60 or 70, but these were of the wealthier class. Many of the pharaohs died young. A few lived to the age of 50, and although Pharaoh Ramses II lived until he was over 90, he had suffered from calcified temporal arteries in the head, which must have resulted in him making incoherent decisions. Although Herodotus stated that next to the Libyans the Egyptians were the "healthiest of men," a fact that he attributed to their climate and their diet, they had other problems.[31] The chief reason for the low life expectancy among the general population was probably the different standards of diet and general care, combined with poor hygiene, the prevalence of larvae of parasitic worms, the high incidence of epidemic diseases, and the general inability of doctors to provide cures. Much the same might be said for the rest of the ancient world.

In Britain two tombstones record the ages of Julius Verens, a veteran of the Second Legion, stationed at Caerleon, who lived to be 100, and his wife, who lived to be 75, but as it is unlikely that they knew when they were born, these ages must be regarded with some skepticism.[32] More reliable evidence comes from excavation in cemeteries. A report on the Winchester (Lankhills) cemetery states that the evidence "is consistent with that of tombstones and other excavations in suggesting that life in Roman Britain was indeed short." Out of a possible 290 burials in a Roman cemetery at York, "a mere handful" lived beyond the age of 45. The excavators of that cemetery probably speak for the whole of the Roman Empire and possibly the ancient world when they reported soberly that "there is compelling evidence that the majority of the denizens of second, third and fourth century York could not expect long to survive their fortieth year."[33] Indeed, the conclusion of this report is that 77 percent of them died before then.

NOTES

1. Juvenal, *Satires* 6, 430–433.

2. Seneca, "De Consolatione ad Helviam," in *Epistulae Morales* 10.3.

3. Persius, *Satires,* translated and edited by P. Grean (Harmondsworth, England: Penguin Press, 1973), 3.98–103.

4. Galen, *AF* 6.498–499.

5. Herophilus, *On Eyes,* fragment 260; Herophilus, *The Art of Medicine in Early Alexandria,* translation with essays by Heinrich von Sraden (Cambridge: Cambridge University Press, 1989).

6. Roy Davies, "The Roman Military Diet," *Britannia,* 2 (1971): 130.

7. Lindsay Allason-Jones, "Health Care in the Roman North," *Britannia,* 30 (1999): 133–140.

8. Galen, *AF* 6.749–750.

9. Athenaeus, *D* 55a.

10. Quoted in C. Reeves, *Egyptian Medicine* (Princes Risborough, England: Shire Publications, 1992), 11.

11. T. James, *Pharaoh's People: Scenes from Life in Imperial Egypt* (London: Bodley Head, 1984), 113.

12. Soranus, *Gynaecology,* translated by O. Temkin with the assistance of N. J. Eastman, L. Edelstein, and A. F. Guttmacher (Ann Arbor, Mich.: University Microfilms International, 1982), 2.46.

13. Galen, *Hygiene,* a translation of *Salens Hygiene (De Sanitate Tuenda)* by Robert M. Green (Springfield, Ill.: Charles C. Thomas, 1951), 10.3.1.

14. Pliny, *NH* 30.21.65–68.

15. Galen, *De Simplicium Medicamentorum Temperamentis ac Facultatibus (On the Properties of Simples),* vol. 2., text and translation by Mark Grant (London: Routledge, 2000), 6.663–670. Hereafter *SF.*

16. Galen *SF* 12.310.

17. Caesar, *De Bello Gallico* 5.12.

18. Plutarch, "De Iside et Osiride," in *Moralia,* vol. 5, 352.5.

19. Herodotus, 2.37.4.

20. Plutarch, "De Iside et Osiride," in *Moralia,* vol. 5, 6.

21. Herodotus, 2.37.

22. Plutarch, "The Roman Questions," in *Moralia,* vol. 4, 289e–f.

23. Quoted in Ricardo Caminos, *Late Egyptian Miscellania* (Oxford: Oxford University Press, 1954), 197.

24. Lucretius, *On the Nature of the Universe,* translated by R. Latham (Harmondsworth, England: Penguin Press, 1951), 3.690–95; Seneca, "De Beneficiis," in *Epistulae Morales,* vol. 3, translated by J. W. Basore (London: Loeb Classical Library, 1935), 2.7.1.

25. Horace, *Satires* 1.5.86–89.

26. Juvenal, *Satires* 10, 200–202.

27. A. Mcwhirr, L. Viner, and C. Wells, *Romano-British Cemeteries at Cirencester: Cirencester Excavations II* (Cirencester, England: Cirencester Excavation Committee, 1982), esp. 135–202.

28. Oribasius, *Medical Compilations* 4 3.2–3.

29. Gildas, *De Excidio et Conquestu Britanniae* 22; *The Ruins of Great Britain and Other Works,* translated and edited by M. Winterbothom (London: Phillamore, 1978).

30. Eugen Strouhal, *Life of the Ancient Egyptians* (Liverpool: Liverpool University Press, 1996), 256.

31. Herodotus, 2.77.

32. R. G. Collingwood and R. P. Wright (eds.), *The Roman Inscriptions of Britain,* vol. 1, *Inscriptions on Stone* (Oxford: Clarendon Press, 1965), nos. 363, 373.

33. L. P. Wenham, *The Romano-British Cemetery at Trentholme Drive, York.* Ministry of Public Buildings and Works, Archaeological Reports no. 5 (London: HMSO), 147–148.

SELECTED BIBLIOGRAPHY

GENERAL REFERENCE

Alcock, Joan P. *Food in Roman Britain*. Stroud, England: Tempus Publishing, 2001.

Amouretti, M.-C., and J. P. Brun (eds.). *La Production du Vin et de l'huile en Méditerranée*. Athens: École Française D'Athènes, 1993.

André, J. *L'alimentation et la Cuisine à Rome*. Paris: Libraire C. Klincksieck, 1961.

Boatwright, Mary T., Daniel J. Gargola, and Richard J. A. Talbot. *The Romans: From Village to Empire*. New York: Oxford University Press, 2004.

Brewer, Douglas J., Donald B. Redford, and Susan Redford. *Domestic Plants and Animals: The Egyptian Origins*. Warminster, England: Aris and Phillips, 1993.

Brewer, Douglas J., and Emily Teeter. *Egypt and the Egyptians*. New York: Cambridge University Press, 1993.

Brothwell, D., and P. Brothwell. *Food in Antiquity*. London: Thames and Hudson, 1969.

Brun, J.-P., and A. Tchernia. *La Vin Romaine Antique*. Grenoble, France: Glénat, 1999.

Dalby, Andrew. *Empire of Pleasures: Luxury and Indulgence in the Roman World*. New York: Routledge, 2000.

———. *Food in the Ancient World from A–Z*. New York: Routledge, 2003.

———. *Siren Feasts: A History of Food and Gastronomy in Greece*. New York: Routledge, 1995.

Darby, William J., Paul Ghalioungui, and Louis Grivetti. *Food: The Gift of Osiris*. 2 vols. London: Academic Press, 1977.

Davidson, Alan. *The Oxford Companion to Food*. New York: Oxford University Press, 1999.

Erman, Adolf. *The Ancient Egyptians: A Sourcebook of Their Writings*. New York: Harper and Row, 1966.

Flower, Barbara, and Elisabeth Rosenbaum. *Apicius: The Roman Cookery Book*. London: Harrop, 1961.

Frank, Tenny. *An Economic Survey of Ancient Rome*. Vol. 5, *Rome and Italy of the Empire*. Baltimore, Md.: John Hopkins University Press, 1940.

Garnsey, Peter, and Richard Saller. *The Roman Empire: Economy, Society and Culture*. London: Duckworth, 1987.

Grant Mark. *Roman Cookery: Ancient Recipes for a Modern Kitchen*. London: Serif, 1999.

Kiple, Kenneth F., and Kriemhild Coneé Ornelas (eds.). *The Cambridge World History of Food*. Cambridge: Cambridge University Press, 2000.

Morris, Ian, and Barry B. Powell. *The Greeks: History, Culture, and Society*. Upper Saddle River, N.J.: Pearson Prentice Hall, 2005.

Nicholson, P. T., and Ian Shaw (eds.). *Ancient Egyptian Materials and Technology*. Cambridge: Cambridge University Press, 2000.

Toynbee, Jocelyn. *Animals in Roman Life and Art*. Baltimore, Md.: John Hopkins University Press, 1996.

Wilkins, John, David Harvey, and Mike Dobson (eds.). *Food in Antiquity*. Exeter, England: Exeter University Press, 1995.

Zohary, Daniel, and Maria Hoft. *Domestication of Plants in the Old World: The Origin and Spread of Cultivated Plants in West Asia, Europe and the Nile Valley*. Oxford: Clarendon Press; New York: Oxford University Press, 1993.

CHAPTER 1

Beloch, Karl J. *Die Bevölkerung der Griechisch-Römischen Welt*. Leipzig, Germany: Dunker and Humblot, 1886.

Burford, A. *Land and Labor in the Greek World*. Baltimore, Md.: John Hopkins University Press, 1993.

Casson, L. *Periplus Maris Erythraci (The Periplus of the Erythraean Sea): Text, Translation and Commentary*. Princeton, N.J.: Princeton University Press, 1989.

Crawford, Dorothy. "Food: Tradition and Change in Hellenistic Egypt." *World Archaeology*, 11.2 (1979): 136–146.

Drinkwater, J. *Roman Gaul: The Three Provinces, 55 BC–AD 260*. London: Croom Helm, 1983.

Erman, Adolf. *Life in Ancient Egypt*. 1894. Reprint, New York: Dover Books, 1971.

Flacelière, Robert. *La Vie Quotidienne en Grèce en Temps de Périclès*. Paris: Hachette, 1959.

Forrest, W. G. *A History of Sparta 950 BC–AD 260*. London: Bristol Classical Press, 1995.

Garnsey, Peter, Keith Hopkins, and C. R. Whittaker (eds.). *Trade in the Ancient Economy*. London: Chatto and Windus, 1983.

Grant, Michael. *History of Rome*. London: Weidenfeld and Nicolson, 1978.

Greene, K. *The Archaeology of the Roman Economy*. Berkeley: University of California Press, 1991.

Isager, S., and J. E. Skydsgaard. *Ancient Greek Agriculture: An Introduction*. New York: Routledge, 1992.

James, Simon. *Exploring the World of the Celts*. New York: Thames and Hudson, 1993.

Kruta, V., O. Frey, B. Raftery, and M. Stabo (eds.). *The Celts*. New York: Rizzoli, 1991.

Lichtheim, Miriam. *Ancient Egyptian Literature: A Book of Readings*. Vol. 3, *The Late Period*. Berkeley: University of California Press, 1980.

Ling, Roger. *The Insula of the Menander at Pompeii*. Vol. 1, *The Structures*. Oxford: Clarendon Press, 1997.

Littman, R. J., and M. L. Littman. "Galen and the Antonine Plague." *American Journal of Philology*, 94 (1973): 143–255.

Maiurii, A. *La casa del Menander e il suo tesoro di argenteria I*. Rome: Libreria dello Stato, 1933.

McNeill, W. H. *Plagues and People*. City Garden, N.Y.: Anchor Press, 1976.

Miller, J. L. *The Spice Trade of the Roman Empire*. Oxford: Clarendon Press, 1969.

Murray, Oswyn. *Early Greece*. 2nd ed. London: Fontana, 1993.

Powell, T.G.E. *The Celts*. New York: F. A. Praeger, 1958.

Préaux, Claire. *Les Grecs en Égypt d'après les Archives de Zénon*. Brussels: Fondation Égyptologique Reine Élizabeth, 1947.

Reynolds, Peter J. *Iron-Age Farm: The Butser Experiment*. London: British Museum Publications, 1979.

Ross, Anne. *The Pagan Celts*. London: Batsford, 1986.

Salway, Peter. *Roman Britain*. New York: Oxford University Press, 1981.

Sparkes, Brian A. (ed.). *Greek Civilization: An Introduction*. Oxford: Blackwell Publishers, 1998.

Strouhal, Eugen. *Life of the Ancient Egyptians*. Liverpool: Liverpool University Press, 1996.

Wilkinson, A. *The Garden in Ancient Egypt*. London: Rubicon Press, 1998.

CHAPTER 2

Alcock, Joan P. "Flavourings in Roman Culinary Taste with Special Reference to the Province of Britain." In H. Walker (ed.), *Spicing up the Palate: Studies of Flavourings Ancient and Modern: Proceedings of the Oxford Symposium on Food and Cookery*, 11–22. Totnes, England: Prospect Books, 1992.

———. *Food in Roman Britain*. Stroud, England: Tempus Publishing, 2001.

Andrews, A. C. "Alimentary Use of Hoary Mustard in the Classical Period." *Isis*, 34 (1942): 161–162.

———. "Alimentary Use of Lovage in the Classical Period." *Isis*, 33 (1941–42): 514–518.

———. "The Carrot as Food in the Classical Period." *Classical Philology*, 44 (1949): 182–196.

———. "Melons and Watermelons in the Classical Period." *Osiris*, 12 (1956): 368–375.

———. "The Opium Poppy as Food and Spice in the Classical Period." *Agricultural History*, 26 (1952), 152–155.

———. "Oysters as a Food in Greece and Rome." *Classical Journal*, 43 (1948): 299–303.

———. "Thyme as a Condiment in the Graeco-Roman Era." *Osiris*, 13 (1958): 127–156.

———. "The Turnip as Food in the Classical Era." *Classical Philology*, 53 (1958): 131–152.

———. "The Use of Rue as a Spice by the Greeks and Romans." *Classical Journal*, 43 (1948): 371–373.

Arndt, Alice. "Silphium." In H. Walker (ed.), *Spicing Up the Palate: Studies of Flavourings Ancient and Modern: Proceedings of the Oxford Symposium on Food and Cookery*, 28–35. Totnes, England: Prospect Books 1992.

Boardman, J. "The Olive in the Mediterranean: Its Culture and Use." In J. Hutchinson (ed.), *The Early History of Agriculture*, 187–196. London: Philosophical Transactions of the Royal Society of London, 1976.

Brewer, Douglas J., and Renée· F. Friedman. *Fish and Fishing in Ancient Egypt*. Warminster, England: Aris and Phillips, 1989.

Brewer, Douglas J., D. B. Redford, and S. Redford. *Domestic Plants and Animals: The Egyptian Origins*. Warminster, England: Aris and Phillips, 1994.

Casson, Lionel. "Cinnamon and Cassis in the Ancient World." In Lionel Casson, *Ancient Trade and Society*, 225–246. Detroit, Mich.: Wayne State University Press, 1984.

Charles, M. P. "Onions, Cucumbers and the Date Palm." *Bulletin on Sumerian Agriculture*, 3 (1987): 1–21.

Coin, J. "Carob or St John's Bread." *Economic Botany*, 5 (1951): 82–96.

Crane, Eva. *The Archaeology of Beekeeping*. London: Duckworth, 1983.

Crawford, Dorothy. "Garlic-Growing and Agricultural Specialisation in Graeco-Roman Egypt." *Chronique Égypt*, 96 (1973): 350–363.

Curtis, Robert I. *Garum and Salsamenta: Production and Commerce in Material Medica*. New York: Brill, 1991.

De Brisey, K. W., and K. A. Evans. *Salt: The Study of an Ancient Industry.* Colchester, England: Colchester Archaeological Group Publications, 1975.

Drachmann, A. G. *Ancient Oil Mills and Presses.* Copenhagen: Leven and Munksgaard, 1932.

Dumont, J. "La Pêche du Thon à Byzance à l'époque Hellénistique." *Revue des Études Anciennes,* 78–79 (1976–77): 96–117.

Étienne, R. "A Propos du 'Garum Sociorum.'" *Latomus,* 29 (1970): 297–313.

Flint-Hamilton, K. B. "Legumes in Ancient Greece and Rome: Food, Medicine or Poison?" *Hesperia,* 68 (1999): 371–385.

Frayn, Joan. *Sheep-Rearing and the Wool Trade in Italy during the Roman Period.* Liverpool, England: Cairns, 1984.

Frost, Frank. "Sausage and Meat Preservation in Antiquity." *Greek, Roman and Byzantine Studies,* 40 (1999): 241–252.

Gallant, T. *A Fisherman's Tale: An Analysis of the Potential Production of Fishing in the Ancient World.* Micellanea Graeca Fasciculus 7. Ghent, Belgium: State University Press, 1985.

Grant, Mark *Dieting for an Emperor: A Translation of Books 1 and 4 of Oribasius' Medical Compilations with an Introduction and Commentary.* Leiden, the Netherlands: Brill, 1997.

Grimal, P., and T. Monod. "Sur la Véritable Nature du Garum." *Revue des Études Anciennes,* 54 (1952): 27–38.

Gunther, R. T. "The Oyster Culture of the Ancient Romans." *Journal of the Marine Biological Association,* 4 (1897): 360–365.

Helttula, Anne. "Truffles in Ancient Greece and Rome." *Arctos,* 30 (1996), 33–47.

Houlihan, Patrick F. *The Birds of Ancient Egypt.* Warminster, England: Aris and Phillips, 1986.

Hyman, P., and M. Hyman. "Long Pepper: A Short History." *Petits Propos Culinaires,* 6 (1980): 50–52.

Jasny, N. *The Wheats of Classical Antiquity.* Baltimore, Md.: John Hopkins University Press, 1944.

Jones, J. E. "Hives and Honey of Hymettus." *Archaeology,* 29.2 (1976): 80–91.

Kuény, G. "Scénes Apicoles dans l'ancienne Égypte." *Journal of Near Eastern Studies,* 9 (1950): 84–93.

Laufer, Berthold. "Malabathron." *Journal Asiatique,* 11 Ser. 12 (1918): 5–49.

Lindsell, Alice. "A Note on Greek Crocus." In J. E. Raven, *Plants and Plant Lore in Ancient Greece,* 49–54. Oxford: Leopard's Head Press, 2000.

Mattingly, David J. "First Fruit? The Olive in the Roman World." In Graham Shipley and John Salmon (eds.), *Human Landscapes in Classical Antiquity,* 213–253. New York: Routledge, 199.

Moritz, L. A. *Grain Mills and Flour in Classical Antiquity.* Oxford: Clarendon Press, 1958.

Nelson, Max. *The Barbarian's Beverage: A History of Beer in Ancient Europe.* New York: Routledge, 2005.

Peacock, D.P.S. "Amphorae and the Baetican Fish Industry." *Antiquaries Journal,* 54 (1974): 232–243.

Ponsich, M., and M. Tarradell. *Garum et Industries Antiques de Salaison dans la Méditerranée Occidentale.* Université de Bordeaux et Casa Velásquez. Bibliothèque de l'école des Hautes Etudes Hispaniques Fasc. 36. Paris: Presses Universitaires de France, 1965.

Purcell, N. "Wine and Wealth in Ancient Italy." *Journal of Roman Studies,* 75 (1985): 1–19.

Rossiter, J. J. "Wine and Oil Processing on Roman Farms in Italy." *Phoenix,* 35 (1981): 345–361.

Seltman, C. *Wine in the Ancient World.* London: Routledge and Kegan Paul, 1957.

Servienti, Silvano. *La Grande Histoire du Foie Gras.* Paris: Flammarion, 1993.

Stol, M. "Garlic, Onion, Leek." *Bulletin on Sumerian Agriculture,* 3 (1987): 23–92.

———. "Milk, Butter and Cheese." *Bulletin on Sumerian Agriculture,* 7 (1993): 99–113.

Witteveen, Joop. "On Swans, Cranes and Herons." *Petits Propos Culinaires,* 24 (1986): 22–31; 25 (1986): 50–59; 26 (1987): 65–73.

———. "Peacocks in History." *Petits Propos Culinaires,* 32 (1989): 23–34.

———. "Preparation of the Peacock for the Table." *Petits Propos Culinaires,* 36 (1990): 10–20.

CHAPTER 3

Cubberley, A. "Bread-Baking in Ancient Italy: *clibanus* and *sub testu* in the Roman World." In John Wilkins, David Harvey, and Mike Dobson (eds.), *Food in Antiquity,* 55–68. Exeter, England: Exeter University Press, 1995.

Firebaugh, W. C. *The Inns of Greece and Rome and a History of Hospitality from the Dawn of Time to the Middle Ages.* Chicago: Frank M. Morris, 1923.

Gauthier, P. "Notes sur l'étranger et l'hospitalité en Grèce et à Rome." *Ancient Society,* 4 (1973): 1–21.

Jashemski, W. F. "The Caupone of Euxinus at Pompeii." *Archaeology,* 20 (1967): 36–44.

———. *The Gardens of Pompeii, Herculaneum and the Villas Destroyed by Vesuvius.* 2 vols. New Rochelle, N.Y.: Caratzas Brothers, 1979, 1993.

Kleberg, T. *Hôtels, Restaurants et Cabarets dans l'antiquité Romaine.* Uppsala, Sweden: Almquist and Wiksells Boktryekeri AB, 1957.

Liversidge, Joan. "Roman Kitchens and Cooking Utensils." In Barbara
    Flower and Elisabeth Rosenbaum, *Apicius: The Roman Cookery Book*,
    29–38. London: Harrop, 1958.
Nutton, V. "Galen and the Traveller's Fare." In John Wilkins, David Harvey,
    and Mike Dobson (eds.), *Food in Antiquity*, 359–370. Exeter, England:
    Exeter University Press, 1995.
Packer, James. "Inns at Pompeii: A Short Survey." *Cronache Pompeiane*, 4
    (1978): 12–24.
Peacock, D.P.S. *Pottery in the Roman World: An Ethnoarchaeological
    Approach*. New York: Longmans, 1982.
Reynolds, P. *Ancient Farming*. Princes Risborough, England: Shire
    Archaeology, 1987.
Santich, Barbara. "Testo, Tegamo, Tiella, Tian: the Mediterranean Camp
    Oven." In Tom Jaine (ed.), *The Cooking Pot: Proceedings of the Oxford
    Symposium on Food and Cookery 1988*, 139–142. London: Prospect
    Books, 1989.
Sparkes, B. A., and L. Talcott. *Pots and Pans of Classical Athens*. Princeton,
    N.J.: Princeton University Press, 1958.
Sparkes, Brian. "The Greek Kitchen." *Journal of Hellenic Studies*, 82 (1962):
    121–137.
———. "The Greek Kitchen: An Addenda." *Journal of Hellenic Studies*, 85
    (1965): 162–163.

CHAPTER 4

Biel, Jorg. *Der Keltenfürst von Hochdorf*. Stuttgart, Germany: Konrad Theiss,
    1985.
Bowman, A. K., and J. D. Thomas. *The Vindolanda Writing Tablets*. London:
    British Museum Press, 1994.
Collis, J. *The European Iron Age*. London: Batsford, 1984.
Crawford, D. J. "Food, Tradition and Change in Hellenistic Egypt." *World
    Archaeology*, 11 (1979–80): 136–146.
Davies, Roy W. "The Roman Military Diet." *Britannia*, 2 (1971): 122–142.
———. *Service in the Royal Army*, D. Breeze and V. Maxwell, editors. Edin-
    burgh: Edinburgh University Press, 1989.
Dayagi-Mendels, Michel. *Drink and Be Merry: Wine and Beer in Ancient
    Times*. Jerusalem: Israel Museum, 1999.
Emery, W. P. *A Funerary Repast in an Egyptian Tomb of the Archaic Period*.
    Leiden, the Netherlands: Nederlands Institut voor het Nabije Ooosten,
    1962.
Jones, Gwynn, and Thomas Jones. *The Mabinogion*. London: Dent, 1975.
Lesko, Leonard H. *King Tut's Wine Cellar*. Berkeley, Calif.: B. C. Scribe
    Publications, 1977.

McGoven, P., S. J. Fleming, and S. H. Katz (eds.). *The Origins and Ancient History of Wine.* Amsterdam: Gordon and Breach, 1995.

Morenz, S. *Egyptian Religion.* Ithaca, N.Y.: Cornell University Press, 1973.

Quirke, Stephen. *Ancient Egyptian Religion.* London: British Museum Press, 1992.

Strouhal, Eugen, *Life in Ancient Egypt.* Cambridge: Cambridge University Press, 1992.

Zahran, M. A., and A. J. Willis. *The Vegetation of Egypt.* London: Chapman and Hill, 1992.

CHAPTER 5

Alcock, J. P. "The Funerary Meal in the Cult of the Dead in Classical Roman Religion." In Harlan Walker (ed.), *The Meal: Proceedings of the Oxford Symposium on Food and Cookery 2001* (31–41). Totnes, England: Prospect Books, 2002.

———. *Life in Roman Britain.* London: Batsford/English Heritage, 1996.

Calza, Guido. *La Necropoli del Porto di Roma nell' Isola Sacra.* Rome: Libreria dello Stato, 1940.

Cherpion, N. "Le Cone d'onguent." *Bulletin de l'Institut Français d'archeologie Orientale,* 94 (1994): 76–106.

Cross, Tom P., and Clark Harris Slover. *Ancient Irish Tales.* New York: Henry Holt and Company, 1936.

Davidson, James N. *Courtesans and Fishcakes: The Consuming Passions of Classical Athens.* New York: HarperCollins, 1997.

Donahue, John F. *The Roman Community at Table during the Principate.* Ann Arbor: University of Michigan Press, 2004.

Dunbabin, Katherine M. D. *The Roman Banquet: Images of Conviviality.* Cambridge: Cambridge University Press, 2003.

El Mahdy, Christine. *The Pyramid Builder.* London: Headline, 2003.

Erman, Adolf. *Life in Ancient Egypt.* 1894. Reprint, New York: Dover Books, 1971.

Faulkner, R. O. *The Ancient Egyptian Coffin Texts.* Warminster, England: Aris and Phillips, 1973.

Foreman, Werner, and Stephen Quicke. *Hieroglyphs and Afterlife in Ancient Egypt.* Norman: University of Oklahoma Press, 1996.

Gold, Barbara K., and Donahue, John F. (eds.). *Roman Dining: A Special Issue of American Journal of Philology.* Baltimore: Johns Hopkins University Press, 2005.

Jameson, M. H. "Sacrifice and Ancient Husbandry in Classical Greece." In C. R. Whittaker (ed.), *Pastoral Economics in Classical Antiquity,* 87–119. Cambridge: Cambridge University Press, 1988.

Kemp, Barry. *Ancient Egypt: Anatomy of a Civilization.* London: Routledge, 1989.

Leon, E. F. "Cato's Cakes." *Classical Journal,* 38 (1943), 213–221.

Lindsay, Hugh. "Eating with the Dead: The Roman Funerary Banquet." In I. Nielsen and H. S. Nielsen (eds.), *Meals in a Social Context: Aspects of the Communal Meal in the Hellenistic and Roman World,* 67–80. Aarhus, Denmark: University Press, 1998.

Lissarrague, François. *The Aesthetics of the Greek Banquet: Images of War and Ritual.* Trans. A. Szegedy-Maszak. Princeton, N.J.: Princeton University Press, 1990.

O'Rahilly, T. F. *Early Irish History and Mythology.* Dublin: Dublin Institute for Advanced Studies, 1946.

Peet, T. G. *Cemeteries at Abydos.* Vol. 2. London: Egypt Exploration Society, 1913–14.

Pritchett, W. Kendrick. *Ancient Greek Military Practices Part I.* [Originally published as *The Greek State at War Part I.*] Berkeley: University of California Press, 1971.

Rathbone, D. "Italian Wines in Roman Egypt." *Opus,* 2 (1983), 81–98.

Raven, J. E. *Plants and Plant Lore in Ancient Greece.* Oxford: Leopard's Head Press, 2000.

Richardson, I. "Water Triclinia and Biclinia in Pompeii." In R. Curtis (ed.), *Studia Pompeiana et Classica in Honor of Wilhelmina Jashemski,* vol. 1, *Pompeiana,* 305–312. New York: Orpheus Publishing, 1988.

Ross, Anne. *The Pagan Celts.* London: Batsford, 1986.

Slater, William J. (ed.). *Dining in a Classical Context.* Ann Arbor: University of Michigan Press, 1991.

Spencer, A. J. *Death in Ancient Egypt.* Harmondsworth, England: Penguin, 1982.

Stead, Ian, J. B. Bourke, and Don Brothwell (eds.). *Lindow Man: The Body in the Bog.* London: British Museum Press. 1986.

Toynbee, J.M.C. *Death and Burial in the Roman World.* London: Thames and Hudson, 1971.

Whittaker, C. R. (ed.). *Pastoral Economics in Classical Antiquity.* Cambridge, England: Cambridge Philological Society, 1988.

Winlock, H. E. *Models of Daily Life in Ancient Egypt from the Tomb of Meket-Ré at Thebes.* Cambridge: Harvard University Press, 1955.

CHAPTER 6

Bryan, Cyril P. *The Papyrus Ebers with an Introduction by Professor G. Elliot Smith.* London: Geoffrey Bles, 1930.

Craik, Elizabeth. "Diet, Diaita, and Dieticians." In A. Powell (ed.), *The Greek World* (387–402). London: Routledge, 1995.

De Ligt, L. *Fairs and Markets in the Roman Empire: Economic and Social Aspects of Periodic Trade in a Pre-Industrial Society.* Amsterdam: Gieben, 1993.

Farwell, D. E., and Molleson, T. I. *Excavations at Poundbury—Volume 2: The Cemeteries.* Dorset Natural History and Archaeological Society Monograph Series, no. 11. Dorchester: Dorset History and Archaeological Society.

Ferro-Luzzi, A., and S. Sette. "The Mediterranean Diet: An Attempt to Define Its Present and Past Composition." *European Journal of Clinical Nutrition,* 43 suppl. 2 (1989): 13–39.

Frayn, Joan. *Markets and Fairs in Roman Italy.* Oxford: Clarendon Press, 1993.

———. "Wild and Cultivated Plants: A Note on the Peasant Economy of Roman Italy." *Journal of Roman Studies,* 65 (1975): 32–39.

Garnsey, Peter. *Food and Society in Classical Antiquity.* Cambridge: Cambridge University Press, 1999.

Garnsey, Peter, and C. R. Whittaker (eds.). *Trade and Famine in Classical Antiquity.* Cambridge, England: Cambridge Philological Society, 1983.

Jouanna, J. "Le Vin et la Medicine dans la Grèce Ancienne." *Revue des Études Greques,* 109 (1996): 410–434.

Leca, Ange-Pierre. *La Médecine Égyptienne au Temps des Pharaohs.* Paris: Roger Dacaosta, 1971.

Majno, G. *The Healing Hand: Man and Wound in the Ancient World.* Cambridge: Harvard University Press, 1975.

Manniche, L. *An Ancient Egyptian Herbal.* London: British Museum Press, 1989.

Reeves, Carole. *Egyptian Medicine.* Princes Risborough, England: Shire Publications, 1992.

Singer, Charles, and Underwood E. Ashworth. *A Short History of Medicine from the Greeks to Harvey.* 2nd ed. Oxford: Clarendon Press, 1962.

Wenham, L. P. *The Romano-British Cemetery at Trentholme Drive, York.* Ministry of Public Building and Works Archaeological Reports, no. 5. London: HMSO, 1968.

INDEX

About the Author

JOAN P. ALCOCK is retired from and an Honorary Fellow of the National Bakery School and the author of *Life in Roman Britain* (1996) and *Food in Roman Britain* (2004), among other works.

LaVergne, TN USA
14 September 2010
196860LV00001B/1/P